Your Death Would Be Mine

Your Death Would Be Mine

Paul and Marie Pireaud in the Great War

MARTHA HANNA

HARVARD UNIVERSITY PRESS
Cambridge, Massachusetts
London, England

For Bob and Beth
with love

Printed in the United States of America

First Harvard University Press paperback edition, 2008.

Library of Congress Cataloging-in-Publication Data
Hanna, Martha.
Your death would be mine : Paul and Marie Pireaud in
the Great War / Martha Hanna.
p. cm.
Includes bibliographical references and index.
ISBN 978-0-674-02318-5 (cloth : alk. paper)
ISBN 978-0-674-03051-0 (pbk.)
1. Pireaud, Paul.   2. Pireaud, Marie.   3. World War, 1914–1918—
France—Biography.   4. Soldiers—France—Biography.   5. Army spouses—
France—Biography.   I. Title.

D544.H36 2006
940.4′124092—dc22
[B]   2006043521

ACKNOWLEDGMENTS

*W*hen I went to Paris in June 2000, I had no idea that I would spend the next six years writing a book about a peasant couple from the Dordogne. My intention was to write a general study of letter writing and its cultural significance in wartime France. My discovery of the letters of Paul and Marie Pireaud, deposited in the French military archives in Vincennes in 1995 and, as far as I can tell, unread thereafter, changed my plans almost overnight. Thus began the first of several research trips to Vincennes, where the archives staff was invariably helpful and, it sometimes seemed, rather amused by my painstaking reading, day after day, week after week, of these letters. My research also took me to the departmental archives of the Dordogne, Charente, Gironde, and Rhône. On each occasion, archivists helped me identify remnants of institutional memory from the Great War. The completion of this project owes a great deal to their professional expertise.

Annual research trips to France would not have been possible without the generous financial support of the Graduate Committee on the Arts and Humanities at the University of Colorado, Boulder. In 2003–04 I was also fortunate to receive a research fellowship from the National Endowment for the Humanities, a visiting fellowship at Clare Hall, Cambridge, and a Faculty Fellowship from the University of Colorado, Boulder, all of which allowed me to devote an entire year to writing. The intellectually stimulating environment of Clare Hall gave me the opportunity to discuss my work with, and benefit from the insights of, scholars from around the world. Marta Garcia Ugarte listened patiently as I rehearsed the story of Paul and Marie Pireaud, chapter by chapter; Peter and Christine Alexander offered critical insights and enthusiastic support; and the Arts, Social Sciences, and Humanities colloquium provided a congenial setting for discussing my project.

I have also benefited from the intellectual expertise and critical analysis of many professional colleagues and friends who read the manuscript over the past two years. Virginia Anderson responded to each chapter with analytical acumen and gratifying encouragement; Michael Neiberg, Sophie de Schaepdrijver, and Leonard V. Smith offered invaluable suggestions based on their deep knowledge of the First World War. Alex Dracobly brought his familiarity with the history of medicine in France to his reading of the manuscript and coordinated a faculty seminar at the University of Oregon that allowed me to learn from the insights of all participants. Ann Carlos, Peter Boag, and Susan Kingsley Kent graciously agreed to read those chapters that touched most directly on their areas of scholarly expertise. Countless conversations with two graduate students, William Miller and Bryan Miller, deepened my knowledge of heavy artillery and the Battle of Champagne. As chapters became a manuscript and a manuscript became a book, I have been fortunate to work with Lisa Adams of the Garamond Agency, and Kathleen McDermott and Susan Abel at Harvard University Press. Each in turn has applied a sharp eye—always tempered by genuine enthusiasm for the story of Paul and Marie Pireaud—to the project, improving it immeasurably. I am indebted to everyone who has read, commented upon, and made suggestions for improving the manuscript. All deserve my most sincere thanks.

Ultimately, this is a story about family and familial affection. It is fitting, therefore, that I acknowledge here the important contributions, tangible and intangible, made by family and friends. Wendy Jager read the manuscript not as an expert on the First World War, but as a loving mother intrigued by the

Pireauds' story and especially sensitive to the challenges that Marie confronted. Léon, Rita, and Lisa Luengo—at home in France and America alike—have been steadfast friends. Arlette and Robert Durand welcomed me into their home in Nanteuil-de-Bourzac, fed me abundantly, shared with me their knowledge of the community and the Pireaud family, and introduced me to friends and neighbors who helped me understand more fully the village and its past. I think of the days I spent in Nanteuil and the conversations I had with Mme Durand and M. Rémy Lachaise with abiding affection. Closer to home, my brothers, Josh and Peter Barber, applied their extraordinary knowledge of military history and military organization, based on direct knowledge of life in uniform, to their careful reading of the manuscript; my nephew, Daniel Barber, and my sister-in-law, Sherry Knettle, tracked down research guides (available only in Canada, it seemed) to departmental archives. No one has offered more to this project, however, than my husband, Bob, and my daughter, Beth. Bob has read every word of every draft and has never wavered in his enthusiasm for this project or his confidence in my ability to do it justice. Beth has taught me that nothing in life surpasses the love a mother has for her child. I dedicated my first book to two soldiers of the Great War but promised that the next one would belong to Bob and Beth. A book about love, family, and the importance of both is my gift to them.

CONTENTS

Introduction

*I*n a small and tranquil village more than three hundred kilometers southwest of Paris, Marie Pireaud wept quietly as she watched the young men of Nanteuil-de-Bourzac leave for war in August 1914. Among those immediately mobilized were most of the boys she had grown up with, several cousins, and her husband, Paul. Married only six months, the newlyweds had hoped that their years of separation caused by compulsory military service were behind them. Paul, they both believed, had already done his bit for France: born in 1890 and thus a member of the military class of 1910, he had been away from home since October 1911, when he had begun his two years of service. After being assigned first to barracks in the provincial city of Limoges—a town renowned for its fine porcelain but with little to recommend it to young men in uniform—he was sent in September 1912 to Morocco. Service in North Africa, where local tribesmen vigorously challenged France's colonial ambitions, exposed him to tropical fevers, outbreaks of the plague, and occasional bouts of bloody combat. Letters from his loving fiancée and the sure knowledge that his military service would soon be over were all that sustained him in his loneliness and involuntary exile. Expecting to be headed home by the end of the year, he wrote confidently in September 1913: "Once I am home there will be nothing but happiness for us because after having suffered so much it is only right that the happiness that awaits us should be perfect and like you I hope that nothing will ever separate or divide us again but death."[1]

Death spared Paul and Marie Pireaud, but the uneventful life of which they had dreamed was not to be. The First World War kept Paul away from home for almost five years. He saw action in some of France's bloodiest and most commemorated battles—Verdun, the Somme, and the Nivelle offensive of 1917—served in northern Italy, and went home for good only in July 1919. Marie joined forces with her parents and in-laws to tend the farm that had been left in their care and sought companionship with the many other local women whose husbands had been mobilized. Confined for most of the war to her village in the Dordogne, she did what she could to remain informed about military developments that would either bring her husband quickly home or place him in great danger, and she focused her energies on nurturing the affection and passion that sustained her marriage. When opportunity presented itself, she traveled long distances (visiting places she had previously only heard about) to spend time with her husband behind the lines; when they were compelled to live apart, she sent him lovingly assembled parcels of warm clothing and local delicacies that conjured up memories of home. But more than anything else, she wrote to him, and she in turn received letters from him. For almost five years, Paul and Marie Pireaud—modestly educated peasants with no pretensions to literary accomplishment—conducted their marriage by correspondence.

Scribbled in pencil from an artillery battery at Verdun; written, in a shaky hand, from childbed; decorated with a toddler's scrawl, adorned with a pressed flower, composed in tiny script to make the maximum use of scarce paper or in a large, round hand; indifferent to spelling and punctuation—the wartime correspondence of Paul and Marie Pireaud tells a story of both combatant and civilian life in wartime France that is exceptionally detailed, unabashedly romantic, and extraordinarily revealing. As Paul endured year after year of combat, he and Marie wrote of their daily lives, their innermost anxieties, and their abiding love. Topics as momentous as the Battle of Verdun and as mundane as the availability of dairy cattle mattered to these two; they mingled intimate confessions of sexual longing with discussions of crop prices and harvest prospects. Anticipating the birth of their first child (who was born in July 1916), they discussed how best to care for a pregnant woman and, after the birth, for the mother and her sickly infant. Paul confessed his fears, acknowledged his moments of deep depression, and confided that the love he and Marie had for each other and the joys of fatherhood were all that sustained him in the face of relentless adversity. Marie's letters, in turn, reassured him of her love, recounted stories of village life, and relayed news of other local men away at war. The Pireaud correspondence thus constitutes an extraordinary source for observing the First World War from the vantage point of the French peasantry; for analyzing the impact of the conflict on rural France; and for resurrecting the human face of war.

Marie, the younger daughter of Bernard and Hortense Andrieux, celebrated her twenty-first birthday in May 1913 and married in February 1914. She was, by the standard of the time, a young bride, and one perhaps more determined than most to marry a man of her own choosing—whatever her parents and sister might have to say about the matter. Having set her sights on Paul Pireaud since at least 1911, she let nothing sway her judgment or weaken her resolve to wed. She found allies in Paul's parents, who thought she would make a fine wife for their only son. She was, everyone agreed, a young girl of impeccable virtue, and her family, which had deep roots in the community, was well regarded. Her own parents, however, were much more skeptical about the match. Her sister, Rosa, and brother-in-law, Louis, opposed it from the outset. And village gossip that circulated in the fall of 1912, insinuating that Paul might have fathered an illegitimate child, seemed to confirm their suspicions that their would-be brother-in-law was undeserving of Marie's affection. Marie's parents heard other disturbing rumors: when news reached them that Paul was one of only fifteen soldiers from his regiment sent to Morocco, villagers were quick to suggest that he must have volunteered for service there. If so, Bernard and Hortense feared, it would seem that he was intentionally distancing himself from their daughter. Only a heartfelt letter in which Paul denied adamantly that he had volunteered for foreign service, vowed that he was a man of honor with no intention of breaking his engagement and no desire to do so, and proclaimed his love for their daughter calmed their apprehensions. Now converted to Marie's cause, her parents prepared for their daughter's wedding by buying the couple's first wedding present: a new bed.[2]

By spring 1913 it was agreed that the marriage would take place; the date remained to be determined. That summer, as Paul approached the end of his second year in uniform, the French parliament debated and then passed the Three-Year Law, extending the period of peacetime service from two years to three. If the law had been applied retroactively to the class of 1910 (as some proposals recommended), Paul would have had to spend an additional year under arms. His relief was palpable when the Chamber of Deputies abandoned that unpopular proviso and allowed the class of 1910 to return home as scheduled at the end of its two-year stint. His marriage plans could now move ahead. Marie's sister and brother-in-law remained opposed, but everyone else had been won over. Paul's mother found her future daughter-in-law to be a lovely girl,

and the two fathers, both elected in 19
nicipal council, found ample opportu
upcoming wedding, to debate the pros
young couple a parcel of land availa
Nanteuil's most socially distinguished f
the advantages of merging two well-r
means affluent local families.

Represented by eight separate families in the commune, the
Andrieux clan was well known and long established. Marie's father, who had been born in Nanteuil in 1854, and his siblings
and cousins had landholdings—some owned outright, others
rented—scattered throughout the commune. Bernard had inherited from his father the Lescure farm, with its lovely stone
cottage and rolling terrain, where Marie had lived throughout
her childhood and would live for the first decade of her married
life. Bernard Andrieux's sisters must have inherited cash, rather
than land, for one sister who married a local man and had a
large family appears to have owned no land. At the beginning of the century, perhaps as many as half of all residents of
Nanteuil-de-Bourzac owned the farms they operated; the other
half were tenant farmers or sharecroppers. Those who owned
land were more likely than those who only rented to stay in the
commune from one generation to the next: of the thirty-six in-
dividuals who worked their own land in 1901, sixteen had been
resident in Nanteuil for at least the previous ten years, and
another five were direct heirs of the previous landholder. By
contrast, tenant farmers moved into and away from the commune with relative frequency: fewer than half those listed in
1891 as tenant farmers still resided in the commune ten years
later; and many new families, including the Pireauds, had arrived in Nanteuil in their stead.[3]

When Paul's parents moved to Nanteuil-de-Bourzac from
the neighboring commune of Saint-Martial-Viveyrol in the

ars of the nineteenth century, Jean Pireaud found work
ially as a carpenter at the flour mill at Moulin du Pont,
where he would live for the rest of his life. Like many young
families setting out, the Pireauds were hardworking but far
from wealthy. Although Paul's father would eventually save
enough to give up carpentry, purchase land, and become self-
sufficient, in the early years he and his wife supplemented their
family income by taking in a foster child. Charlotte Mazeau,
born in Bordeaux in 1892 and orphaned or abandoned at an
early age, was legally defined as an *enfant de l'hospice*. But like
many rural foster children, she was effectively, if not legally
speaking, an adopted child, and she developed close bonds
with the family that had saved her from the orphanage.[4] Charlotte thought of Paul as her brother, and Paul's mother, at least,
seemed to think of her as a daughter. When her adoptive
parents became sufficiently prosperous to become landowners,
Charlotte would have helped her mother, whose responsibilities consisted primarily of running the household and farmyard, canning fruit, curing meat, making sausage, and tending
the poultry. Working with his father in the fields, Paul would
have taken on ever more strenuous tasks as he grew from boyhood into adolescence. The family flourished, and over time
Jean Pireaud won the respect of his neighbors. Selected by his
fellow council members in 1912 to serve as mayor of the commune, he was the first man in Nanteuil to learn, in late July
1914, that war was imminent.[5]

The first real evidence that war might interrupt the harvest
and shatter the peace of Nanteuil-de-Bourzac came on 31 July
1914. A telegram from the prefect, the most important administrative authority in the Dordogne, called upon every mayor
in the department to alert all owners of cattle, horses, and
motorcars in their commune to the possibility of imminent requisitioning. Citizens were, the telegram stated, "to be ready to

deliver their animals and their cars to the designated requisitioning centers as soon as the order [was] given." How Jean
Pireaud was to carry out this task while maintaining "the greatest possible discretion," in order to prevent the outbreak of
widespread panic, remained unclear.[6] Many of his neighbors
probably had if anything only a remote inkling of the international crisis that had been escalating since 28 June, when a
Serbian nationalist had assassinated the heir to the Austro-
Hungarian throne in Sarajevo. Those who subscribed to the
regional newspaper, *La Petite Gironde,* might have noted that on
28 July 1914 Austria had declared war on Serbia. But late July
was hardly a time for newspaper reading in rural France: when
crops, their ripening delayed by unseasonably wet weather,
needed to be harvested, farmworkers had little opportunity
and less energy at the end of a long day for evening reading.
And with most newspapers focusing on the murder trial of
Henriette Caillaux, the elegant wife of a controversial national
politician, the intricacies of international diplomacy probably
escaped all but the most attentive reader.[7] Could the good people of Nanteuil have known that following Austria's declaration
of war, Russia, France's only ally, would probably move to defend Serbia and the principle of Slavic autonomy in the Balkans? Could they have suspected that Russian mobilization, announced on 31 July, would provoke a German response and
thus bring about an international war that France could not
escape? The peasant farmers in communities like Nanteuil-de-
Bourzac, a commune of fewer than five hundred residents,
probably understood little of this. But Jean and Rosa Pireaud
knew what the requisitioning alert signified: their only son
would soon be summoned to war. Small wonder, then, that
when the gendarme carrying the official mobilization decree
arrived in Nanteuil on the afternoon of Sunday, 2 August 1914,
asking to be directed to the mayor, Rosa (after hearing him out

and sending him into the fields in search of her husband) began
to cry.

Rosa's son was two months shy of his twenty-fourth birthday when he packed his kit on 3 August and left Nanteuil,
heading once again for Limoges, headquarters for the twelfth
military district of France. During his prewar military service
Paul had served here in the Twenty-first Cavalry Regiment, and
had he been similarly assigned in 1914 he would soon have
seen action in Belgium and northern France. As luck would
have it, however, he drew a better straw: he served for the first
year of the war in the third company of the Twelfth Squadron
of the Army Service Corps, a supply company that did nothing
more dangerous than bake bread.[8] Why he enjoyed such a
cushy position, when so many from his military class were sent
almost immediately to the front, remains unclear. Paul believed
that his combat service in Morocco had secured him a temporary exemption from frontline service, but it is also possible
that poor health kept him behind the lines: he had been injured
in his first year of military service and had contracted a tropical
fever in Morocco that left him enervated and lethargic. Whatever the cause, he and Marie knew that a military posting that
required him only to feed, groom, and stable the company's
horses was the best they could hope for and better than many.
There was no glamour in the Army Service Corps, but there
was no danger either. The loneliness of enforced separation
could be endured, if only they could write to each other on a
regular basis.

Paul and Marie Pireaud were by no means the only French couple compelled to carry on their marriage by correspondence.
Indeed, France during the First World War became a nation of
letter writers. When nearly all young men and women were literate, letter writing was a possibility for almost everyone; given

that eight million men would be conscripted (almost half of whom were married), it would become the fundamental means of expressing familial affection. Four million letters made their way from or to the front every day, more than ten billion in all.[9] In the army, where censorship was erratic before 1916 and difficult to enforce thereafter, troops ignored the rules the censors sought to impose, gambled on the likelihood that their letters would not be intercepted, and established codes and subterfuges to thwart the censors and nullify censorship's numbing effect. Because letter writing was the means by which soldiers maintained their civilian identity in the midst of war, and because it kept them in contact with the reassuring familiarity of home, they turned to it eagerly and often. But letter writing was by no means a one-way street. The novelist Jules Romains observed, "Most of the men exist on letters and parcels from home."[10] Marie Pireaud, who like many other young wives applied herself to the task of corresponding regularly, endeavored to write at least one letter every day. Sometimes circumstances made it next to impossible to do so: illness, the exigencies of agricultural work, or the unpredictability of the postman's schedule occasionally conspired against her. At the front, circumstances considerably more dire made regular communication simultaneously a challenge and an urgent necessity: in 1916, while under relentless artillery fire at Verdun, Paul sometimes wrote two or more short letters in the course of a day. How else could he reassure his wife that he was still alive? Recognizing that regular correspondence was the lifeline that kept their marriage vital, Paul and Marie exchanged upwards of two thousand letters over the course of the war.

One of the few complete collections of wartime letters written by French peasants, the Pireaud correspondence offers rare glimpses into the cultural beliefs, social customs, and economic challenges of a rural world turned upside down by war. Called in disproportionate numbers to defend the nation, the men of rural France—and the families they left at home—paid a heavy price between 1914 and 1918: the peasantry comprised 41 percent of France's working population in 1914 and accounted for 44 percent of wartime casualties. In predominantly rural regions, like that encompassed by the military district of Limoges, 20 percent of all the men who were mobilized died.[11] This basic truth is acknowledged in all scholarly studies of France during the First World War. But the scarcity of sources generated by rural communities themselves has meant that few scholars have been able to discern exactly what it was like to live from day to day in an agricultural society heavily dependent upon male labor, in which half the labor force was absent for more than four years and a fifth of all those who served did not come home.[12] Novelists have offered us powerful images of rural France at that time—of the hardships imposed by arduous work and ubiquitous mourning, and of the sexual weaknesses, appetites, and frustrations that beset men and women separated by war.[13] Among the most haunting of these works is Jean Giono's description of village life in *Le Grand Troupeau* (*To the Slaughterhouse*), in which a war widow consoled by the empathy of her neighbors, a child forever bereft of a father's love, and farm women in love with men destined for the infantry all experience the emotional anguish caused by war, separation, and the ever-present threat of death or permanent disfigurement. The Pireaud correspondence reveals how closely Giono's portrait of village life captured the reality of rural French life between 1914 and 1918. In Nanteuil-de-Bourzac, as in Giono's alpine village, war permanently marked the soldiers who went off to fight and the families they left behind.

Because Paul survived the war, the letters he and Marie exchanged also allow us to see close-up how this conflict, which touched France more deeply than it did any other principal combatant, affected one couple—along with the military and civilian communities in which they lived—for the duration, from the outbreak of hostilities in August 1914 until the armistice in November 1918, and well beyond. Many collections of wartime letters have come to light over the years: some appeared in print during the last phases of the war itself or in the first decade of the interwar years; others have been published more recently, as families have unearthed packages of letters sent long ago by young men to wives or parents. But in nearly all cases, these collections of letters have preserved and memorialized the experiences of men who served and died in combat: moving, eloquent, and haunting though they are, they are also of necessity incomplete. The Pireaud correspondence stands out in part because it includes the letters of a man fortunate enough to have survived, but also, and just as significantly, because it includes those of his wife.

Letters from civilian France were often lost amid the mud and mayhem of frontline service. Soldiers, who had to carry everything from rifles to groundcloths, from the bottle of cheap wine to family photographs, on their backs, often found it almost impossible to ensure the safe-keeping of the letters they received from home. They abandoned them reluctantly, for most men in uniform lived for the loving reassurance that a letter usually brought with it, and they would have held on to these cherished mementos of home if they had had the means to do so. But a damp, overladen knapsack was a poor place to preserve letters and postcards. As Paul's own letters testify, sometimes he had no choice but to burn the letters he would have preferred to keep. Thus, the wartime correspondence of civilian France has not survived in the same abundance and rich variety as that of combatant France. Although Marie Pireaud's was by no means the voice of all French civilians, it is a voice, heretofore muted, that deserves to be heard.

Paul and Marie had learned the rudiments of letter writing as schoolchildren. The young men called to war in August 1914 and the women they left at home were, as many scholars have observed, the first generation of French peasants to be fully literate. Many peasants in the nineteenth century had a rudimentary knowledge of reading, but mastery of writing—a much more difficult skill, as any schoolteacher can attest—was by no means universal. This was especially true of women: 25 percent of all French brides in 1880 could not so much as sign their name to the marriage register. By 1910, however, only 3.2 percent of brides were deemed completely illiterate, and 86 percent of all male conscripts could both read and write.[14] This could not have happened without the educational initiatives of Jules Ferry, who as minister of public instruction in the early 1880s was committed to free, secular, compulsory schooling for all children between the ages of six and thirteen. The Ferry laws guaranteed that the young boys of Nanteuil and similar rural communities, who before 1881 had had access to primary education but little appreciation of its practical value, would henceforth be compelled to attend school regularly; and the same laws made education for the young girls of the commune a reality for the first time. Indeed, Nanteuil had no girls' school before the passage of the Ferry laws. In August 1881 a report prepared for the administrator responsible for public education in the Dordogne noted that the commune, which numbered 687 residents, was in violation of the new law that required schools to be made available to all children in every commune of at least five hundred residents. Calculating that a school for girls would provide elementary education for approximately

fifty local children, the school inspector urged the state to sub-
sidize the costs of construction.[15] When the new school was
complete and a young woman was hired to teach the girls of
the village, Nanteuil-de-Bourzac could at last educate all its
children.

Louise Chazeau and Jean Camus taught reading, writing,
and simple arithmetic. Camus would have impressed upon his
young charges their patriotic responsibilities to love France,
fulfill their duties as citizens, and defend the nation in times of
danger. Mlle Chazeau's lessons would have urged the young
girls of Nanteuil to be compassionate to the poor and dutiful to
their parents. Boys and girls alike were taught that in the event
of extended separation they should become faithful, honest,
and conscientious correspondents, for the elementary curriculum placed great emphasis on mastering the art of family correspondence. Letters (and letters alone) enabled family members
separated by circumstance to stay in contact with one another.
When young boys moved away from home—whether to pur-
sue an advanced diploma, to work in an office, or to fulfill their
military-service obligations—they and their families were expected to correspond regularly and describe to the best of their
abilities the minutiae of daily life. Teachers impressed upon
their students that family correspondence be informal in struc-
ture, conversational in tone, and honest in spirit.[16]

The wartime correspondence of Paul and Marie Pireaud
suggests that they learned some of these lessons well. Their letters reveal little respect for French grammar, an insouciant disregard of punctuation, and an imperfect grasp of spelling. Both
Paul and Marie fell victim to the welter of homonyms confusing to unwary writers of French. Like many a writer of English
who easily substitutes "their" for "there," Paul and Marie—and
Marie more than Paul—often exchanged one identical-sound-

ing word for another: *ces* ("these"), *sait* ("knows"), and *c'est* ("it is") appear interchangeably in Marie's letters. However painful to the eye of the strict orthographer—however embarrassing they would perhaps have been to the village schoolteacher, who surely had drilled her young charges in the art of correct spelling—these common errors of composition never compromised the gist of the letters themselves. More important still, they never inhibited Paul and Marie's ability to write with an impassioned honesty and an honest passion that many a more educated reader might envy.

Paul and Marie had first practiced the art of intimate correspondence during their courtship and engagement. Although Marie's letters from that period have not survived, it is evident from Paul's letters that they became comfortable correspondents during that time, when they were first forced to live far apart. It is also clear that the most frequently repeated lessons of the letter-writing curriculum had made an impression upon him. Letters, like acts of confession, were to be honest avowals of personal conviction or (when warranted) admissions of personal weakness, even if such admissions cast the letter writer in a less than admirable light. They should moreover be artlessly frank when written to one's peers but might justifiably be somewhat more reserved when addressed to one's parents. And the rules of composition that governed family correspondence—letters should be written on stationery rather than notepaper, for instance—should be observed when possible but could be set aside under extraordinary circumstances. Paul was embarrassed in early September 1913 to send Marie a letter on a sheet of paper he had torn from his notebook and begged her indulgence: "I hope that you will excuse me as you say between us such things aren't important if I were in France I would be sickened to find myself in such a situation but here you get used to everything and I find it completely normal."[17]

In fact, much that he came reluctantly to regard as normal in the course of his military service helped inure him to the hardships of life in wartime. Military service was, in his experience, an amalgam of boredom, enforced servility toward mindless martinets, and moments of sheer terror. As he confided to Marie shortly after he first reported for duty in Limoges, army life consisted in the main of pointless aggravation inflicted on hapless young men by an overbearing, self-important officer corps. The new recruits, denied time either to shave or to eat, were, he lamented, up from four in the morning until eleven at night. Like many a new soldier unaccustomed to the rigors of military life, he could not understand why a bed inspection that failed to meet the reviewing officer's exacting standards, or a soldier's inadvertent failure to salute a commanding officer, could bring about a cancellation of Christmas leave. As he complained of petty injustices and incomprehensible regulations, he recognized, "It is certainly wrong to tell you about my weakness and my discouragement but I love you too much not to open my heart to you." And so he risked the wrath of his captain, who forbade his men to take time out of their day to write home, and hid himself away in dimly lit stairwells to commune with his beloved. He begged her—in tones in which self-pity and passionate confession commingled—to write back: "When I see my colleagues reading letters from their parents and friends I can't help crying have pity on me write to me often I beg of you don't forget me I have nothing else on earth to comfort me but the love and confidence that I have in you."[18]

If the tedium of barracks life prompted Paul to pour out his heart to Marie in letters that were confessional, passionate, and wistful, life on the front lines of colonial conflict inclined him toward a frankness of expression when writing to his fiancée that was notably absent in letters he sent to his parents. Encouraged by her repeated request that he not hide anything from her, he described how his encampment had come under sustained rifle fire from Moroccan insurgents and how the regiment was in danger of contracting the plague that had caused French reinforcements recently arrived from Casablanca to be quarantined. Because he did not tell his parents such unsettling news, Marie wondered what precisely conditions were like in North Africa. Judging from the news that Paul's mother shared with her, all was well in the desert hinterland of Morocco. Could this possibly mean that Paul would happily stay on beyond his assigned tour of duty? To such fanciful imaginings, Paul could only reply: "You don't seem to believe what I write you when you see the consoling letters that I send to my parents you really must understand that to avoid giving them anything to worry about I prefer to hide everything that happens here, how can you ask me if I would prefer to stay in Morocco or return to France where I could see you several times a month where I would have nothing to fear from rifle fire fever and the other dangers that threaten us here."[19]

Military service thus trained Paul not only in the ways of army life, but in the practice of letter writing. Before his departure for Limoges in September 1911, he would have had little need to write letters, for everyone he knew lived within easy walking distance of his family's farm. Nor would he have needed to write long, impassioned love letters to the beguiling young Marie Andrieux, who could be wooed much more directly on those precious evenings when she evaded her parents' vigilance and the young couple lingered in the country lanes of Nanteuil-de-Bourzac. Writing, a skill only intermittently employed in prewar rural society, became a fundamental feature of life in wartime France. And the motifs evident in Paul's prewar correspondence—an insatiable hunger for news from home, a grudging resignation to military routine, and a willingness to describe his experience of combat—would recur as a plaintive refrain in his wartime letters.

The story of Paul and Marie Pireaud helps us understand in new ways aspects of the First World War that have previously been viewed only through a wide-angle lens. Three topics fundamental to the way we think about the war achieve sharper definition when observed close-up, through a microscopic lens: the alienation among frontline troops, the indifference on the home front to the suffering of those at war, and the hardships of rural life in wartime. Scholars of the war have often maintained that a profound cognitive divide separated those who fought, and thus knew the war firsthand, from those who did not and thus remained ignorant of its horrors. At the heart of this thesis is a belief, long maintained as canonical and only recently challenged, that combatants rarely told civilians what the war was really like. Anxious not to overburden their wives and mothers with a knowledge that could only be distressing, they chose instead to remain silent. This heroic silence had, however, two unfortunate consequences. First, it alienated the men who fought from the civilians who did not. Exposed to the unutterable conditions of trench warfare, soldiers grew ever more resentful that civilians neither shared the experience nor appreciated the sacrifices of frontline duty. Those who survived, the story ran, returned home disaffected and embittered. At the same time, the soldiers' stoic resolve not to tell about what they knew insulated the home front from both direct experience and secondhand knowledge of the war. As a result, the home front held fast in large part because civilians did not know and thus could not understand the reality of the war as lived and experienced at the front.

The Pireaud correspondence points to an entirely different truth. Paul was not as alienated, and the citizens of Nanteuil-de-Bourzac not as ignorant, as the usual interpretation would have us believe. Like almost all his comrades-in-arms, Paul was angry or embittered from time to time: any evidence of female sexual infidelity made him furious; signs of civilian indifference to the suffering of men at the front aroused his ire. But he cherished his family, longed for home, thought incessantly of leave and the joys that awaited him in his conjugal bed, and in the long, lonely intervals between periods of leave, valued every token of affection that made its way to the front. Marie's parcels proved that he had not been forgotten; and letters—the longer the better—that he could linger over, read, and reread bore witness to the fidelity, concern, and ardor of his beloved wife. Reassurances of this type were of the utmost importance, especially for married men who often viewed the war as a struggle to protect the people they loved from the devastation of defeat, the ignominy of invasion, and the atrocities associated with enemy occupation.

Connected to home by bonds of affection that withstood distance, separation, and marital misunderstanding, Paul was also willing to share with Marie much of his lived experience at the front. Not every letter was filled with heart-rending descriptions of bloody combat and bodily dismemberment, but there were enough letters of this type to convey something of the intermittent but very real terror of life at the front. And as the correspondence makes evident, Paul was not the only young man to write such letters, and Marie was not uniquely privileged in her access to such information. Knowing that newspapers did not tell the truth, that the army was notoriously slow in relaying information to families about the fate of their loved ones, and that letters were often subject to arbitrary delays, villagers in Nanteuil shared whatever news came their way, pooled their intelligence, and thus gleaned precious nuggets of otherwise unavailable information from one another. By sharing news explicitly intended for public consumption (while keeping secret the intimate avowals that concluded many a letter), residents of Nanteuil transformed their village into an informal communications depot to which information about the war was conveyed and from which it was then relayed, first to other local residents and from them back to the front. This kept the village informed and the war omnipresent. Without doubt these villagers had only an imperfect, secondhand knowledge of the war. They did not live with death as their menfolk at the front did. But their understanding of the war was more vivid and more visceral than we might suspect. To the extent that they continued to support the national war effort, they did so not because they were ignorant of its horrors but in spite of what they knew of its harsh reality. Theirs was an informed consent, like that of the soldiers with whom they remained in contact.

Or was it, as many urban commentators and some soldiers suggested at the time, merely a consent grounded in peasant greed? Everyone acknowledged that peasant conscripts paid a heavy price and that their wives and parents worked tirelessly to bring in the harvest of 1914. Many citizens contended, however, that after 1914 the civilian peasantry took advantage of economic circumstances to profit handsomely from the war. Some enterprising spirits, it was alleged, would have been happy for the war to last forever, so abundant were the opportunities for financial gain. The avaricious peasant, intent only on lining his pockets at the expense of the poor soldier (immortalized in *Under Fire*, Henri Barbusse's best-selling, prize-winning novel about life at the front), thus became the archetype of civilian greed and callous indifference.[20] City folk, who felt the pinch of inflationary prices and scant supplies during the last two years of the war, were no kinder in their assessment: possessing food to spare, French peasants, they were convinced, were profiting from other people's hunger and misfortune. (Peasants, in turn, denounced the high wages and exemptions from military service that many skilled laborers enjoyed.) The reality was considerably different.[21] Life in the cities was not as carefree, affluent, and untouched by mourning as many country critics believed. And life in rural France was harder than many in the cities were willing to admit. Certainly there was more money circulating in the countryside than ever before, and peasants made no apologies for selling their surplus products at whatever price the market would bear. But rural life was marked neither by indolence nor by indifference. Peasant families used much of their newly acquired cash to send money and parcels to the front, to soften as best they could the hardships of life under arms, and to reassure those who fought that their families had not forgotten them. For peasants whose lives were dominated by heavy labor, debilitating anxiety, and persistent sadness, no benefit was to be gained from a war without end.

Your Death Would Be Mine teases out the broader significance of the Pireaud correspondence by placing the individual story of Paul and Marie within its local, regional, and to a certain extent national context. It is possible to do this by imagining both of them as situated at the center of a set of ever-broadening concentric circles, each of which can be reconstituted by reference to available sources. After a year of service well behind the lines, Paul went to the front in late 1915, where he served in the First Battery of the newly created 112th Heavy Artillery Regiment (Régiment d'artillerie lourde, or RAL). His regiment saw action in Picardy in the early months of 1916, at Verdun, and on the Somme; thereafter, it served in the Tenth Army, which held down the right flank in the ill-fated Chemin des Dames offensive of 1917 and later made up the core of the French expeditionary force to Italy in late 1917. Although the operational logbooks (*Journaux des marches et opérations*) of Paul's battery have not survived, logbooks from other batteries in the 112th Heavy Artillery Regiment make it possible to situate Paul's particular experiences in the broader context of his regiment. Furthermore, the voluminous records compiled by the army's postal censorship office (which starting in late 1916 reviewed on a weekly basis a random sample of all letters sent from or to the front) shed light on the dissatisfactions, aspirations, and preoccupations of men who served in other regiments assigned to the same military sectors as the 112th. These records are especially valuable for understanding the sentiments of men serving in the French expeditionary force in Italy, a facet of the French war effort that has otherwise been little studied.[22]

It is also possible to compare Paul's daily correspondence with the few collections of letters written by peasant soldiers that have survived. The collections that do exist suggest that Paul's was not the lone voice of impassioned honesty and intense affection. Fernand Maret, a young peasant who wrote regularly to his parents in the Mayenne from the time of his mobilization in 1915 through the end of the war, shared with them his horror, anguish, and intense anger at what he took to be the military mismanagement of the war. Germain Cuzacq, a poor tenant farmer from the southwest frontier, imparted advice to his wife on child-rearing and (like Paul) sent home hand-drawn maps of the sector at Verdun where he served (and unlike Paul, died) in 1916. These collections, when read in conjunction with the records generated by the postal censors, suggest that many soldiers of modest background from regions all across France were willing to speak more openly about the war than their military superiors would have liked.[23]

Marie, too, lived at the center of a ring of concentric circles, which, like ripples in a pond, become more diffuse and hence less clearly visible the farther they are from the center. That which she knew best (and which we can know most precisely because of the detailed nature of the correspondence) was her immediate family life, centered on her home at Lescure; but her life was embedded in that of the village, which in turn was situated in a wider community of villages within walking distance of Nanteuil. These were the places she knew directly. Her village was also situated within the arrondissement (or subprefecture) of Ribérac, the department of the Dordogne, the region once (and now again) known as Aquitaine, and, of course, the nation of France. Documents that describe daily life within the vicinity of Nanteuil, the region of Ribérac, and the department of the Dordogne are unusually detailed and fortuitously rich. Daily and weekly reports from the first month of the war reveal the effects of mobilization on this rural society, and monthly reports prepared by subprefects, prefects, and police commissioners during the last two years of the war catalogued material conditions and assessed local morale in rural communities. Schoolteachers' accounts of village life add depth and local nuance to the regional picture that emerges from those sources.

In 1916, the French Ministry of Public Instruction called on all primary school teachers to respond to a detailed questionnaire about life in their village, from the declaration of mobilization onward: what effect, Paris wanted to know, did the war have on economic conditions, religious practice, school attendance, access to medical care, attitudes toward the poor, and respect for public order? Many of these reports—including those prepared by schoolteachers in the Dordogne—have not survived. But daily life in Nanteuil, which is within walking distance of many villages in the department of the Charente, can be reconstructed in part by reference to teachers' reports from those nearby villages. When read alongside reports prepared by the subprefect in Ribérac, the prefect in Périgueux, and the police commissioner for the Dordogne (who was especially attentive to the impact of the war on rural life in 1917 and 1918), these documents show how the experiences of one couple and one village found resonance within the region as a whole.

To imagine Paul and Marie as situated at the center of two distinct sets of concentric circles is to capture one reality of family life in wartime France and to obscure another. Two sets of concentric circles inscribed on the flat territorial surface of France—like the ripples created when two stones are thrown into a pond at some distance from each other—inevitably suggest distance and separation. And there is truth in this, for physical separation was the painful reality husbands and wives endured as long as the war lasted. Physical separation did not, however, necessarily entail affective separation or cognitive alienation. Indeed, the most persistent message to emerge from the letters of Paul and Marie Pireaud is one not of separation and alienation but of connection and compassion. The concerns and anxieties of the one became, through regular, frank correspondence, the concerns and anxieties of the other. As the following chapters reveal, for long stretches of time domestic life and its daily tribulations dominated their correspondence: for most of 1915, before Paul went to the front, and following the birth of their son in July 1916, their letters concentrated primarily on family matters and village life. There were also, not surprisingly, long stretches when the traumatic character of combat dominated their daily musings: while Paul served at Verdun in particular, but also during the Chemin des Dames offensive of 1917 and in the last months of the war in northern Italy. At no time, however, did the distinct worlds of combatant and civilian that Paul and Marie inhabited exist in isolation from each other. Marie was as eager to know about combat (however unsettling the knowledge had to be) as Paul was to know about child care. Thus, it is more appropriate to imagine these two sets of concentric circles—the home front and the military front—not as stretched out at great distance from each other in two-dimensional space, but as two discs with a common center point, intersecting each other in three-dimensional space. From 1914 through mid-1919 Paul and Marie found themselves at the center of two distinct but intersecting worlds: each was unfamiliar with much that occurred at the outer edges of the other's temporary universe, but at the same time each remained cognitively, although not physically, immersed in, attentive to, and fascinated by the other's immediate reality.

The wartime experiences of one young peasant couple from a small village far from the firing line were not, of course, those of every French citizen. Religious identity and regional origins, economic occupation and political affiliation, marital status and military duties: all shaped the way civilians and soldiers alike perceived the war, defined what they were fighting for, and reconciled themselves to its sacrifices. In a nation that mobilized more than eight million men, suffered the invasion and occupation of ten departments, and boasted both large, elegant cities and small country villages, it could not have been otherwise. Young women who lived in the occupied zone were entirely deprived of the luxury of daily correspondence that Marie Pireaud came to take for granted. They went for four years with no word from, and no ability to communicate with, husbands or fiancés serving in the French army.[24] French civilians accustomed to fast-paced urban life, the labor agitation of industrial trade unions, and the cultural modernism of the big city experienced a war different in many regards from that of the villagers of Nanteuil-de-Bourzac. And peasants from more devout regions, such as Brittany, where piety was the norm no doubt found greater reassurance in their religious faith than did Marie and Paul, whose faith was in the one case lukewarm and in the other completely nonexistent.

Perhaps most important, soldiers who served in the infantry—which accounted for 85 percent of all French casualties
and lost 29 percent of all men assigned to its regiments—experienced a war different from and in many respects even more
horrific than that which Paul knew firsthand. Conditions in the
artillery (and especially in the heavy artillery situated well beyond the reach of murderous machine-gun fire) were, indeed,
so superior to those experienced by the poor infantryman—the
poilu of French national memory—that many infantry soldiers
depreciated those who served in the heavy artillery as shirkers
who did not really know what war was like.[25] Their disdain was
perhaps understandable, but it was not entirely fair. Paul spent
two months at Verdun, came under direct fire many times, and
more than once counted himself fortunate to be alive. Nonetheless, he escaped the war unscathed. He survived in part because he served behind the lines for the first year of combat,
when France suffered more than a million casualties; in part because the mortality rate in the artillery was one-fifth that of the
infantry; and in part because he was just plain lucky.

Your Death Would Be Mine is the story of one young peasant
couple caught up in the maelstrom of the First World War. A
love story set against one of the most monumental, terrifying,
and historically important events of the twentieth century as
well as a chronicle of daily life both at the front and behind the
lines, it allows us to see how the Great War—an event that top-
pled governments, ended empires, precipitated revolution, and
redrew the map of Europe—also imposed itself on all aspects of
everyday existence and in the process transformed the lives of
ordinary people. Paul's experience of the Great War was not
identical in all details to that of every other French soldier mobilized in defense of the nation; Marie's was not that of every
young woman waiting at home. But theirs is a story—rich in
detail, passionate in its expression—that is worth retelling.

My beloved Paul

Now that Italy has mobilized do you believe that the war will be finished
soon I saw in the paper yesterday that Greece Romania and Bulgaria are
all going to get into the war during the summer if only this could bring us
an end because as you know everything is bothering us we have lots of work
my mother is almost always at Coutancie and my father too. So you can
see what I mean . . .

Anyway we are only doing what we can the most urgent. We are in the
midst of haymaking that's going pretty well soon we will move over to the
meadows at la Conterie.

The wheat is beautiful now with long stalks I don't really know but I
think that lots of fodder crops and wheat are going to be lost imagine all the
houses where there is only a woman and the children.

How sad the countryside is. When will we learn that these horrible
things are finished Until then receive from your wife all her best kisses and
her gentlest caresses love and kisses from the one who will love you forever

Marie to Paul, 27 May 1915

ONE

How Sad the Countryside Is

As the men of Nanteuil-de-Bourzac left for war in August 1914, the women who remained behind contemplated their departure with trepidation and, in some cases at least, mute disbelief. In the village of Salles-Lavalette, only a short distance from Nanteuil, women wept unabashedly as their menfolk gathered to hear the reading of the mobilization order. And those who had held back their tears in public probably wept in the privacy of their homes that evening, as men assembled their supplies and summoned their courage for the task ahead. On the next morning, 3 August, wives and mothers watched in silence as their men began a ten-kilometer march toward the nearest railway station and, from there, to war. The scene was similar in the nearby commune of Juignac, where villagers greeted the news of mobilization "with sadness but resignation." At this point, many believed that diplomacy would defuse the crisis and that men now departing would soon be returning home.[1] When it became evident that the moment for diplomacy had passed, these and countless other peasant families resigned themselves to the grim truth that France really was at war.

As yet unaware that a fifth of all those who left would not come home, wives and parents set themselves a task, simple in conception but less so in execution: they would work the land that had been left in their care, so that when the war was over—in six weeks if all went well, in three or four months if unanticipated delays disrupted the army's best-laid plans—their menfolk would return to farms still fertile and productive. The initial objectives, based on the premise that the war would be over by Christmas, were therefore short-term. The harvest had to be completed and the soil prepared for the next sowing (a task usually undertaken in October or early November). Beyond that there was no need to plan. The men would be home in time to take on the heavy labor of spring planting, haymaking, and summer harvesting. When victory eluded the Allied forces in the spring of 1915, however, peasants braced themselves for another season (surely the last) of exceptional effort. But because the war deprived the small, unsophisticated farms of southwest France of essential manpower, draft animals, and chemical fertilizers, the challenges of agricultural life in 1915 were greater, the accomplishments less deserving of national acclaim, and the conditions of everyday life more difficult.

Although the deprivations of war made working the land increasingly arduous, it remained a familiar task. Keeping in touch with men at the front and staying abreast of military developments were new tasks, unique to a nation at war, to which young peasant women and aging parents soon accustomed themselves. Determined to alleviate as best they could the misery of military service, they put together parcels of food, warm clothing, and loving mementos of home; they sent money to men underpaid and facing a winter campaign; and they wrote letters. Despite their meager schooling, parents fatigued by days of backbreaking labor wrote newsy, semiliterate letters to absent sons. Wives sent letters or postcards, often on a daily basis. Pages filled with detailed accounts of work in the field, crop yields, and of course the weather assured distant husbands that their land was not being neglected; affectionate, often passionate words carried with them the promise that wives remained faithful, their husbands beloved. To learn what they could of where local men were serving, to assess the dangers that they confronted, and to calculate their chances of a safe return, villagers read newspapers, shared private information, and compared notes on the nation's military fortunes. In the early weeks of war, when published news was carefully vetted, letters were delayed in postal clearinghouses all across France, and real news was often trumped by rumor, this was no easy task. But it was of the first importance, for civilians young and old longed to learn what they could of the fate of their men in the face of danger. Far from being indifferent to the plight of soldiers far from home, the citizens of rural France were avid for any reassurance that their men remained, for the moment at least, unharmed.

Marie neglected none of these tasks. She worked the land, shared information with friends whose husbands were also in uniform, labored with her mother-in-law to prepare packages filled with home-cooked food and warm clothing, and found solace in correspondence. Because any disruption in the delivery service caused annoyance or outright alarm, she promised to write a card or a letter every day and implored Paul to do the same: "Write to me every day," she begged in January 1915, "and I will be happy."[2] The only thing that made her happier still was physical reunion with her husband. Throughout the war, some fortunate couples successfully conspired to spend time together in run-down inns or seedy hotels near the front lines. These conjugal visits were illegal: army regulations repeatedly prohibited wives, girlfriends, and other women from traveling to or within the military zone. Such regulations had little effect, however, and they certainly did not deter Paul and Marie, who enjoyed at least three such visits in the first year of the war.

Like most of the Dordogne, where more than 80 percent of the population lived in small villages or hamlets and even the de-

Photo of Paul and Marie Pireaud, 1915. Service historique de la défense, France.

partmental capital Périgueux was a modest town of fewer than 35,000 residents, the commune of Nanteuil-de-Bourzac was first and foremost a farming community. Of the 485 residents recorded in the census of 1901 (the last year before the war for which annotated census records exist), fewer than 50 lived in the village of Nanteuil itself, which counted among its inhabitants two blacksmiths, two grocers, two teachers, and a few families (one of which could trace its noble ancestry to long before the French Revolution) who lived off their investments. More than 400 men, women, and children lived in the surrounding hamlets and farms. Although a handful of rural artisans—a stonecutter, a cobbler, a tailor, and several millers— were resident in the outlying communities, the great majority of adults worked the land. They were, by their own definition, peasants: subsistence farmers who engaged in small-scale cultivation. Unlike farmers in some parts of France whose rich arable land and proximity to major markets allowed them to engage in commercial, monocultural production, the peasants in the northwest of the Dordogne and those who lived in neighboring communes of the Charente grew wheat predominantly, but also oats, clover, beets, potatoes, and corn; raised enough cattle to supply themselves with animals to work the land; cultivated a few vines (though not nearly as many as their ancestors had in the years before phylloxera had destroyed most of the local vineyards); and labored not to supply some distant market but to feed their families and provide fodder for their cattle.[3] In an age before widespread availability of agricultural machinery, farms depended first and foremost on the raw strength of men and of harnessed animals: fields were plowed and sown with animal-drawn plows; harvests were reaped and grain threshed with human muscle power.

By depriving villages of men and animals alike, war disrupted the established routines of rural life. Nanteuil sent

seventy-one men to war from 1914 through 1918.[4] Some of
these men—including Georges Carteaud, who was born in 1898
and died before his twenty-first birthday—were too young in
1914 to have been mobilized; others were old enough to serve
but too old to be mobilized immediately. Thus Marie's brother-
in-law, Louis Chaboussie, who was thirty-eight when the war
broke out, reported for duty not in August but in mid-September. It is likely, however, that at least fifty men left the commune immediately after mobilization was decreed. It fell to the
women, teenage boys, and older men who remained behind to
complete the harvest, which at this latitude in France was usually well under way by late July. They were not found wanting.
The prefect of the Dordogne, reporting to his superiors in
Paris, noted that the people of his department had done their
duty admirably. Even though mobilization had "called up the
strongest and healthiest of our farmers," those who remained at
home had "redoubled their efforts" and had done what was necessary to bring in the harvest.[5] On the parcels of land that
Paul's and Marie's families tilled, the harvest of 1914 was bountiful. Marie reported in late September that they had amassed
thirty-nine sacks of wheat from the acreage at Lescure, and another twenty-nine at Moulin du Pont.[6] This would become the
standard against which all subsequent wartime harvests would
be judged and invariably found wanting.

Urban commentators, who were quick to celebrate the "mi-
raculous" harvest of 1914, often did not understand how difficult it would be to repeat it in the years to come. Those who
worked the land, however, knew that the singular success of
1914 had depended not only on their own patriotic zeal but
also on the foregoing efforts of men now mobilized: before the
women and the elderly finished the harvest of 1914, younger,
stronger men had cleared the land, tilled the soil, fertilized the
crops, and weeded the fields. Without this manpower and the

assistance lent by draft animals now caught up in the net of military requisitioning, the peasants who remained at home would be hard-pressed to match the production standards that had been the norm before the war.

The prefect's telegram that Jean Pireaud received on 28 July made it clear that the army would need not just men but farm animals—horses especially, but beef cattle as well. To feed the nation in arms, the army would requisition almost 750,000 cows and bulls in the first five months of the war alone; to move supplies, gun carriages, and essential provisions, it would "conscript" hundreds of thousands of horses and mules.[7] Although the subprefect for Ribérac assured the prefect as early as 3 August that the requisitioning of horses was taking place "in the most favorable conditions possible," the process wrought havoc in the countryside.[8] By late October, when Jean Pireaud left the village to take yet another consignment of horses to the nearby town of Verteillac, Marie reported that the army was so desperate for horses that it was taking brood mares and colts as young as a year. Farmers were far from pleased. Claiming that the necessary funds had been delayed in transit from Paris, the authorities had been slow to compensate peasants whose animals had been taken from them— and the army's ongoing requisitioning of animals boded ill for farmwork the following year.[9] Without men or animals, work in the fields would be backbreaking.

In the Dordogne, mobilization also brought with it a temporary food crisis. Ever cognizant of Napoleon's famous adage that an army marches on its stomach, the army requisitioned, in addition to cattle and horses, much of the new wheat crop, monopolized significant salt supplies, and mobilized thousands of millers and bakers. Because inclement weather had delayed the harvest, damp grain recently harvested remained unmilled in early August, when mobilization took millers and bakers off

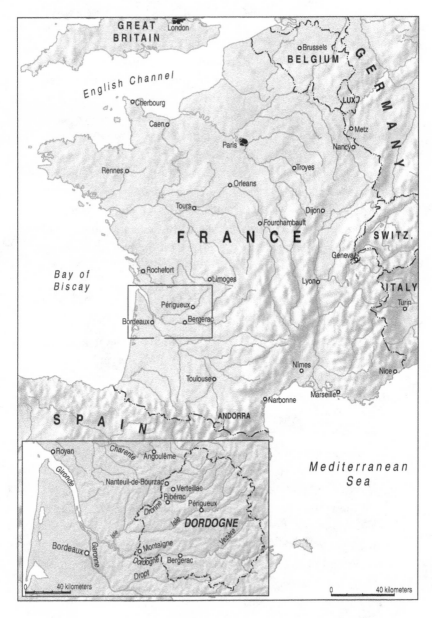

France (with inset of the Dordogne). Map by Philip Schwartzberg.

to war. Now deprived of millers to grind the flour and bakers to guarantee the bread supply, the department's largest towns—Périgueux and Bergerac—confronted real food shortages in the first weeks of August. To compound the problem, the price of flour rose exponentially as soon as war was declared, prompting bakers and consumers alike to believe that greedy peasants and mercenary millers were stockpiling supplies in hopes of reaping windfall profits. By 5 August the prefect believed that the department's bread supply could be assured only through the end of the month. But unlike many city dwellers, who customarily blamed all food shortages on peasant greed, he understood that the situation was more complicated than that. Not only were rural mayors obliged by law to help the army meet its almost insatiable need for grain, but they also had to reserve an adequate seed supply for the next planting. In the rocky soil of the Dordogne, this meant that perhaps as much as a quarter of the harvest had to be put aside as seed for the next crop. Only when these two needs were met could farmers think about selling their surplus to city folk.[10]

It was not just city dwellers who went hungry in August 1914. With more than three million men in uniform, the army's appetite for bread was so voracious and supplies of flour and salt so limited that the food crisis soon disrupted village life, too. In a community only a few miles northeast of Nanteuil-de-Bourzac, the baker had to suspend production of bread for lack of salt. An emergency shipment from Ribérac, with a promise of more to come from Angoulême, temporarily solved the crisis. But salt shortages persisted through the end of the month, disrupting daily life in some villages and most major towns and cities.[11] If, as seems likely, Nanteuil-de-Bourzac escaped the worst of the bread crisis, it is probably because at least one of the local millers was too old for military service and the villagers, who must have baked their own bread (for the census records show that there were no bakers in the commune), relied on their food cooperative for basic supplies.

Although the peasants of Nanteuil did not suffer physical hunger in the weeks following the outbreak of war, their appetite for news of military developments was as keen as any other civilians'. Few had greeted the war with any enthusiasm, but once resigned to its inevitability, all were determined to learn as much as they could, as quickly as possible, about developments that directly affected the men they loved. News, however, was scarcer than salt in the first weeks of the war. The French state was determined to thwart the circulation of any information that might cause panic. There thus emerged, from the earliest days of the war, a tension between what the civilian population wanted to know and what the state through its official intermediaries was willing to divulge. On 3 August the mayor of Ribérac asked the subprefect to share with him any news or official telegrams originating in Périgueux, so that his electorate could be fully informed of developments as they occurred. Although it was a simple matter to post news bulletins in Ribérac, where the subprefect was in daily telephone contact with the prefect, relaying news to outlying communities (even those relatively close to Ribérac) was more difficult, though politically just as necessary, for village mayors soon made it clear that their communities too were avid for news. To accommodate this deep-seated desire for information, the subprefect arranged for the printing and comprehensive circulation of daily *Bulletins de communes*. Reliable and regular distribution was, however, anything but assured. The bulletins were mailed from Ribérac, and given the near anarchy that reigned in the postal service at the beginning of the war, many went astray en route. To appease the anger of rural mayors, who consistently objected that their communes were being deprived of important information, the subprefect arranged for *Bulletins* to be posted in the railway stations of a dozen regional towns, including Verteillac, the closest town to Nanteuil-de-Bourzac.[12]

There was, of course, little to report in the first week of the war, when troops all over France were still in transit. And so, in the absence of real news, rumors abounded. Rumor was nothing new in this region of rural France. Rumors that brigands paid by antirevolutionary aristocrats were wandering their roads in the summer of 1789 had given rise to the Great Fear, during which the mob burned and ransacked the households of the nobility, destroying the seigneurial records that had forced the peasants to forfeit significant portions of their harvest each year to their aristocratic landlords. Eighty years later, the outbreak of the Franco-Prussian War generated a new wave of antiaristocratic rumors. In the commune of Hautefaye, only a few miles from Nanteuil-de-Bourzac, Alain de Monéys met a grisly fate in August 1870, when the assembled marketgoers, outraged by rumors that he was sympathetic to the enemy cause, tortured and then murdered him.[13] Antiaristocratic rumors persisted through 1914, when some peasants insisted that the Kaiser himself had taken up residence in a nearby château.[14] How he and his retinue had made their way from Berlin to southwest France remained unclear, or at least unexplained. Stories of this sort had to be contained, for experience showed that public order could easily be jeopardized if rumors went unchecked.

Very few residents of the Dordogne seem to have believed that the Kaiser was in their midst; but many were willing to accept that less distinguished enemy agents were everywhere. All foreigners were suspect, only occasionally with good cause. Police brought charges against an Austrian resident of a small town for cutting the telephone lines. But in more cases than not, the patriotic search for spies was driven by panic or xenophobia. Thus a crowd of close to five thousand enraged citizens ransacked the shop of a German clockmaker in Périgueux on 4 August 1914, believing that he had had the lack of restraint to proclaim, "Long live Germany." If mobs of five thousand unruly patriots bent on vigilante justice operated only in large towns, suspicion of strangers was rife throughout the department. The subprefect of Ribérac reported on 5 August that a young German girl, employed as a maid in Paris, was on vacation with a French girl in the tiny commune of Faye. It would be best, everyone concurred, to keep the suspicious young Fräulein under close watch, meanwhile intercepting any letters sent on to her from Paris. And just to be on the safe side, when an Italian nun visiting the Dordogne failed to file the appropriate declaration of residency, the local priest quickly brought this alarming irregularity to the attention of local authorities.[15]

Townspeople were particularly suspicious of anyone affluent enough to drive a car and, once a curfew restricting automobile travel to daylight hours went into effect, of anyone rash enough to drive at night. The subprefect of Ribérac noted on 8 August that drivers in several local towns had been set upon by angry crowds, all too ready to take them for spies. In Nanteuil-de-Bourzac, where no foreigners had resided for decades and local residents had only two years earlier had to go to Verteillac to find a car, strangers—especially those driving cars in the middle of the night—would have been viewed with wary eyes. It seems unlikely that the residents of Nanteuil would have been any more temperate in their judgments than their neighbors in the commune of Montignac-le-Coq, where the local schoolteacher noted wryly, "At the beginning of the war spies were seen everywhere." To protect themselves from suspicious travelers, a group of conscientious villagers set up a roadblock outside the village inn. While the self-appointed guards played cards inside, the road was barricaded by a chain swung

from lamppost to flagpole. When a similar setup in a neighboring commune caused an accident, the good citizens of
Montignac-le-Coq dismantled their defensive barrier. Dis-
missing the zealous, sometimes comical responses of their
neighbors, mayors throughout the region assured the police
commissioner that there was no reason to suspect the loyalty of
foreign residents in their communes. If spies were afoot, they
were not residing within the purview of vigilant, observant, and
patriotic mayors. Thus reassured, the police commissioner ran
announcements in newspapers urging the local population to
give no further credence to rumors of espionage.[16]

As rumor abated, real news made its way by telephone and
letter, through personal testimony and the pages of the press,
back to the Dordogne. The first news worth reporting occurred
on 7 August 1914, when French troops reclaimed the Alsatian
city of Mulhouse for France. Happy to tell his readers that
French victory had at last effaced the humiliating defeat of
1871, the editor of the *Avenir de la Dordogne* rushed the story into
print. But when the prefect got word that the French victory
was going to be prominently celebrated in the regional newspaper, he ordered the press run stopped and made certain that
the good news was purged from the paper's pages. Like the military commandant in Limoges, with whom he was in close
communication, the prefect feared that if civilian France knew
of every unexpected victory or unanticipated setback, excessive enthusiasm and excessive alarm could produce panic, mayhem, and disorder. His intervention was, however, in vain. The
mayor of Périgueux, as eager as the local editor to share the
good news, had authorized the distribution throughout the
town of posters announcing France's first victory. When the local citizenry read or heard the news, they broke into spontaneous celebration.[17]

The dancing in the streets was premature. Not only would

the French quickly lose their toehold in Alsace, but they would lose thousands of men in the process. And word soon surfaced in the Dordogne that all was not well on the eastern border. In a telephone call overheard by an inspector of the Postal and Telegraphic Service, a government official temporarily resident in Paris told his wife in the south of the Dordogne that France had suffered twenty thousand casualties during its advance into Alsace. Once Mme Roche had learned this dismal truth, how quickly would word spread among her friends and their acquaintances? Anxious to stifle such stories and the unease that inevitably accompanied them, the military commandant in Limoges issued a public call for calm: "Let us close our ears to false news, exaggerated in one way or another, and let us welcome only that news whose official provenance guarantees its authenticity." It was, he continued, the duty of private citizens as much as of the press to avoid the temptation to spread rumors that would "give rise to either premature hopes or unjustified alarm."[18]

Justified alarm was, presumably, another matter entirely. The French army suffered setbacks so severe and casualties so daunting—more than three hundred thousand French soldiers died in August and September alone—that fully a fifth of all French deaths suffered in more than four years of war were sustained in the first five weeks of combat. And even if the precise toll exacted in these early campaigns remained unknown at the time, civilians had more than an inkling of the unfolding disaster. An official communiqué, dated 28 August 1914, announced to an astonished nation that France held a line that extended from the Somme to the Vosges, thus admitting that Germany now occupied a significant swath of northern France. But many families in the Dordogne, whose men had been sent into Belgium in mid-August, learned a day before the government

communiqué conceded as much that the French were in retreat. On 27 August a convoy of wounded soldiers returned
to Périgueux, having seen action on the Belgian frontier. These
men soon told their families of the hard and bloody fighting France had recently endured: German forces had broken
through Belgium, repelled the French Fifth Army on the
Sambre River, and forced it into a 120-kilometer-long strategic
retreat. So vivid were the soldiers' tales, and so unsettling to
families whose men remained at the front with the Fifth Army,
that the prefect recommended that wounded troops no longer
be sent to their home base to convalesce. The effect of their
eyewitness accounts was too demoralizing and disturbing to
parents and neighbors.[19]

When it became evident that the French campaign into Belgium had failed utterly, civilians in the Dordogne openly criti-
cized the high command and questioned the commanders' professional judgment. Why, they wondered aloud, were so many
territorial troops being sent home on short-term leave when
the very future of France was hanging in the balance? Ignoring
the fact that many of the middle-aged men benefiting from
these temporary leaves were bakers, millers, and farmers—the
very men needed to address the food crisis that afflicted their
own villages and towns—disgruntled citizens insisted that all
able-bodied men be sent to the front immediately. It is probably just as well that Joseph Joffre, the French commander in
chief, was unmoved by the wisdom of these armchair strategists, for the reserves were to prove France's salvation in early
September. Unlike Germany, which had deployed most of its
reserves immediately, "France was able to make up its losses. By
not having used all its reserves from the outset, and by falling
back on to its lines of communications, it could bring over
100,000 men from the depots to fill its depleted ranks."[20]

The wisdom of this strategic thinking eluded many civilians far removed from the front in late August 1914. Knowing only that France had suffered a series of defeats—from Alsace in early August to the Ardennes, and westward to the Sambre on August 21—and being unable to anticipate the victory on the Marne that would halt the German advance in early September, they naturally feared that the debacle of 1870 was repeating itself. As the German army marched toward Paris and the French government relocated to Bordeaux, anxiety escalated. Presumably the Dordogne was safe enough, for surely the government would not establish headquarters in the adjacent department of the Gironde if there was reason to believe that southwest France would fall into German hands. But in these uncertain days, the prefect met with all mayors in the department to impress upon them the importance of maintaining calm in their communes. Their duties were clear: they had to guarantee the food supply, provide care for the wounded and shelter for civilian refugees fleeing Belgium and the now occupied departments of northern France, and cultivate in their communes an atmosphere of stoic resolution, uncompromised by alarmist rumors and pessimistic predictions.[21] This, then, was the message that Jean Pireaud took away from the meeting the prefect convened in Verteillac. He had to assure his wife, his daughter-in-law, and many others whose sons or husbands were in more direct danger than Paul that the fortification of Paris, the German occupation of northern France, and the apparent disarray of the French army were not causes for alarm. As good patriots, citizens were to have faith in their commanders and trust in their men. The calm demeanor with which they had confronted the declaration of war was as important now, in the early days of September, as ever.

As the prefect himself realized, however, maintaining the

stoic resolve of the rural population depended in large part on their ability to communicate regularly with their men at the front. In this regard, the experience of the first month of the war had been anything but reassuring. With the immediate mobilization of almost three million men and with every train given over to the transport of troops, the efficient and timely delivery of letters was, perhaps understandably, a low priority in the army's grand scheme of things. And when the mayhem of retreat combined with the constant movement of troops, the regular delivery of mail became even more difficult. Because men were always on the move and the front was in dangerous flux, civilian letters were often held back at distribution points, to be forwarded to their intended recipients perhaps once a week. Letters destined for the home front, sorted in departmental capitals and then sent on to their ultimate destination, were also subject to irksome delays. Mayors of towns and villages in the Dordogne had to contend with angry residents, some of whom "vigorously demonstrated their dissatisfaction" when letters that arrived in Périgueux were not delivered to outlying communities until the next day.[22]

Whatever the causes, the inefficient and unpredictable delivery of mail was unacceptable to civilians, soldiers, and state officials alike. When civilians received letters from the front that were vague and unfocused, they could not understand why their correspondents failed (or, as it seemed, refused) to respond directly to questions posed in previous letters. Did these silences signify indifference or, more alarming still, grave injury? Unaware that the letter that had posed the still unanswered question was probably sitting in a depot far behind the lines, families at home feared the worst and—in the judgment of the departmental prefect—often gave in to "a profound malaise that had to be put to rest." Men in uniform were equally disconcerted by long delays in mail delivery that kept them out of touch with home for weeks on end.[23] Even men located well behind the lines, as Paul was throughout the turmoil of August 1914, found the mail system infuriatingly unpredictable. In his first letter home, dated 9 August 1914, he begged for news of home and, sounding much like the young recruit who had first donned a uniform three years earlier, shamelessly begged Marie to write him often: "Write to me as soon as you can you will certainly make me cry to read your letters because I see the other guys crying when they receive letters from home." It would be two weeks, however, before he received a windfall of correspondence: four letters, three cards, and a food package. Although one of these letters had been sent only two days earlier, cards Marie had sent as early as 7 August and a letter written two days later had taken more than a week to make their way to Troyes, where Paul was temporarily (and very safely) stationed. His realization that Marie was fully occupied with the harvest prompted him to forgive what looked from his vantage point like a failure to write on a daily basis. At the same time, however, several consecutive days without word from home made him fear that he had already been forgotten in her affections. Only her letters, late arriving and grammatically flawed though they were, offered the reassurance that he craved: "I know that you love me still as much as I love you."[24]

As Paul fretted in Troyes, anxious to hear from his beloved "marquise," Marie struggled with the difficulty of getting news from Nanteuil to his depot. Thus when she received a card on 25 August in which Paul lamented, yet again, that he had not heard from her for ages, she walked five kilometers to the nearest post office, in the village of Salles-Lavalette, determined to get something through to him: "This morning I sent off two postcards because I am upset that you are receiving nothing I went to Salles to send you a telegram they didn't want to send it to Troyes. They sent it by way of Limoges. I think that you will get it. Before I leave I will write you this letter and will send it by registered mail I think that you will receive something."[25]

From her contact with other wives whose husbands were also in uniform, Marie knew by mid-August that many local men were on their way toward the Belgian border (where they would engage the enemy in ill-fated battle on 21 August). Such developments made her fear that Paul would soon be transferred to a frontline regiment. Paul admitted that many regiments temporarily based in Troyes were heading north, but he reassured her that his company was in no such danger. By the end of August, however, with the Germans pushing deeper into France, Marie suspected that Paul's regiment, still far behind the front lines, would soon be engulfed in the general retreat: "Only one thing I fear that when you receive my letter you will have already left Troyes the Prussians are advancing through the department of the Aisne and are heading toward Paris so unless the French push them back you will not remain where you are you will be forced to retreat." The situation seemed to grow ever more serious: on 4 September she noted that Paris was building fortifications to protect itself from enemy bombardment and that the Germans were now occupying "the Ardennes, the Aisne, the Vosges, the Meurthe." Well-informed though she was, Marie was interested only in how military developments would affect the security of her husband's situation: Was he safe, would he continue to be so, and would his company be forced into retreat? Her intuition that Troyes would soon be too close to the front lines to function efficiently as a supply depot was well founded: on 5 September, as the French prepared to stand their ground at the Battle of the Marne, Paul's company headed southwest from Troyes deep into the interior of France and temporarily set up camp in the tiny town of Fourchambault, in the department of Nièvre.[26]

When Marie wrote in mid-September, she confessed that she was "desperate that you have not received any letters because I write every day a card or letters and you tell me that you receive nothing. Today I am sending you a military card and I think that you will receive that . . . I hope that you will receive these two little words that I am sending you and that you will receive all my letters you will have something to read I assure you that I write every day." With the stabilization of the front that occurred after the Battle of the Marne, irregular mail delivery became something of a rarity. Although the postal service sometimes lost mail, and intentionally held it back in advance of major offensives (so that the enemy could not intercept letters containing clues to troop movements and concentrations), for the most part it functioned with extraordinary efficiency: mail often arrived at the front within three days. The establishment of a regular and reliable postal delivery system, strongly recommended by the prefect of the Dordogne in September 1914, went a long way toward calming the fears of civilians and soldiers alike. If family correspondence, replete as it was with unsettling stories and unexplained silences, did not succeed fully in setting minds at rest, it did make conversation with those far away a reality for the nation at war.

In the aftermath of the Battle of the Marne, the opposing armies slowly dug themselves into trenches that would extend from the English Channel to the Alps: thereafter, the stalemate of trench warfare—the tragic signature of the Great War—replaced the fluidity of the first six weeks of the war. This stalemate would haunt military commanders, who tried in vain to devise a strategy of offensive warfare that would break the deadlock, and frontline troops, which witnessed the deaths of thousands sacrificed in these unsuccessful assaults. When it became evident that the short war that both sides had anticipated was not to be, civilians as well as soldiers had to adapt to this new reality. In rural society, this meant that the young women, teenage children, and elderly men who remained at home had to assume responsibility for the long-term operation of the farms left in their stewardship.

No sooner was the harvest of 1914 complete than work began on the winter seeding. Teenage boys and older men assumed principal responsibility for the arduous task of preparing the soil, but with so many men at war, women were no longer exempt from heavy agricultural labor. In peacetime they were expected to care for their children, maintain their household, take charge of the farmyard, the orchard, and the vegetable garden, and help with the harvest; plowing and tilling the soil had remained men's work. From 3 August 1914 onward, those more taxing tasks often fell to women whose husbands were away at war, whose children were too young to help, and whose parents were themselves overburdened by the demands of daily life. Although it remained exceptional (if not unknown) for women to take charge of the plow,[27] all other tasks fell within their competence. In mid-September Marie reported that her father was "working in the fields every day and we should be able in spite of the bad weather to sow everything." By late October, however, bad weather, the bane of every farmer's existence, threatened to thwart their best efforts. To make up for time already lost, Marie joined forces with her father to get the beet and potato crops into the ground. While he harnessed two of their cows to plow the beet field, she took

the other two into the potato field. After this hard day in the
fields, she still found the time—and the energy—to write a
long and very affectionate letter. Having summarized her day's
activities, she closed: "I don't have much else to say except that
I think of you and that I wish that you could come back to me
because believe me I find this waiting long . . . To give myself
courage I tell myself that everyone else is the same and that I
am in fact better off than most because you are not in danger
and so many others are facing life and death. If only you could
stay with the bake ovens I would be happy."[28]

Even in the depth of winter, which in early 1915 was bit-
ingly cold as far south as the Dordogne, the daily tasks of farm
life were unceasing. At forty-seven years old, Paul's mother,
Rosa, was not supposed to be breaking her back threshing
grain. But the war left her little opportunity to take life easy, as
she noted in a poignant letter penned in mid-January 1915.
"My dear son I am taking advantage of this little moment of
tranquility to write you because we have been threshing today
and I assure you it's a real bother I promise you your poor
wife and I have had lots of work these last few days to prepare
everything because the folks from Montignac brought their
wheat here to be threshed with ours . . . They had 18 sacks and
we had 19 you see how things are." Judging that "the army is
bad for everyone," she stoically resigned herself to her lot:
"One must endure that which one can't prevent." In closing, she
reassured Paul that everyone sent love and best wishes and
asked that he overlook the sorry state of her letter: "You will
forgive me for not writing on the lines—in the evenings I don't
see too well and during the days I don't have time [to write]."[29]

Rosa was grateful that Marie's brother-in-law, Louis, who
had been home for a week, had been able to help with the
threshing before heading back to the front. But it soon became

obvious that prospects for the spring planting season and the summer harvest were bleak. As the army prepared for offensive campaigns in the region north of Arras and farther east in Champagne, few men would be eligible for agricultural leave to help on their family farms. Nor would it be easy to enrich the soil in preparation for the summer growing season. In late February 1915, Marie noted that nitrate fertilizer, a staple agricultural commodity by the early twentieth century, was now being "mobilized," and she opined, "If this is true it will be a pretty business my father is going to go to Verteillac on Sunday to see about this he doesn't want to clear the stubble because he says that if no one has any nitrate that it won't be worth the bother that the wheat will be nothing and he says that it is too late for this year." Although Bernard was able to order four balls of nitrate (only two of which were eventually delivered), neither he nor Marie believed that this would meet their needs. And if, as rumor had it, the state was going to requisition two of their four cows, there would be little manure to make up the shortfall.[30] Deprived of chemical and animal fertilizers, the crops, she feared, were going to be meager at best.

Marie took little consolation in knowing that it was the same for everyone, given that the land clearing done in October had not been as effective as in previous years. "Let us hope," she wrote at the beginning of March, "that the nitrate will fix everything and that all will work out because the soil is good. How long it seems till you can come home to take up your work again *and our caresses.*" As if loneliness, inadequate supplies, and anxieties about low crop yields were not worrisome enough, in the first week of March the weather turned foul: heavy rains, which threatened to flood out the low-lying land surrounding Moulin du Pont, then turned to hail and snow that, when combined with a sharp wind, made it feel like early

January. Work, however, continued. At the beginning of April, Marie noted that weather notwithstanding, they were not too far behind with their crops: the potatoes were seeded, the vines trimmed and fertilized, and the beets were coming along. Perhaps all would be well, but Marie, who had a good head for business, saw some unsettling signs on the horizon. Nitrate that had cost thirty-one francs in March was selling for forty-five francs a month later, when a quintal of wheat sold on the open market for only twenty-four francs and fifty centimes. Marie made no apologies for selling their surplus wheat at the local fair for more than the army would pay if it were requisitioned: if they sold their grain to the army at twenty-three francs they "would lose too much." By the end of May, when the villagers were busy mowing the hay meadows, she was optimistic that Italy's recent entry into the war would bring a quick and decisive Entente victory: "If only this could bring us an end because as you know everything is bothering us we have lots of work . . . In any event, we will only do that which we can the most urgent." Although the wheat crop looked "beautiful," it seemed likely that "lots of fodder crops and wheat are going to be lost imagine all the houses where there is only a woman and the children . . . How sad the countryside is."[31]

By the spring of 1915, it was evident that even those who could call on the help of an extended family had reached the limits of their endurance. Marie's parents had to work their own land while also helping their older daughter and Marie. She, in turn, did what she could to help her parents, her sister, and her in-laws. It was especially irksome, therefore, that Charlotte seemed to begrudge the time she spent helping Paul's parents at Moulin du Pont. There was certainly no love lost between Marie and Charlotte, who was not only Marie's sister-in-law but also the wife of Marie's cousin, Joseph Bardy. True, Charlotte had her own land to worry about, but Marie believed that she could be doing more to help the parents who had taken her in and given her a real home. In these hard times, cooperation was surely the order of the day. When Paul inquired in early June whether Charlotte was volunteering to work on his parents' land, Marie responded caustically: "She says that she doesn't give any more effort to the others than at Moulin and that at least she isn't working for the others. Because every time that she does the least bit of work at Moulin she says that I am [off] working for others . . . She doesn't like me, I can tell you, but I believe that I have never hated and detested anyone the way she does."[32]

However willing (or unwilling) family members were to help one another, they could not escape the harsh reality that there were by the spring of 1915 too few hands and too much work. Although women whose families owned or held long term-leases on land did what they could to keep their farms under cultivation, day laborers who had no land to call their own were likely to abandon farmwork when their labor contracts expired.[33] Whether they gave themselves over to a life of idleness (as the prefect suspected) or sought lucrative jobs in the munitions factory in Bergerac, they had no reason to stay in the country. This meant that the families who did remain on the land had fewer and fewer workers to help bring in the harvest. Teenage boys too young for military service were available, if one could afford their wages. Marie reported that her sister had recently hired a fifteen-year-old to help with her farm. He would work three days a week, earning 2 francs 50 a day (a year earlier a day laborer had earned, on average, only 1 franc 56). This would, Marie judged, make everyone's life easier: "I assure you that this will be good for us because having cut the hay and wheat at her farm, they will be able to gather it up while we cut our own."[34]

Nonetheless, the bigger picture was disconcerting. When

Paul inquired whether the village had pulled together in a spirit of fraternity to bring in the crops, Marie had little good to report. "As for goodwill, what can one say, it's like all the other years . . . The war changes nothing and nobody helps anyone else now . . . If one poor person suffers a misfortune then the others laugh behind her back, so let's not talk about it any more because it's shameful we were harvesting the same day as my sister she had 22 men and 10 women [to help her] you can see that she found a lot of people the next day I went to Coutancie to help Nadal's wife, she was harvesting with 9 men and 21 women ask yourself how that happens. As for us, we had 19 men and 9 women. To get men, you have to go a long way to look for them."[35]

Men were in short supply, but so were animals. Many had been requisitioned, and pregnant and lactating cows were unfitted for the heavy work of plowing and powering the village threshing machine. Marie noted in July, "We are badly off when it comes to animals. One of them has her calf and Barotte is now in labor. My father says that he wants to keep this calf because she is going to be fatter than the other one . . . We won't be able to raise both of them in this season because the mothers won't have enough milk." When inadequate fodder crops reduced the cows' milk supply and cows set to heavy labor in the fields could not produce enough milk to support a calf, it seemed foolish to keep both calves. Marie happily reported that she had been able to sell one of them for 80 centimes per livre—a significant improvement on the prewar price of only 50 centimes—which put 172 francs in her purse. Harvest news was not so encouraging, however: whereas Lescure would ordinarily have harvested forty quintals of wheat, the farm realized only twenty-eight in 1915. When all the crops were in, the Pireaud and Andrieux lands had yielded only forty-four quintals of wheat and ten of oats, a poor showing by comparison with those in previous years. Knowing that Paul would be disappointed, Marie counseled resignation: "Console yourself it's the same everywhere and how many will there be who will not have enough to live."[36]

Recognizing that mobilization brought real financial hardship to many families, the French state moved quickly in August 1914 to introduce military allowances for households whose principal breadwinner, whether a son or a husband, had been mobilized. Each household that could demonstrate financial need was entitled to receive one franc twenty-five per day, for the duration of the war, with an additional daily allocation of fifty centimes for each dependent child. Given that the soldiers themselves received the paltry sum of only twenty-five centimes a day, this was a program with real heft: as many commentators at the time and many have subsequently observed, the French countryside was soon awash in cash. Administering the allowances was, however, no simple task, and disputes about eligibility, rumors of malfeasance, and suspicions about the rectitude of the administrators and the honesty of the applicants made for interesting gossip, hard feelings, and lingering resentment. Shortly after the law was promulgated on 5 August, the prefect of the Dordogne called upon every mayor in the department to begin processing applications for military allowances. When several local mayors complained that the application process was unnecessarily cumbersome, requiring several separate pieces of documentation to establish eligibility, the subprefect of Ribérac assured them that the program could be administered very simply: each mayor had only to write down the specific circumstances of each applicant on a piece of blank paper and forward this to the regional committees that were ready by late August to review the applications.[37]

Perhaps this uncharacteristic informality contributed to the allegations of favoritism that beset the program from the start. Women whose applications were denied were quick to complain if their neighbors' were approved. Recognizing that the state stood to gain very little if the rural population was disaffected, the prefect urged local review committees to be prompt and generous in their adjudications. Consequently, negative decisions originating from the earliest weeks of the war, when the principle of economic hardship was most rigorously applied, were often overturned on appeal. This seems to have been true in the Dordogne and the neighboring Charente, where, for example, the allocation committee responsible for the town of Montmoreau reversed on appeal all thirty-six of its original negative judgments.[38] Welcome though these adjustments were, they did not solve all the problems identified with the military allowance program. In some parts of the country, women complained that the administrators were—like the notorious shop owner who came to a grisly end in Zola's *Germinal*—all too prone to extort sexual favors from women when they went to collect their monthly check.[39] Others complained that the program discriminated against some, while giving a financial advantage to others. If, for example, parents claimed their son as their principal breadwinner (as they were entitled to do) and his wife (justifiably) made the same claim, only one household would receive the allowance. Nor could parents receive more than one allowance, even if they had two or more sons in uniform. At the same time, however, two married women—whether mother and daughter, two sisters, or mother and daughter-in-law—who decided to share the same household for the duration of the war could receive two separate allowances if both had husbands in uniform. When some seemed to profit excessively from the system, while others profited not all, it was easy to see injustice afoot.[40]

In Nanteuil-de-Bourzac Jean Pireaud administered the military allowance program with a generous hand, admirable efficiency, and personal rectitude. Marie noted in the spring of 1915 that all the applications he had processed for women in the commune had been approved. As a result, some women were living better than ever and made no apologies for doing so. One woman, of whom Marie spoke bitterly, "happily eats her" daily allowance; others remarked "that never had they been so happy" as they were in the summer of 1915. Comments of this type made Marie furious, in part because she could not imagine being happy while her husband was away at war, in part because she received no military allowance. Jean Pireaud, aware of rumors that village mayors often favored their own when reviewing applications for the military allowances, was determined that no one would say such things about him, and he thus refused to approve Marie's application. Paul, much to Marie's dismay, seconded his father's judgment. Indeed, had Paul insisted, his father would have submitted Marie's application to the review board. Paul refused to press the case. Convinced that the war would soon be over, he believed that it would be inappropriate to accept the government's money for the duration. Marie's fury—directed at her father-in-law and Paul alike—was unbounded: their scruples deprived her of the independence that other women now flaunted.[41]

With so much cash flowing into the countryside, distant observers wondered whether the allowance system was not in fact too generous. Critics charged that peasant women could now indulge in luxuries that had theretofore been available only to women of more refined and affluent background.[42] More worrisome still was the belief that the allowance system encouraged laziness. Would women who were guaranteed ten francs fifty a week bother to work the land at all? To put paid to this fear, the prefect of the Dordogne reported in May 1915: "The great majority of beneficiaries of the allowances are farm families . . . Among the owners and the tenant farmers I have never noticed that the allowances have had the effect of weakening their will either to work or to save, which constitutes one of the most inherent traits of our rural population." Many rural school-teachers agreed: there was no evidence of incipient indolence in their villages. Families certainly had more money than ever before, but in communities near Nanteuil "the payment of the allowances did not bring about the cessation of labor on the part of the beneficiaries." The allowances made it possible for women to give their children a few more treats, but no one used the cash payments as an excuse not to work. In the distant department of the Rhône, the prefect came to the same conclusion in March 1916: the cash payments helped rural families face their trials with patience, but they did not entice peasant cultivators to abandon their lands in pursuit of a life of indolence.[43]

Even if the critics were correct and the countryside was being corrupted by unseemly supplies of cash, some (perhaps much) of this newfound wealth was immediately redirected to men in uniform. This, at least, was the considered judgment of the teacher in Vaux-Lavalette, a village a few kilometers from Nanteuil, who observed that the monthly stipends allowed wives and parents to send much-needed money to their menfolk at the front.[44] Getting cash to men in uniform in fact became something of a national pastime. When families learned that the delivery of registered letters to the front was slow and inefficient, they complained mightily to local administrators and demanded immediate improvements.[45] Even families ineligible, for whatever reason, for an allowance did what they could to send money to husbands or sons. As early as September 1914, Marie fretted that Paul was ill equipped for a winter campaign and insufficiently paid to outfit himself adequately. Aware that her friend Emilie had "already sent money twice to her husband," Marie was eager to do the same for Paul. Allowance or no allowance, she could not abide the thought of his suffering from the cold. "I want to know how you are sleeping if you have horse blankets. It seems to me that you must need your wool vest, socks, and flannel underwear. I want to know if you have bought them. I know that you must need money because with the high cost of everything you must need some . . . If you can get it, I promise you that I won't waste a minute in sending you some."[46]

Neither Paul's repeated reassurances that he needed nothing but regular affirmations of his wife's abiding affection nor his insistence that she keep whatever cash she had were of any use. Marie's desire to send him money and warm clothing became a constant refrain throughout the winter and spring of 1915. Thus, in February she wrote: "If you want anything don't hesitate to ask me for it I will be happy if you tell me send me this or that at least I will see that you aren't afraid to ask me for it instead of depriving yourself. I beg you ask, don't be afraid, and I will be happy to be able to send you whatever it is that you want." At the end of May, she promised to send him as much money as he needed: "I will send it to you immediately because I beg you don't deprive yourself of anything . . . as for me here never going out I have no need of it, so don't be afraid to ask for some . . . I understand that those who don't have any money are not happy." And within days of selling the calf, Marie sent Paul twenty francs, the receipt of which he gratefully acknowledged: "I thank you with all my heart I see that you are thinking of me my beloved little wife and I would love to be able to thank you as you deserve and as you would like to be thanked as well but what can be done I can only send you tokens of my love."[47]

Access to cash also made it easier for women to send packages of food and warm clothing to their men at the front. Although letters sent to and from the front lines were delivered without charge, postal rates still applied to packages, much to the indignation of many mobilized men. Paul complained more than once that the state was taking advantage of its citizens by charging what he took to be extortionate rates for parcel post. Others worried that their parents were bankrupting themselves by sending packages to the front. The cost of parcel post—and regulations that prohibited the shipment of liquids, food items, and all perishable goods—offered little deterrence, however, to anyone determined to keep in touch with men at the front: the postal service handled more than two hundred thousand parcels every day.[48] Most were filled with homemade delicacies, meat and fruit, and bottles of alcohol (often disguised as "medicine"). Although not every package arrived in good condition or with the contents fit for consumption, what did weather the journey made a welcome change from the monotony of mess food, and in a nation renowned for the rich variety of its regional cuisines, the packages were much-appreciated reminders of home.

Marie, her mother-in-law, and her sister worked together to guarantee that Paul would be well provided for. In the autumn and winter months, when the garden was past its prime and fruit trees were no longer bearing, Marie filled her packages with homemade jams and warm clothing. Having heard that local men were suffering frostbite and, in one case at least, dying of exposure at the front, she could not bear to think of Paul, warmly billeted though he was, unprotected against the cold of early 1915. Nor could she bear to think of him going hungry.

She sent a package in mid-January that included a warm vest, two rabbits (with a little cooking fat, so that they could be properly prepared in the local style), and a bottle of wine. A month later, in anticipation of Mardi Gras, she assembled a package that included a roast chicken, one bottle of wine and another of brandy, a few apples, and more warm clothing. Although the parcel did not arrive in time for Mardi Gras, Paul assured her that he and his mates had enjoyed more than one meal thanks to her bounty. Unlike his good friend, Chavenat, who had received no box of festive delicacies because his wife had taken seriously the warnings in the press about the prohibition on the shipment of food packages, Paul was grateful that his wife was more determined to spoil him than to observe petty regulations punctiliously. He worried, however, that she would soon wear herself out preparing the lavish packages. Marie would not think of abandoning this enterprise, which she took to be a sign of her abiding affection: "You tell me not to send you packages so often that the war will last for so long that I will wear myself out, think about it for you I will never become tired of this and what's more this summer I will not be able to send you very much because it will spoil if I could I would send everything to you, Paul, whom I love and I would leave myself nothing." By early summer, when heat threatened to spoil uncooked meat but fresh fruit and vegetables were abundant, Marie and her mother-in-law sent Paul strawberries from the farm, and she and her sister prepared a package that included new socks, cherries (which, being crushed in transit, ruined the socks), artichokes, and a bottle of cassis.[49]

Paul appreciated the love with which Marie assembled her packages, but feared that she was depriving herself of necessities in order to pamper him with little luxuries. When he received the money she sent at the end of May 1915, he implored her to keep funds for herself, for he knew that however much cash was now circulating in the countryside, life was hard at home: "I thank you from the bottom of my heart for your devotion on my behalf and I would like to be able to thank you directly and to save you all your fears that you must have because I can see from here what our poor countryside must be like each time that we talk about it among my buddies tears come to my eyes. I beg of you keep your money, I have less need of it than you do."[50]

Overworked muscles and underproductive fields were not, of course, the worst aspect of life in wartime. For guardians of the home front, nerves were stretched to the breaking point and life was plagued by relentless anxiety. Men from Nanteuil-de-Bourzac came through the brutal fighting of the early weeks of war relatively unscathed. Some had been wounded, but none seriously. Given that Paul's former regiment had fought at the Marne, this was good news indeed.[51] Within weeks, however, more somber news began trickling back. Several local men who had been taken prisoner had written to reassure their families that they were being well treated. Marie was cautiously optimistic, for rumors of German atrocities circulated freely in the fall of 1914: she wrote, "If only the Germans don't kill them now that they are prisoners then they risk nothing." More distressing was the story of Maria Fabas. A foster child who had grown up in Nanteuil on a farm owned by the Videau family, she had married and settled in the nearby village of Vaux-Lavalette. When "the mayor of Veau [sic] received word of the death of her husband who died in the hospital, having succumbed to his wounds, he didn't have the courage to tell her." So Maria went on hoping, while everyone else knew the truth. Chastened by this tale, Marie resolved "to wait patiently" for Paul's return: "There are many who are more unfortunate than I."[52]

The Videau family must have sympathized over Maria's loss, but with two sons at the front, Léon and Henri, the parents had more immediate cares, too. Léon was one of Paul's closest friends; two years his senior, he was someone in whom Paul often confided. Indeed, he wrote to Léon so often that Marie warned her husband to be careful what he said. In February 1915 everyone in Nanteuil believed that Paul and his friend Chavenat were now on the front lines, and Marie was not eager to disabuse them of this belief. But the truth would quickly circulate if Paul was not careful in what he wrote to Léon, who—Marie noted a touch disdainfully—told the "old folks" everything. When so many other village men were on the front lines, Marie wanted to preempt ugly rumors to the effect that Paul was not doing his bit. The Videaus already resented the fact that both their sons were in direct danger, while others were threatened only by bedbugs and chilblains. Within days, their anxieties and no doubt their animosities intensified, when they received word that Léon had been seriously wounded. Through much of February, rumors circulated in the community that one of the Videau sons had been wounded, but no one seemed to know more than that. Then, on 8 March, Marie wrote: "Yesterday evening, coming back from your parents' place, I met Pierre [Léon's father] he told me that on 17 February Léon was wounded in the head and the shoulder by an exploding shell at the moment the medics took him away he told a friend to write his parents for him, that he would also write his parents as soon as he got to the hospital but since then nothing, no news no one knows where he is without the letter from his friend we would know nothing and his parents are very afraid."[53]

The awful silence that so often signified a death at the front afflicted Marie's extended family as well. In late January, only a few weeks after her brother-in-law, Louis, had been home helping with the threshing, he appeared to have gone missing in action. On 22 January Marie noted that there had been no letter or postcard from him for more than two weeks, and everyone feared that he had been killed at Soissons. Whatever hard feelings Marie might once have harbored toward her brother-in-law had long since been set aside, and she now anxiously awaited word of his fate. When news finally came at the end of the month, Marie was delighted to report that Louis was in fact alive, and assigned for the moment at least to a quiet sector. If the Andrieux family had been spared, the Pireauds were not so fortunate. In late February 1915, Marie took upon herself the sorrowful task of telling Paul that his cousin, Elie, had been killed by a shell on the Somme: "They were on the front line when the shell splinter hit him he died without coming to." A week after Elie's death, his parents had not yet received official confirmation; they had instead heard indirectly, from his best friend. The two young men had done their military service together and, finding themselves in the same unit at the front, had "promised each other that the first one to be killed would be buried by the other in a cemetery with a wreath. That's what he did, took him to the cemetery and buried him there." Knowing that news of his death would devastate his parents, Elie had also asked that his friend first notify Paul's father (Elie's uncle), who would then break the news to the young man's parents. Marie concluded her sad missive: "I will tell you it is a death that has hit a lot of people hard he was killed on 19 February."[54]

News of this type gave Marie much to think about during the dreary, lonely winter of 1915. She considered herself fortunate that Paul was still safely behind the lines, but she also knew that nothing was certain in these uncertain times. A local woman's mournful story made her reflect on the cruel unpredictability of life in wartime. On 14 February Marie confided that she had "just learned a very sad piece of news which pains me a great deal, I feel intensely for poor Marie because she is someone I liked a lot." Her school friend Marie Blois had just learned of her husband's death. He had been wounded some time earlier, had been sent to convalesce in a hospital near the front, and, when he had fully recuperated, had returned to the trenches, where he contracted a severe fever (perhaps typhoid, which raged through the French trenches in the winter of 1914–15). Confined to a hospital in the Pas-de-Calais and probably suspecting that he was going to die, he had sent for his wife. She had made it as far as Angoulême when her parents received word that he had died. Marie Pireaud admitted that news of this sort depressed her, and she begged Paul: "Take care of yourself so that nothing will happen to you." In a subsequent letter, she reflected further on the fragility of their lives: "Recognizing that you are safe and that we alarm ourselves unnecessarily [it is still true that] the war is not over and for as long as it continues one cannot know one's fate. So one can't be happy (as for me, I am not happy ever) and I believe that it's the same for everyone else."[55]

As news circulated in the commune that local men had been taken prisoner, seriously wounded, or killed at the front, Marie knew that her circumstances were better than most: although she worried that Paul's company would be sent to the front or—and this was increasingly likely in the late spring and early summer of 1915—that he would be transferred to a frontline infantry regiment, she could and did take comfort in the fact that in the short term at least he was safe. From Paul's point of view, his situation well behind the lines was welcome for another reason: it made it possible for Marie to visit him for a few days or, if all went well, a few weeks. The stalemated war gave Paul and Marie opportunities to see each other that the army's earlier mobility had denied them. And as long as this remained the case, much of their energy, and a great deal of their ink, went into planning how they could spend a weekend or longer ardently engaged in forgetting the war.

Conjugal visits were essentially illegal. An army regulation dated 28 August 1914 prohibited men assigned to depots from bringing their wives and families to stay with them.[56] Experience would show that this order, frequently reissued, was difficult to enforce, arbitrarily administered, and often completely ignored by the rank and file and their commanding officers alike. Indeed, conjugal visits became something of a cause célèbre in the spring of 1915, when newspapers reported the tragic tale of a tempestuous couple, Captain and Mme Hérail. Determined not to be separated from her husband, who was stationed behind the lines in late 1914, the intrepid and perhaps unbalanced Mme Hérail journeyed to Narbonne, where she, and many other army wives, set up residence. When officers received orders to send their families home, all the other wives accepted without demur, but not Mme Hérail. In the angry confrontation that ensued, Captain Hérail shot and killed his wife. Placed under psychiatric observation in the following months, the now notorious captain went on trial in April 1915; he was acquitted. Echoes of the famous Caillaux trial were inescapable: less than a year earlier, Henriette Caillaux had murdered the editor of a prominent Parisian newspaper to prevent the publication of private correspondence that would have compromised the reputation of her politically ambitious husband; although the evidence against her was incontrovertible, Mme Caillaux emerged from her trial in July 1914 exonerated.

Not quite a year later, the Hérail case suggested that when it came to crimes of passion and honor, men were as likely as women to get off the hook.[57]

If those who read about the Hérail trial in the press had any second thoughts about the merits of conjugal visits, they soon suppressed them. André Kahn, who was serving as a stretcher bearer on the front lines in the spring of 1915, wrote about the trial in one of his letters to his mistress but showed no hesitation in encouraging her to visit him behind the lines.[58] Indeed, so many men, whether permanently situated at the rear or only temporarily relegated to rest camps, assumed that their wives or girlfriends would be able to spend some time with them in the military zone that the army had to repeat its injunction against conjugal visits at irregular intervals for months on end. When officers were blatantly ignoring the regulation—on one occasion, Paul went to town to escort his captain's wife back from the railway station—enlisted men were no more likely to observe it. Some visits were less successful than others (though none was as disastrous as that of Mme Hérail). Paul wrote in February 1915 that one of the men in his unit had found himself in an awkward situation when his wife had arrived in Melun a week ahead of schedule. Far from being delighted by this unexpected good fortune, Paul's comrade seemed seriously inconvenienced: "Madame Debernat arrived last evening and her husband wasn't expecting her for another week and my word . . . [sic]. I don't know." This whiff of scandal intrigued Marie, who wondered whether Debernat had told his wife "what it was that he had or was it hidden as if nothing was wrong. In a word, tell me what you know, I'm interested in all of it and it helps me pass the time." Paul couldn't say for sure, but he believed that "Debernat is cured but perhaps not it's difficult to know what happened between him and his wife."[59]

Perhaps bemused by Debernat's predicament, Paul was nonetheless appalled when women abused the system of conjugal visits: having secured from their local mayor the passes needed for travel to the military sector, they would, he averred, then steal away for an illicit weekend with a new lover. Depot towns provided ample evidence of such misbehavior, but there was also, as Paul well knew, evidence of honest wives' braving everything to be with their husbands, no matter how uncomfortable the conditions or how difficult the enterprise. Train travel was time-consuming, expensive, and unreliable; young women of respectable reputation were not supposed to travel alone; and accommodations in towns near the lines were tawdry and unappealing. None of these obstacles was sufficient, however, to deter Paul and Marie.

Paul had been away from Nanteuil less than a month when he and his army mate Chavenat first made plans for their wives to visit. Now that the company was settled in Troyes and military action still remote, Paul proposed that Marie visit him there as soon as her harvest duties were complete. He calculated that she could safely make the trek across central France, especially if she and Mme Chavenat, who lived near enough to Nanteuil to make the plan practicable, were to travel together. He promised that he would find a reputable hotel where Marie could stay for a week or more. Marie was as excited by this prospect as Paul: "I would be so happy if I could stay with you a little you cannot imagine the joy that I would feel I would brave everything and risk everything to be with you again." Although Marie did not know Mme Chavenat, she welcomed the opportunity to travel with her so that they could both visit their husbands: "If I were sure that she wanted to go there too I would be ready to leave." Nonetheless, she feared that with the German army making steady progress through the north of

France, Paul's company would be forced to leave Troyes before she could make the trip to visit him. "I would be very happy to go and visit you but I'm afraid that when I get to Troyes you will have had to leave what will I do in the middle of all those soldiers and then to come home again that would be even harder for us than the first time I would never be able to come back. How I would like to be able to go and find you and bring you back with me when will this war end which causes so many tears how happy I would be to be able to see you again and embrace you." She calculated, "In a few days if the Germans are forced back how happy I would be to come and find you I would go and see you."[60]

The company's relocation first to Fourchambault and subsequently to Melun proved Marie right: this was no time for romantic trysts. Even Paul, who rarely saw obstacles serious enough to thwart his plans, had to concede as much when he found himself on the very margins of the Marne battlefield. In the aftermath of the battle, the Germans were only twelve kilometers away, all locals had been pressed into service burying the German and French dead, and support troops were strictly forbidden access to the town. This prohibition did not stymie one of Paul's friends, who successfully met up with his wife at Melun, but it did stir the wrath of the company captain: henceforth the scofflaw soldier was not allowed to sleep in town. Whether his punishment was commuted in mid-September, when Paul reported enthusiastically that all married men, of whatever rank, were allowed to sleep in town and have their wives visit, remains unclear. What is clear is that Paul was now determined that Marie should visit as soon as possible. All impediments had now vanished: the crops were harvested, the Germans were in retreat, and the army was, for the moment at least, unusually cooperative. All Marie had to do was buy a train ticket. But just in case she had any lingering doubts about the propriety or safety of such an enterprise, Paul played what he hoped would be his winning card. If Marie were to come to Melun, she would save him from the discomfort and the dangers of sleeping rough: "You could help me avoid sleeping on straw which I am beginning to find pretty hard and you could also help me avoid getting sick because I am already coughing quite a bit." How could she resist? Within the week, Marie prepared to depart for Melun.[61]

The romantic, erotic plans of the recently married young couple ran afoul, however, of the hard-headed realism and moral scruples of middle-aged parents. As a young woman, only recently married and still childless, Marie retained much of the dependent status that traditionally accrued to unmarried women. Peasant culture held that a woman was her father's dependent until marriage, her husband's thereafter, and only fully adult in the eyes of the village community upon the birth of her first child.[62] Protecting the virtue of a married but childless woman, and hence the legitimacy of the family inheritance, was not only a husband's concern, but also the concern and responsibility of his extended family. Thus Marie found herself in an unusual state: married but economically and to a certain extent physically constrained by the will of her in-laws, who in the absence of their son assumed responsibility for protecting his wife's honor and his patrimony. Paul's father took these responsibilities seriously. Adamant that Marie not travel alone on trains thronged with undisciplined soldiers, he resolved to chaperone her on the journey to Melun. When he learned from the local stationmaster that the trip would take at least a week—in which time Paul's company might have been relocated yet again (as in fact it was)—he vetoed the trip entirely. Marie was furious: "I am not happy I wanted to go there by myself, never am I mistress of my own life, neither with my parents or with yours, they didn't want me to go saying that it was too dangerous . . . I curse myself for having been so weak and not to have left in spite of everything." Determined that interfering in-laws would not come between her and her husband again and distraught at the idea that Paul might consider her absence a sign of indifference, she reassured him that she still loved him immeasurably: "While waiting to receive word from you soon that you still love me and that you forgive me, I send you my very best kisses your wife who loves you and will never forget you. Receive all these marvelous caresses goodbye my dear little husband whom I love so much when will this martyrdom end when will we be able to live happily together and resume once more our interrupted happiness, while hoping for that day let us be brave as before and we will succeed."[63]

Paul, having suspected that his parents were at fault, did not blame Marie for having missed their assignation. He did, however, do everything he could to persuade her to venture out without a parental chaperone. Not only did he emphasize that he would "prefer it if [Marie] were to come alone," but he insisted that whatever his parents might think, a young married woman could safely and respectably travel alone—"I tell you again that you could have come by yourself, there are plenty of women who are traveling right now by themselves, all those who are young and alone and then there is always someone from whom you can ask directions." Paul's parents were not easily persuaded, however, for his father did accompany Marie when at last she set off in early October for Fourchambault, where the company was once again headquartered. They were away from Nanteuil for only a few days and returned with letters for local families that had sons or husbands also serving with Paul's unit, and with verbal reassurances for Emilie, Marie's friend and confidante, that she had nothing to fear as long as her husband remained at Fourchambault. Marie came home in a calmer frame of mind, too: "I was happy to have seen you because I now know how things are with you and that you are not too unhappy. Only I feel very much alone now, more alone than before going to visit you; in any case, if only this would all end quickly and you could come home to me, what a joy that would be."[64]

No sooner was she home than they made plans to meet again. Several circumstances thwarted their plans temporarily—the death of Paul's grandmother, which kept Marie in mourning and close to home; the return of Paul's company to Melun, and the prospect that it might soon move farther east toward Metz; and the new regulations to the effect that "officers, noncommissioned officers, brigadiers, and soldiers are prohibited from receiving visits from their wives," which Paul cited in a letter home.[65] By the end of the year, however, once Marie's obligations to her in-laws had been met, Paul's company was in no immediate danger of relocation, and no one seemed to be heeding the military regulations, Marie spent several weeks with Paul in Melun. When she left for home in early January, taking advantage of the opportunity to visit Paris on the way, Paul looked around their little hotel room and wrote plaintively: "How all alone I feel now in this bedroom which you left yesterday without hope of returning." Marie felt much the same. Although she enjoyed stopping in Paris—"we went to the law courts, the mayor's office, the city hall, the cathedral"—she too longed to retrace her steps to Melun. "On Monday I will leave for Melun if you want me to in your letters you seem decided that I should come back for me too to embrace you again would be my greatest happiness. Otherwise I will take the train for Verteillac you only have to tell me what you want and I will be happy to obey."[66] It seems likely that Marie did return to Melun, for she did not arrive in Nanteuil-de-Bourzac until two weeks later.

When Marie arrived home in mid-January 1915, both she and Paul hoped—and expected—that she was pregnant. A fortune-teller in Paris, whom Marie visited one evening after a day of sightseeing, had intimated as much: promising her a life of happiness, the card reader told Marie that she would have a baby boy and that her husband would return home safely. Given that this same woman had correctly foreseen the death of another woman's husband, Marie was loath to underestimate her power to predict the future. Perhaps suspecting that Paul would scoff at such superstitious indulgences, she conceded that the visit to the fortune-teller was nothing more than a diversion on an evening out, but she held fast to the prediction that she would have a child. Writing from Angoulême, where she stopped for a day en route to Nanteuil, she told Paul: "You know that the fortune-teller told me that I was going to have a baby boy. Since I must have a son you can console yourself that you will come back to me because this time I'm not pregnant I am only sick. Therefore, to have a baby we will have to see each other again."[67] With the hard work of spring planting awaiting Marie at home and the prospect of yet another move hanging over Paul's company, it was not entirely clear, however, that another opportunity would soon present itself.

At the end of March, after several false alerts, delayed starts, and unsubstantiated rumors, Paul's unit relocated to Rampillon, a small town slightly to the east of Paris and a relatively short distance from Melun. Once the move was over and the most disturbing rumors (that the company would move to the eastern frontier) laid to rest, Paul turned his thoughts once more to the possibility of Marie's traveling to join him. Several factors conspired, however, to make another visit logistically difficult, most unsettling of which was the fragile state of Marie's emotional well-being. By April 1915 the villagers of Nanteuil-de-Bourzac, and, indeed, the women of France in general, had plenty that might make them susceptible to depression. Victory was nowhere in sight, and casualties were already in excess of half a million men killed or wounded. It was evident that the short and victorious war to which their sons and husbands had so resolutely set off was not within reach. Victory might yet be secured, but the war would not be short; nor would it leave Nanteuil unscathed. As Marie and others kept a mournful tally of the commune's losses—this young man killed by a shell, another seriously wounded, a third taken ill in German captivity—the grim statistics weighed on them, darkening their thoughts and depressing their spirits. Even family members who knew that a husband or son was temporarily safe found their equilibrium affected by others' losses. Marie remarked, "When we learn of the death of one today, of another tomorrow even though they are young guys who mean nothing to you, it hits you even so." The cumulative weight of collective grief was indeed overwhelming: "There are so many dying now that it makes you tremble," Marie confessed, and she begged her husband, "Oh do all that you can to avoid all danger because your death would be mine."[68]

To compound her misery and intensify her melancholy, Marie heard nothing from Paul for days on end in May 1915. This was especially troubling because he remained in contact with his parents, making it unlikely that the postal service had been interrupted, as was sometimes the case, by military order. Having received neither a letter nor a postcard for almost a week and reasonably certain that he was in no direct danger, Marie confessed that the silence was destroying her peace of mind:

"How I worry on days when I receive nothing [from you]. What weariness I don't want to do anything but cry when will this all end how long I find the days . . . This separation has made me realize even more how dear you are to me. If only you could stay with the supply company so that you would be safe and could come back to me." Five days later, worried that he had taken amiss something she said in a previous letter, she berated herself in bitter self-recrimination: "I see quite clearly that you are angry with me one of my letters must have annoyed you which one I don't know but whichever one it was burn it destroy it . . . Was it the one about the allowances but if it is that one which is most likely well then let it be I couldn't care less about money if I have to be deprived of your love and friendship. Whatever it is no matter what I tell you that I am beside myself I hide myself away and cry. But this cannot go on because I am at the end of my tether if it is the letter where I told you that I couldn't leave for the time being, well that is completely true because I am so weak that I couldn't undertake a journey right now."[69]

As Marie wept anguished tears, convinced that Paul had abandoned her, he feared that she was on the verge of suicide. In a letter written some time earlier that has not survived, Marie seems to have made an indistinct but nonetheless dire threat: "You will regret this one day, God willing it will not be too late." When Paul heard nothing from her thereafter, he feared the worst. Only the arrival of a letter on 19 May reassured him that she still lived, and he responded with a passionate letter, intense with expressions of paralyzing anxiety and unwavering love: "My beloved my adored one it is impossible to tell you how happy I am . . . The suffering that I have endured is nothing next to the joy that I am now feeling if I had received nothing from you this morning I believe that I would have gone

mad. I would have gone to N. to telegraph my parents all night
long I had a fever I couldn't sleep for five minutes it seemed to
me always that I saw one of those telegrams that they bring to
you one of those slips of blue paper which generally announce
sad news now that I have received your letter of the 17th it
seems to me that it is impossible but last night I saw over and
over again that fearful phrase 'You will regret this one day God
willing it will not be too late.' How you made me suffer . . . Tell
me my dear Marie my beloved you whom I adore tell me that
you will never think such thoughts again even if you don't get
any word from me because you must know that whatever might
happen I will love you forever you must know how much I love
you and how much I cherish you even if you hear nothing from
me for a month or two whether because of the postal service or
something else . . . Why do you not believe me when I tell you
that I adore you that I will love you forever whatever happens
that nothing can deprive you of my love not even death because should I die I will die thinking of you."[70]

By late May, mail service was back to normal—a letter and
three postcards arrived at the Lescure farmhouse on 21 May—
and Marie's emotional crisis had subsided. Assuring Paul that
she had never thought of suicide, she noted nonetheless, "Sadness could kill almost as quickly," and confided that a week earlier she had been so weak as to be almost incapable of standing
up. This, she feared, was a symptom of the anemia that plagued
her every spring. Now that she was receiving medication, she
felt revitalized. This did not mean, however, that she was free
to join Paul anytime soon. With the most strenuous work in the
fields ahead of them, it would be impossible for her to leave
Nanteuil before August. And even then it was not clear that she
would be able to afford the expense. In mid-June she wrote,
"You seem to have decided that I should come to see you in Au-

gust and I would be so happy too, what happiness it would be to see you again But I don't dare hope for it because it would take so much money that I'm afraid that I wouldn't be able to go." This frugality drove Paul mad. There were, he reminded Marie, many other women "who have nothing and who find the means to come and see their husbands." Why could she not do the same? He feared that Marie's penny-pinching ways were in fact being imposed on her by his parents, who were reluctant to part with the hundred francs such a trip would cost: "So tell those who want to save everything that if they don't want to give you the money you will do it without them."[71]

If only she could have done as Paul suggested. But without a military allowance, she lacked the financial independence that other women now enjoyed. "You tell me that there are those who have nothing and who find the means to go and visit their husbands. But those you talk about are like the women in Nanteuil they have their 480 francs per year . . . I can understand that they don't need to overdo it to be able to pay for their trips and stay for a long time with their husbands." Unlike the women who cavalierly spent their military allowances going to visit their husbands, she had to save whatever money she could (from the sale of the calf, for example), because, as she ruefully reminded him, "right now there is not a lot to be earned from agriculture." The economic reality remained that she could afford another trip only if she were to deprive Paul of the parcels and necessities of life that made life away from home something other than pure misery. In response to Paul's angry letter that she was more interested in saving money than in visiting him, Marie lamented: "I beg you please don't believe that it is for lack of desire because you must know that I still love you madly and that my greatest happiness would be to be with you always. Only I know that you deprive yourself that you do without things and I don't want that I would prefer to send you money that I would otherwise spend so that you can take care of yourself."[72]

Paul, though, had no patience with penny-pinching and did not hesitate to use emotional blackmail to make his case. In mid-June he described a military funeral at which he had served as an honor guard: "Oh how sad it was the poor young guy was married and father of an 18-month-old child he was 27 years old . . . His widow, father, mother, sister, and child were at the burial it was painful to see their grief . . . The commandant made a short speech at the graveside I was right near by but when the poor widow and his parents came forward to shake his hand their distress was painful to see the widow cried out I had to turn my back so as not to see her that's how much it touched me." To drive home the moral of this sad tale, he concluded: "Listen to me my love . . . don't bother yourself about saving money because if it should happen that one or the other of us should disappear the one who remains will be sorry for a long time for having wanted to save money."[73]

Terrified that she would never see her husband again, Marie resolved to resist her parents and in-laws and make the trip, come what might. She asked Paul to find them a room with a bed, because she had no desire to walk back and forth from the farm where he was billeted to the nearest town every day; but realizing that this might not be possible, she reassured him that if they had no bed, they could still make do with a secluded spot in the countryside.[74] Tantalizing though these thoughts were, Marie knew that she would not be able to leave Nanteuil until after the crops were harvested, in mid-August at the earliest. Illness then delayed her departure until early September, when military developments that threatened to relocate Paul's company to the Balkans almost scuttled their plans completely.

The much-delayed, much-desired journey finally took place in September 1915. By the time Marie returned to the village, she was pregnant and Paul was on his way to the front. The days of baking bread were now behind him for good; he was off to serve in the newly formed 112th Heavy Artillery Regiment.

Letter of an eyewitness: Verdun is impossible to describe. It is about 7 or 8 kilometers from here to Douaumont. Not a trench, not a communications trench, nothing but shell holes one inside another. There is not one piece of ground that is not turned up. To see what has been done here one could not imagine all the shells of all calibers that have been used. The holes made by the 300 [-millimeter shells] could hold fifteen horses. There are no more woods. Shattered trees resemble telegraph poles. It is complete devastation. Not one square of land has been spared. One would have to come here to understand it. One cannot imagine such a thing.

Everything has been brought together on this part of the front. The cannon are mouth to mouth and never cease firing there is not one second when the cannon cease. There are no attacks right now but still there are losses. Shells fall and mow down everyone and everything without pity.

One can only go out at night to work this land that has been churned up a hundred times. The cadavers of swollen horses infect this immense battlefield. We make a trench, a shell lands, everything has to start over again if one is among the survivors. Attacks become impossible. When a troop wants to go out the artillery takes aim at it. There are too many guns everywhere. For as long as they are here both advance and retreat are impossible.

You can be sure that Verdun will not be taken. Here it is extermination on the ground without seeing the enemy. Soon we will be relieved. I wonder how I am still standing after all of this one is completely numb.

Men look at one another with wild eyes. It takes a real effort to hold a conversation.

Paul Pireaud, 23 May 1916

TWO

Here It Is Extermination on the Ground

For the first year of the war, Paul Pireaud led a protected albeit dreary life. Unlike so many of his acquaintances who had seen action from the earliest days, and unlike his best friend, Léon Videau, who died from his wounds in the spring of 1915, Paul had been spared the worst of the war. His life in uniform was lonely, to be sure, uncomfortable on occasion, but never dangerous. All of this changed in the aftermath of the failed Champagne offensive of September 1915. Assigned in late 1915 to the newly created 112th Heavy Artillery Regiment, Paul had to learn the rudiments of artillery work before being sent to positions north of Arras, where his battery first confronted the enemy in February 1916. Thereafter, he served for more than two months at Verdun. In this, the most ferocious, most destructive, and later most commemorated battle of the war for the French, Paul's regiment came under fire so intense and merciless in late May and early June that he believed he would never make it home alive. He would die, he feared, without witnessing the birth of his first child, without finding bliss once more in his wife's arms. Compelled by his circumstances to acknowledge that he might not survive the hell on earth that was Verdun, he did not seek consolation in religion (as many French soldiers reawakened to their Catholic faith did); nor did he, at least overtly, face combat armed with patriotic fervor.[1] He survived Verdun because he was lucky; he persevered because he believed that defeat—and the destruction

it would visit on his home and family, on his wife and unborn child—were intolerable, and anything but victory unimaginable.

The Champagne offensive of September 1915 was supposed to end the war. Its failure, indisputable by early October,
forced the French high command to derive what lessons it
could from the battle's inconclusive outcome. Conceived as the
major thrust of a two-part offensive (in the second part French
and British troops attacked in the Artois), the Second Battle of
Champagne was designed to break through the German lines
and bring the war to a decisive end. Despite early gains, won
in forbidding territory in inclement weather and with horren-
dously high casualties, in the end the efforts of those first days
went for naught. As the French advanced uphill without benefit
of cover, the German army exploited its superior situation to
launch a withering counteroffensive that quickly erased all the
preliminary advantage of the French. The French general staff
extracted two lessons from this failure: heavy artillery was effective, and France did not have enough of it. Although the
French had amassed more than eight hundred heavy-caliber
guns on the Champagne front (in addition to 1,100 of their
much more celebrated 75 millimeter [mm] field artillery
pieces), even this concentration of firepower proved insufficient.[2] In those sectors of the line that employed the still
novel tactic of the antecedent barrage—in which heavy guns
pummeled the enemy lines for days in advance of the infantry
attack—the French forces had made real (though temporary)
gains. But the army had been unable to deploy enough heavy
guns in the field to make a real difference at every point along
the line. When advantages won in the early days were effaced
by subsequent setbacks, it became evident that the French
army could not conduct a successful campaign without substantially increasing its heavy artillery.

The role and value of heavy artillery had been much debated in French military circles before the war. Some experts insisted on the advantages to be gained by a mobile heavy artillery force, equipped with guns larger than those of the field artillery but not so unwieldy as to be suitable only for siege warfare—a force that could match Germany's gun for gun. But insofar as the dominant attitude toward military planning in France up to 1914 had stressed the advantages of waging an offensive, mobile war, for which it was claimed only the smaller-caliber guns of the field artillery were well suited, efforts to expand the heavy artillery bore little fruit. When the war broke out in August 1914, France had only 308 guns of sufficient caliber to merit the designation "heavy artillery" yet mobile enough to be used in the field; the Germans, by contrast, had two thousand guns of comparable range and caliber.

Within months of the outbreak of war the folly of prewar biases became evident: confronting the stasis of trench warfare, the French general staff recognized the need to increase the size, function, and quality of its heavy artillery substantially. Plans set forth in October 1914 inaugurated this process, allowing for a greater than fourfold increase in the number of heavy-artillery batteries—from a mere 67 in August 1914 to 272 in the summer of 1915—available for deployment. The Battle of Champagne, at which many of these newly created units and recently acquired weapons went into action, seemed only to reinforce the wisdom of the new course. Much of the new equipment on order since the summer of 1915 was still in production, however, during the Battle of Champagne and would become operational only in late 1915 or early 1916. Anticipating its deployment, the French High Command authorized in October the creation of twenty-five new regiments of heavy artillery. Twenty of these regiments (including the 112th Heavy Artillery Regiment) would be equipped with the smaller-caliber cannon of the heavy artillery arsenal: 105 mm, 120 mm, and 155 mm guns. At a maximum weight of approximately six thousand kilograms (or thirteen tons), even the largest of these could be transported by a team of ten horses; an additional team of ten horses was needed to move the munitions carriage for each gun.[3]

The working unit of every artillery regiment was the battery, equipped with four guns. Like an infantry company (although much smaller), the battery was commanded by a captain who was responsible for executing the orders passed down from battalion (or, in French terminology, "group") headquarters, for maintaining good order and discipline, and for doing what he could to sustain the morale of the men under his command. A young American resident in France when the war broke out, who volunteered for service in a heavy artillery regiment of the French army for the last year of the war, remembered the battery in which he briefly served as much like a family in which the foibles and virtues of all members were both well known and understood; in this family, the captain played the role of the stern but by no means unkind or indifferent father.[4] Two lieutenants, each responsible for supervising the operation of two guns, reported directly to the battery captain. The officers' duties, and to a somewhat lesser extent the duties of the noncommissioned officers who served directly beneath them, required a good head for mathematics, and in particular more than a passing familiarity with geometry. Guns like the 155 mm cannon, which would become the mainstay of the French and, subsequently, American heavy artillery, had a range of ten kilometers. Operating at such a distance from their targets, battery officers could not aim their guns on sight. Instead, they had to apply complex mathematical formulas (set forth in firing tables specific to each gun) that would determine the angle at which a gun should fire, based on the precise locations of the battery and its target, the gun's distance from its designated target, the kind of shell being fired, and prevailing atmospheric conditions. Indeed, mathematical ability was such a necessary skill for all artillery officers that the artillery initially preferred to commission only students who had graduated from the nation's most technically rigorous institutions of higher education. By 1916 this was no longer a luxury the army could afford to indulge in, however, and many artillery officers came from backgrounds less distinguished than the prestigious Ecole Polytechnique. Nonetheless, the technical demands of artillery command limited opportunities for promotion to those with more than an elementary education. Officers and noncommissioned officers assigned to the heavy artillery had to pass through rigorous training schools, created in the fall of 1915, that required candidates to demonstrate at the very least a mastery of elementary geometry.[5]

If the most sophisticated tasks of the heavy artillery required brains, many other tasks, equally essential to the battery's effective operation, required brawn. The shells fired by the 155 mm gun weighed forty kilograms. And in the heat of battle, each gun in a battery might be called upon to fire at a rate of one shell every two minutes. The logbooks of the Twenty-seventh Battery of the 112th Heavy Artillery Regiment indicate, for example, that on one day in April 1916 the battery's four guns fired 130 rounds of poison-gas shells in just over an hour. Several months later, on a particularly active day on the Somme, the same battery fired nine hundred shells (more than two hundred shells per gun) in the course of the day.[6] Although the hectic pace of one round fired every two minutes could not be sustained for long—the gun would overheat, potentially fatal errors in loading would occur, and exhaustion would inevitably set in among the artillerymen—an eight-man gun crew in the midst of battle faced long days of

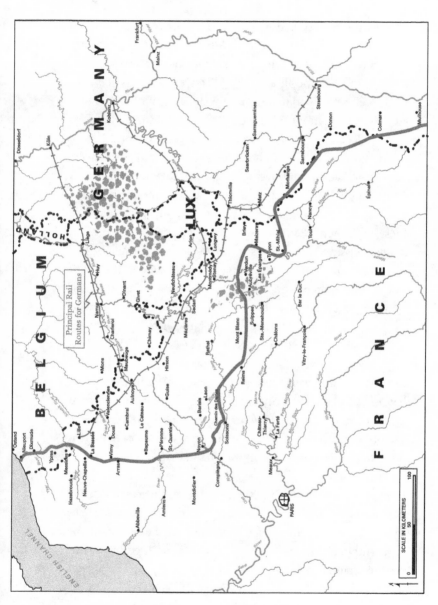

The western front. Map from Robert A. Doughty, *Pyrrhic Victory: French Strategy and Operations in the Great War* (Cambridge, Mass.: Harvard University Press, 2005), 106.

backbreaking physical labor. Moving heavy shells into position, loading them carefully into the breech, and firing guns that rent the air with a din that shook the ground and a heat that scorched all the foliage nearby: these were not tasks for the physically unfit or the faint of heart.[7]

A battery's efficient operation depended, however, on more than the physical stamina and sangfroid of its gun crew. Observation crews, situated a few kilometers in front of the battery itself and charged with determining when and where artillery rounds fell, had to remain in communication with the battery and its officers. Only visual evidence—garnered if the weather permitted from balloons or airplanes, but often available from land-based observation posts alone—could determine whether a gun had fired short, wide, or on target. Telephone lines laid down between the battery and the observation unit could, under ideal circumstances, guarantee prompt communication, but ideal circumstances were rare on the western front, and telephone lines were easily and often broken. Messengers then had to move back and forth between the observation post and the battery. Officers, messengers, observers, and gunners all had to be fed. A cook, supported by men assigned to gather provisions and firewood, was indispensable to the efficient operation of an artillery battery. Finally, the unit could not function without a complement of eighty horses, which needed to be fed and groomed.

The creation in late 1915 of twenty new horse-drawn heavy artillery regiments thus created a demand for men educated in the mathematical sciences, men undaunted by hard, physical labor, and men experienced in the care of horses. In a nation where almost half the population worked the land, it should not have been difficult to find such men, but manpower by October 1915 was in seriously short supply. The Champagne offensive alone had added 145,000 French casualties to the lists of killed and wounded. When these were combined with previous losses, the tally of killed, wounded, and missing in action amounted to almost 2,000,000 men, of whom more than 16,000 officers and almost 600,000 men from the rank and file had been killed. Another 6,000 officers and 400,000 men were missing in action. For a nation of 38,000,000, only two-thirds as large as its principal adversary, losses on this scale were devastating in the extreme. Nor could the artillery hope to find enough men by bringing young conscripts into the field in advance of their established service date. The Ministry of War calculated that the army would need 1,600,000 under arms in 1916, but only 1,200,000 were available for immediate deployment.[8]

When every able-bodied man was essential to the war effort and when heavy artillery regiments were being created out of the whole cloth, it is not surprising that Paul's days of baking bread, grooming horses, and holding romantic trysts far from the front lines were numbered. Rumors that his support company would be disbanded had circulated since the summer of 1915: some had hinted ominously at the men's redeployment to the infantry; others spoke more reassuringly of assignments in the artillery. A posting in the artillery by no means guaranteed protection from enemy fire, but it was distinctly preferable to deployment in the infantry. Men in the heavy artillery did not have to "go over the top," participate in bayonet charges, or undertake nighttime raids into No Man's Land as the infantry did, but Paul's letters and the surviving official logbooks of his regiment make it clear that life in the heavy artillery was not only physically arduous but also often dangerous. Batteries came under direct fire that was intended to neutralize the artillery's firepower; and poison-gas shells fired by the enemy or misfired by their own battery sent men scrambling for gas masks that were not always adequate to the task. Because heavy guns once dug into position were difficult to move, their crews often served for weeks on end in locations exposed to enemy fire. It was for this reason that the First Battery of the 112th Heavy Artillery Regiment found itself at Verdun from early April through late June 1916.

Formed on 1 November 1915, the 112th Heavy Artillery Regiment first saw action in the Artois region of northern France, where it served under the command of the French Fifth Army. The regiment's command post, located in the small village of Auxi-le-Château, northwest of Amiens and approximately forty kilometers inland from the Channel, had authority over batteries situated north of Arras. This area had seen intense, bloody, and fruitless fighting through much of 1915—as the enormous cemeteries at Notre-Dame-de-Lorette and Neuville Saint-Vaast testify to this day—with little appreciable gain for the French and British forces serving in the area. By the end of the year, two massive offensives (one in March and a second in September) had failed to dislodge the Germans from the strategically important high ground at Vimy, which constituted one of the targets of the 112th in early 1916. It was in this region due north of Arras that Paul was first exposed to enemy fire in February 1916. Having completed artillery training in January, during which he had not only cared for the battery's horses but also learned the rudiments of loading, firing, and maintaining the guns, Paul accompanied his battery when it moved north into Picardy in early February. On 6 February he described how he and his comrades, having had nothing hot to eat for almost sixty hours, dug themselves into position. The first task was to install the guns and establish the battery's infrastructure. The cannon had to be camouflaged and deep holes dug for the guns and ordnance. That accomplished, the battery had to establish communications connections with the command post, nearby batteries, and forward observation posts. Finally, the men had to build trenches and dugouts that would, if all went well, afford them protection from incoming fire. In contact with an observation balloon whose task was to alert the battery to incoming enemy shells, the men worked day and night to secure their site. Under these conditions, Paul feared that he would not always be able to write home every day. He assured Marie, however, that she should not take his silences amiss: "You must know how much I love you my poor wife my hope my only thought know well that if I don't write you it will be because I have been prevented from doing so by a force greater than myself."[9]

Now that her husband was in direct danger, Marie was anxious to learn as much as she could about his situation, his responsibilities within the regiment, and his proximity to the front lines. Although military regulations prohibited any explicit mention of the location of troops at the front, the men rarely paid any heed to these rules. Sometimes they used coded allusions and other subterfuges to inform their families of where they were and what conditions were like in their sector. Highly educated men often took cover in literary allusions, as André Kahn, a young lawyer who served as a stretcher bearer for most of the war, did when he told his mistress (who would become his wife) where in northern France he was by making reference to the fourth act of Edmond Rostand's *Cyrano de Bergerac*. But many soldiers adopted a much simpler ploy: they underlined particular letters in successive words of a missive to spell out their position on the line. This was the method preferred by Benjamin Simonet in apprising his wife of his stationing at Ypres in 1914–1915; and of Fernand Maret in writing to his parents in 1917. Paul had developed a similar stratagem as early as spring 1915, when his captain warned that any violation of the army regulation imposing strict secrecy would merit swift and certain punishment. When he moved to the front lines, Paul proposed to Marie that he would place very faint (and now almost indiscernible) crosses under a run of letters that when read in succession would identify his position.[10]

Useful though these simple codes might have been, in most cases they were unnecessary. Censorship was so randomly enforced in the first two years of the war that troops could often get away with writing very openly about where they were and how "hot" their sector was. In March 1916, for example, Marie wrote that one of Paul's letters, in which he had violated a cardinal rule of military correspondence by speaking openly of how the English were about to take over the sector north of Arras, had clearly been intercepted by the censors: the envelope had been ripped open and then resealed, but the letter itself had not been defaced. Even if the censors had held this one letter back, it is very likely that a subsequent letter conveying similar information would have gone through without incident. Therefore, Paul wrote repeatedly in early February in response to Marie's request that he describe his situation. It is evident that some of his letters were intercepted en route, because on 16 February he wrote, with a hint of impatience (directed not so much at Marie as at the postal censors): "Every day you ask me where we are and what we are doing. I have already told you this several times you must not have received my letters. I will give you another description of our military situation." And at this point he ignored all military regulations and told her precisely where they were, what they were up to, and where they were headed. The battery, having disembarked at Auxi-le-Château, had first proceeded northeast to the Somme; camped almost thirty kilometers from Arras, he believed that they were safe enough for the moment, although they could hear the incessant bombardment to the northeast. Once they had finished preparing the battery site, they practiced firing the guns for two hours, to determine the range and trajectory of the guns. This, he confided, was all a ruse to trick the Germans into thinking that medium-range guns were to be permanently installed here, whereas in fact the guns were to be withdrawn almost immediately by the French, abandoning the site they had so painstakingly built to much larger guns.[11]

When word came on 21 February that the battery was to relocate, Paul was painfully aware of the dangers that now awaited him. In a lengthy letter he told Marie where the battery was headed, tried to assure her that it was a better location than many in the region, and hinted that he might not come through his new assignment unscathed. "It's decided we are leaving tomorrow morning at five o'clock to take up a new position tomorrow night. We are going to Saint-Aubin four kilometers to the north of Arras. I was able to buy two cards of the department of Pas-de-Calais and I will send you one you will be able to see where we are and where we are going. I prefer that it be Saint-Aubin and not Arras because yesterday evening they said that we were going to Arras and that's not a good place to be the Germans bombard it day and night and it wouldn't be long before we got a few shells in the face but four kilometers [from the city] there is less danger. I am telling you today where we are going because tomorrow it will be forbidden to do so you can tell my parents and any friends who ask after me." He confessed that he approached the front with trepidation. A few days earlier, when the prospect of action was still uncertain, he had assured her that he could contemplate "with a good heart firing on the Boches," because he would be thinking of his wife who loved him and their baby yet unborn. For Paul, if not for more high-minded patriots who spoke proudly of their love of France, defense of family alone made the war endurable. But even these comforting thoughts could not calm all his fears. As the battery prepared to move forward, he remarked, "The 'music' that we hear from morning to night makes you afraid to go there but what can be done you can't let yourself go to pieces you just have to have courage when you receive this letter I will have had my baptism by fire and will have already fired on the Boches." Knowing the risks that now awaited him, he concluded: "Don't forget if anything should happen to me write to Combe at the same address as me. Tell my parents that I don't have time to write. What a sad life it is."[12]

By early March, Paul's battery was taking fire from two sides and was close enough to the enemy to hear "the whistle of German bullets which proves that we are not very far from them since rifle fire can get right up to us." When his battery "launched a barrage to stop a German attack the horizon was nothing but fire talk about thunder boy it's terrible." Although Marie urged him not to go out at night, he confessed that he had no other option: "When there is work to be done it has to be done at night because one cannot work during the day unless it is foggy." In response to her inquiry about what a battery actually did, he replied, "We fire the guns when we have to and we build a shelter for the gun and for ourselves imagine that to build a gun emplacement and a shelter for eight men it takes more than a month for the gun you have to dig a hole which is ten meters wide and fifteen meters long . . . For our dugouts you have to dig 4 meters long by 3 meters wide and 2.5 meters deep."[13]

Although Paul had to burn most of Marie's letters from this period, for lack of space in his kit bag, it is evident from those which have survived and from his letters home that much of what he wrote was in response to her direct questions. She wanted to learn all she could about his circumstances and the duties that fell to the heavy artillery. She seemed especially concerned about the possibility that Paul's battery was in close contact with poison gas and tear gas. Her fear of poison gas was legitimate, for its devastating effects on men inadequately protected by gas masks were real. By 1916, however, poison gas—especially when directed at opposing batteries—was used primarily to inconvenience and temporarily disable the enemy. A battery exposed to poison-gas shelling could not easily maintain fire, for the gun crew would be so encumbered by gas masks as to make regular operation of the guns extremely difficult. This, at least, was the judgment of tacticians who argued in an artillery training manual that no benefit was to be gained from intermittent firing of "special shells", rather their use should be concentrated and "continuous in order to prolong the threat of asphyxiating effects, which oblige the enemy to wear its masks continually, and thus greatly reduce its freedom of movement."[14] The 112th Heavy Artillery Regiment received and fired poison-gas shells, but Paul made as little of this as possible. He noted that some men were charged with preparing the shells, others with transporting them to the batteries, and yet others with firing them. In a subsequent letter, however, he explained that he had decided to shave his face clean because he feared that if fully bearded he would suffocate under his mask in a gas attack. Knowledge of this sort gave Marie little comfort. Noting how sad the village was when it observed the pre-Lenten carnival in 1916, with so many local men en route to or already in position at Verdun, she confessed: "How I suffer knowing that you are so unhappy. Take heart this will finish well Farewell receive from the one who loves you everything good that she can send you, to you my beloved my tenderest kisses."[15]

Until the end of March, Verdun remained only a vaguely unsettling eventuality for the First Battery of the 112th Heavy Artillery Regiment. Fully occupied as he was in the Artois, Paul paid only passing attention to news that the German army had launched an artillery assault on 21 February of such unprecedented ferocity that it could be heard more than 150 kilometers from the fortified city of Verdun. Germany's plan was neither to capture the city nor to break through the French lines. Whether German forces captured Verdun itself was ultimately of only incidental importance. The real goal of this assault was much simpler: to force France out of the war by seriously depleting its ranks. If Germany could "bleed France white," then the Entente alliance would collapse and Britain, stranded on the western front, would have to sue for peace.

Unaware that this unprecedented and unapologetic exercise in attrition would soon draw his battery away from Arras into a furnace of shellfire unlike anything he had yet witnessed, Paul was initially concerned only that "that business at Verdun" meant the suspension of all leave, regardless of where one found oneself at the front.[16] At this point he had no inkling that the German general staff, under the direction of Erich von Falkenhayn, was calculating—correctly, as it turned out—that the French high command would deploy whatever forces it could muster to hold Verdun, a site so frequently fought over in centuries past that it held a unique symbolic significance in French national memory. Nor did Paul realize that his battery would spend two months there, participating in a battle that would, more than any other, indelibly impress itself on the nation's collective psyche.[17] By the time the Battle of Verdun came to a close in late 1916, almost 80 percent of the French army—more than a million men—had seen action in this blighted sector. Provisioned exclusively via the Voie Sacrée, the only road link between Verdun and the rear, the French lost ground, ceded critical fortresses, and suffered enormous losses before turning the tide of the German offensive in late June. In the end, the French line held, but the cost was almost beyond human comprehension. The French suffered more than 350,000 casualties, the Germans almost as many. Falkenhayn's original calculation that the French would lose three men for every one German fell wide of the mark. The final reckoning would show that almost half of the more than 300,000 men who died at Verdun were German. This was indeed "extermination on the ground." Villages were destroyed, never to be rebuilt. The natural landscape was pulverized and then indelibly pocked by craters and shell holes. Gleaming white crosses now mark the graves of thousands who fell on the ill-fated terrain surrounding Verdun; and the unidentified remains of thousands more, when gathered in the interwar years, filled an ossuary that has dominated the countryside ever since. Witnessed by so many, endured at such cost, Verdun became for all French soldiers the defining event of the First World War.

Verdun was, first and foremost, an artillery duel. Infantry charges and countercharges—to gain land, secure or retake strategically located fortresses, or regain territory that had been lost to the enemy—certainly took place, at great cost and usually to little effect. But the hallmark of the battle was the relentless barrage of guns, aimed with equal ferocity at the almost indistinguishable front lines and at opposing batteries arranged in step formation (with the heaviest guns farthest back) behind the lines. The artillery's task was manifold: dislodge frontline troops, destroy machine-gun nests, and neutralize the enemy's guns. As shells of every caliber, from 75 mm to 310 mm, mercilessly rained down on the landscape of Verdun to murderous effect, heavy artillery regiments like the 112th were destined to play a pivotal role in the unfolding battle.

Simple soldiers like Paul Pireaud who knew only what they

could see from their limited vantage point at the front had little advance warning that 1916 would be marked by the great Battle of Verdun. Indeed, French military commanders, concentrating all their attention on their recently completed plan to launch a huge interallied offensive on the Somme in the summer of 1916, also underestimated the scale and intensity of a German attack on the Verdun salient. Joseph Joffre, the French commander in chief, believed in January 1916 that the Germans might well target Verdun, but he thought that any German attack there would be at most a diversionary enterprise. Military intelligence accumulated through the first weeks of the new year, to the effect that the Germans had something more than diversion in mind, failed to convince him otherwise.[18] It was only in the week preceding the opening artillery barrage that Joffre and Sir Douglas Haig, his British counterpart, agreed to a repositioning of troops that would put the British army in sole charge of the sector north of Arras, thereby allowing for the wholesale transfer of the French Tenth Army eastward toward Verdun.[19]

In early March Paul saw on the ground the consequences of these last-minute strategic negotiations. Having spent weeks digging into position, a task that was still incomplete on 3 March, his battery learned that the English were to take over the sector. Paul tried to deflect Marie's worries by suggesting that his regiment was, according to one rumor, headed to Champagne (now a quiet sector) and, according to another, to the Woevre (where American troops would fight in 1918); but what he knew for certain was "that English are arriving here every day."[20]

Paul did not know for sure but might well have suspected that the two weeks' respite he enjoyed in mid-March was granted as a much-needed breather before his battery was sent to the battle now raging near the northeastern border. There was no rest for Marie, who was seriously worried. Other men from Nanteuil and the surrounding villages were on their way to or already encamped at Verdun; it was, she feared, only a matter of time before Paul's battery moved there, too. "I can't wait to find out where you are going there are a great many from around here who write and say that they are going to Verdun you already know [where you will be sent] but as for me when will I know too. H. hasn't written for more than a week and he usually writes every day Is it the change of location or has something happened to him everyone wants to know." Even more unsettling was the knowledge that men who had recently been in Paul's sector in the Artois were now at Verdun: "B's son who belonged to the Twelfth at Notre-Dame-de-Lorette has been at Verdun for the last week." Thus when Paul reported at the end of March that his battery was preparing to decamp for "an unknown destination" at least a week's journey away, all evidence suggested that it, too, was heading toward Verdun.[21]

By the time the 112th Heavy Artillery Regiment arrived at Verdun in early April, the French had already suffered some serious setbacks. In the very first days of the German offensive, the French—outmanned, outgunned, and outmaneuvered—had lost ground and, perhaps more grievous for national pride, had witnessed the fall of Fort Douaumont on 25 February. The city of Verdun had been fortified since at least the seventeenth century, when Louis XIV's military engineer Vauban had ordered the construction of a citadel at the very heart of this strategically important site. Two hundred years later, in the aftermath of the Franco-Prussian War, the defenses had been significantly reinforced through the construction of a dozen fortresses located to the west, north, and east of the city. Closest to Verdun itself were the forts of Saint-Michel and Belleville on the right bank of the Meuse (a gently meandering river that ran almost due north through the city on its way to Belgium, Holland, and the North Sea) and Fort Chaume on the left bank. A second line of fortifications spread out in a wider semicircle beyond these installations, and a third ring of fortresses completed the city's defenses.

Of all the fortresses that defended Verdun, none was larger or more important than Douaumont. A behemoth capable of holding a thousand men, Douaumont had once boasted some of the largest guns in the French arsenal. By the end of 1915, however, the fortress was little more than an empty shell. Stripped of most of its heavy guns early in the war, when Verdun seemed a sleepy spot in an uncontested sector, and deprived of most of its men, Douaumont was by February 1916 unable to defend either itself or the city that stood almost ten kilometers behind it. When a handful of Germans fell upon the fortress almost by accident on the fourth day of the battle, they found it occupied by only a few French troops, who surrendered in the mistaken belief that they were being surrounded by overwhelming enemy force. Although the fall of Douaumont was a crushing blow to French pride, it did not signify the end of the battle. Not only would the French spend much of the rest of the year fighting to reclaim the fortress, they would also have to try to dislodge German troops from other sites that had been captured in the weeks following its loss and whose significance was, like that of Douaumont, sometimes more symbolic than strategic.

In the early weeks of the battle, most of the formidable German firepower unleashed at Verdun was concentrated to the north and east of the city, on the right bank of the Meuse. In March, however, Crown Prince Wilhelm, who commanded the

German army at Verdun, decided that the time had come to
launch a flanking attack on the city by taking particular aim at
two hilltops that dominated the river's left bank: the tragically
well-designated Mort-Homme (Dead Man) and the more pro-
saically named Côte 304. For infantry regiments located here,
the last days of March and the first week of April were harrowing beyond belief. Augustin Cochin, in command of an infantry company that went into the line with 175 men, was caught
up in the last throes of the crown prince's offensive. On 9 April
1916 Cochin described the mind-destroying mayhem of warfare in the industrial age: "There is a completely relentless rum-
bling, rending the air with piercing whistles and the din of
nearby explosions." His men were at their wits' end, and neighboring companies were in even worse condition. One company
had lost 40 men in one day; another had seen an entire section
destroyed by a single shell. Nor did circumstances improve
from one day to the next. On 11 April an incoming shell buried
alive half the men of an entire section; another killed Cochin's
liaison officer as Cochin stood right next to him. His only hope
was that his company, now reduced to 130 men, would soon be
relieved: "One cannot remain in a trench for two weeks while
losing twenty or thirty men a day." His estimation was correct.
When his company was relieved on 14 April, he counted his
losses: of the 175 who had moved into position, only 34 remained, more than half of whom were, Cochin conceded, off
their heads. The devastation he and his men had witnessed was
daunting. Trenches were completely destroyed, corpses lay everywhere, and commanding officers could do nothing more
than line them up along the inside wall of the parapets.[22]

And yet the crown prince's offensive failed. On 10 April, in
a famous message to the troops, General Philippe Pétain con-
gratulated the soldiers of Verdun for their valiant stand against

the German assault and insisted—in a phrase that would become synonymous with the battle itself—"*Courage. On les aura!*" Perhaps some battle-weary skeptics in the French ranks greeted Pétain's words with cynical disenchantment, but Paul Pireaud was not one of them. A new arrival at Verdun—the First Battery of the 112th Heavy Artillery Regiment had moved into position on 3 April—Paul took pride in Pétain's rousing words of praise. Writing home only four days later, he quoted the order of the day almost verbatim: "Today they read us a letter of congratulations from General Pétain for the armies that so successfully repelled the terrible attack of the crown prince on the day of the 9th infantrymen, artillery all rivaled one another in heroism." Like Pétain, who had also predicted, "The Germans will no doubt attack again," Paul knew that the battle was far from won, but he expressed a confidence in the final outcome that would have warmed the general's heart: "Last Tuesday, the 11th, they launched an attack such as no one has ever seen before it was repulsed this means that now the Germans will not succeed anywhere but it's terrible."[23]

It was terrible indeed. After having been safely behind the lines as recently as 3 April, the First Battery of the 112th Heavy Artillery Regiment found itself in the thick of the battle a week later. In a quick card dispatched on 10 April, Paul could say only that although the weather was glorious, conditions were dire. Responsible for ferrying food from field kitchens to the battery, Paul made his way across the pock-marked landscape two or three times a day. The incessant cannonade that characterized this monstrous battle often made even that simple task hellish. As he would report the next day, the Germans had targeted the 112th's sector, and Paul and his companions were exposed to direct bombardment. "We had gone only 1 kilometer when a shell landed 400 meters from us on the edge of the road we stopped and lay flat on the ground three more fell around us and then we got up and rode away farther along at a gallop . . . Two more fell but big ones only 150 meters to our right . . . We heard another six but they fell farther away. An airplane tried to hit our lines but it was forced back." Paul took heart at the thought that he and his companions had faced this mortal threat with courage and sangfroid. Several even joked, while lying flat out on the ground with shells exploding around them; others mocked the Germans when some of their shells proved to be duds. This collective bravado notwithstanding, he had to confess: "It is impossible to imagine the agony that you feel while waiting for a shell to explode." Astonished by the intensity of the German bombardment, he found comfort in the thought that soon the enemy would have to let up and would then taste some of its own medicine. By 16 April this had indeed come to pass, much to Paul's relief. He remained convinced, however, that another attack was a real possibility; given the ferocity with which the Germans had attacked earlier, anything could happen.[24]

A hand-drawn map, combined with other internal clues, shows that the First Battery of the 112th Heavy Artillery Regiment was situated on the right bank of the Meuse, equidistant from the two forts of Saint-Michel and Belleville, with Douaumont and Fort Vaux straight ahead. This sector would be bitterly contested between April and June, as the German army pushed forward, laying siege to Fort Vaux in late May, capturing it in early June, and then advancing ever closer to the forts of Saint-Michel and Belleville. Only in late June would this advance be halted near the village of Fleury; thereafter, the tide of battle turned—slowly, to be sure, but noticeably nonetheless—in France's favor. But during much of the worst of it— from early April, when Paul's battery entered the line, through

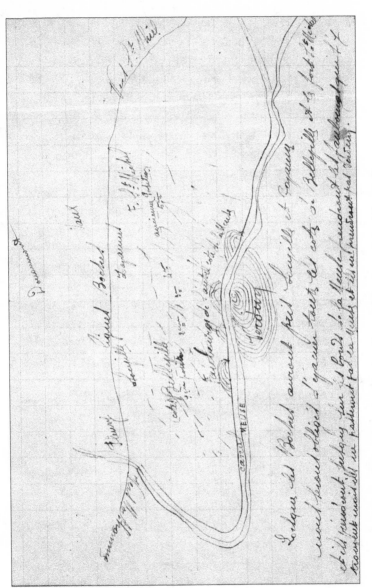

Paul Pireaud's map of the battlefield at Verdun. Service historique de la défense, France.

20 June, when it left Verdun—it was never relieved: firmly dug in, exposed to intense German artillery fire, it was subjected to more than sixty days of relentless, agonizing battle. This, Pétain knew, was hardly ideal: the guns became clogged with mud, the men demoralized, the batteries inefficient. In a memo sent to Joffre on 24 April, he suggested that heavy artillery batteries located elsewhere on the western front be rotated into Verdun to give the batteries already in position some much-needed relief.[25] That did not happen. The Twenty-seventh Battery of the 112th Heavy Artillery Regiment, for example, served at Vaux-Varennes, north of Reims and several kilometers from Verdun, from the beginning of April through mid-July, when it moved to the Somme.[26] By contrast, Paul's battery remained at Verdun. Equipped with guns that the high command recognized as essential to French success in this bitterly contested sector, the battery could not be spared until the German lines had been pushed back. But for as long as the German army was advancing, placing its own guns beyond the range of the field artillery's 75s, only France's larger-caliber guns, and especially the 105 mm and the Long 155 mm, had the range, the trajectory, and the accuracy needed to do real damage to the enemy's artillery.

Even the lull that Paul's battery enjoyed in mid-April was only relative. The difficulty in moving about made it next to impossible for Paul to visit with any of the men from Nanteuil-de-Bourzac who were, Marie assured him, close by. As he noted by way of apology: "To find them in these conditions is not easy." In fact, the conditions were so miserable that by the time he returned to the battery one evening, having successfully procured provisions, Paul was soaked to the skin and encased in mud. He feared that if by some stroke of unexpected fortune he were to head home on leave, no one would recognize him:

"Since it has been raining every day it has been impossible for me to get clean . . . I am unrecognizable no one would dare touch me we have no clean water for shaving or washing, only the muddy water in the shell holes. I can't wear my galoshes the mud is deeper than they are." Several days later, when the dreary weather was temporarily behind them and everyone was, for the moment at least, in the best of spirits, he explained how he came to be so dirty as to be beyond recognition: "5, 6, 10 times a night we had to lie flat out often in water or mud 50 centimeters deep to avoid the explosions and dirty and completely soaked through we had to sleep like that in a shed where it rained as if we were outdoors."[27]

And then life got even worse. In a series of letters written in the last week of May, Paul put pen to paper to bear witness to the apocalyptic misery of Verdun. The frequency and intensity of the letters suggest that he was convinced he would not survive the battle; every letter, written under the grimmest circumstances imaginable, tried to convey something of the unutterable horror of life under constant artillery fire. It was during this week that he composed the "Letter of an eyewitness" that opens this chapter, and several other heart-rending descriptions of near misses and lethal hits. Indifferent as ever to military regulations, he wrote on 23 May that it was "about 7 or 8 kilometers from here to Douaumont." In the space that separated his battery from the fortress, there were "nothing but shell holes one inside another. There is not one piece of ground that is not turned up. To see what has been done here one could not imagine all the shells of all calibers that have been used. The holes made by the 300 [-millimeter shells] could hold fifteen horses. There are no more woods. Shattered trees resemble telegraph poles. It is complete devastation. Not one square of land has been spared. One would have to come here

to understand it. One cannot imagine such a thing." That being
said, he nonetheless tried to describe that which all other
witnesses agreed defied ordinary description: "Everything has
been brought together on this part of the front. The cannon
are mouth to mouth and never cease firing there is not one second when the cannon cease. There are no attacks right now but
still there are losses. Shells fall and mow down everyone and
everything without pity. One can only go out at night to work
this land that has been churned up a hundred times. The cadavers of swollen horses infect this immense battlefield. We make
a trench, a shell lands, everything has to start over again if one
is among the survivors. Attacks become impossible. When a
troop wants to go out the artillery takes aim at it. There are too
many guns everywhere. For as long as they are here both advance and retreat are impossible." From this bitter reality he extracted what comfort he could: "You can be sure that Verdun
will not be taken." But the impregnability of the city owed less,
it seemed, to the valor of French soldiers than to the inescapable truth: "Here it is extermination on the ground without seeing the enemy." Holding to the universal hope, "Soon we will
be relieved," he closed: "I wonder how I am still standing after
all of this one is completely numb. Men look at one another
with wild eyes. It takes a real effort to hold a conversation."[28]

On the same day that he wrote his self-styled "testimony,"
he composed two other letters. This practice, common to soldiers under especially heavy fire, suggests that when from hour
to hour there was little likelihood of survival, each letter would
signify that at the moment it was written, at least, the soldier
was still alive. Thus, on 23 May Paul wrote, "I am taking advantage not of a calm moment to write to you on the contrary it's
falling so thick and fast that we are obliged to stay flat on our
stomachs so I'm taking advantage of this to write to you, lying

between two other guys . . . [The shells] are falling some only 15 meters from us this covers us with dirt and smoke but they can't trap us because there is a small embankment in front of us if they fall in front of that because it is higher than we are we risk nothing. If they fly over the embankment they have to fall between 12 and 20 meters from us so lying flat out we risk nothing but it's pretty terrible no one who has not seen it could imagine what it is like . . . I will always do what I can to send you word every day. The proof of this is that I am writing you in this wretched position surrounded by a din the likes of which I have never heard before tell my parents that I will not be able to write them very often."[29]

However hazardous the conditions were, Paul learned (presumably at the end of the day) that he was being moved "into position for good . . . At the very least I will be closer to the Boches and I will see a bit more of the machine guns." Having been responsible for bringing provisions to the battery, a task that carried its own dangers, he would henceforth have to stay with the guns, for he was now assigned to the gun crew of the 155 mm long-barreled guns. Knowing that his new responsibilities would be physically exhausting and often dangerous—a shell incorrectly loaded could explode in the gun barrel, thereby destroying the gun and often injuring or killing members of the gun crew—Paul promised that he would try to write every day, circumstances permitting, but he forewarned Marie that he might be too busy or too tired to do so. On 24 May 1916, his first day manning the cannon, he wrote: "I am in position now and farewell for you to long letters and farewell for me to any spare time we have to work from 5 in the morning until 10 at night and go to bed without any light and so I am obliged to write you in between firing the gun I can do it a bit but too often the Boches force me to lie flat on my stomach I can tell you one thing it is terrible, very terrible, you see such sad things even the hardest hearts are softened by it I assure you that this evening they made me cry with their tear gas in spite of the fact that they have sent us a lot of stuff we have done good work."[30]

The French, he believed, had retaken Douaumont. In fact, the assault launched two days earlier to regain the fortress had been only temporarily successful. The Fifth Infantry Division had penetrated the fortress on 23 May, but for lack of reinforcements could not hold it and fell back on the following day. In truth, the assault on Douaumont, which brought the Fifth Infantry Division more than five thousand casualties, failed miserably, and this prized possession would not be restored to French hands until late October, eight months after it had been captured.[31] But it is not likely that Paul wrote to mislead Marie, for when he learned subsequently that the French had not recaptured the fortress, he set the record straight: "Douaumont was retaken, then lost, then retaken that's inevitable because the two opposing artilleries have so totally turned it upside down demolished it that anyone could take it, the difficult thing is holding on to it there are no longer any trenches, any barbed wire, everything is annihilated by the rain of steel that falls night and day." This passage suggests that rumor, battlefield confusion, and overly optimistic official pronouncements could mislead even frontline combatants. Paul wrote what he did know for certain: "Shells are falling everywhere in front above behind to the right and to the left it is beginning to rain we will not be able to walk in the mud."[32]

Long, wearying days of firing the guns did not, however, prevent him from writing seven letters in the last week of May, at a time when it seemed ever more likely that he would not survive the battle. These were not the carefully composed letters that soldiers wrote on the eve of battle, to be sent to their next of kin in the event that they died in action; rather, they were hastily scribbled cards written as circumstances allowed. Anxious that Marie not be tormented by the doubt, uncertainty, and unrealistic hope that plagued so many families when a soldier's death at the front was reported merely as "missing in action," Paul reminded her that whatever happened, his friend Combe could be counted on to tell her the truth. He knew that Marie would be shattered by news of his death, but it was better for her to know the truth than to live in false hope.

Finally, in a more detailed letter he described at some length the circumstances in which he found himself. Recalling that Marie had often told him that she wanted to know the truth, he urged her to summon up her courage, for what he had to tell her was grim and unsettling in the extreme. The battery found itself on the edge of a crest of land, completely surrounded by massive shell holes: "There is one that is in front of the gun, 8 meters to the right and 14 paces from us which is 24 meters in diameter. I measured it and it is 3.5 meters deep tonight a 150 mm Boche shell fell on our shelter, and another one fell before I got here which penetrated 1.8 meters into the ground . . . It wounded four men at the gun emplacement." He confessed, "Spectacles such as these are so numerous they no longer move me, any more than the shells." Nonetheless, he urged Marie not to fret, for he stayed in the underground dugout whenever possible. Sometimes, however, duty or necessity forced him out of doors. Certainly the guns could not be fired from deep within a dugout, and so the men would leave their "damp, black holes . . . on the run to fire the guns and then [would] hide away again" as soon as they were finished.[33]

On a more prosaic level, they had to escape the close quarters of a dugout to relieve themselves. Most soldiers rarely spoke to civilians of this unpleasant but unavoidable fact of life at the front. Paul was in this respect something of an exception, for he did describe the very real embarrassment of having to relieve himself in a shell hole while under constant fire. "What's really annoying is that when you have to go you really don't know where to go everywhere is dangerous and so you hold it as long as you can but at some point you just have to go. I am telling you this because this morning at one thirty I wanted to go and I got myself into a shell hole that was two meters deep. I just got there and right away there was a shell whistling by me I lay flat out and right away three more followed one of which exploded in a hole just 30 meters in front of me I grabbed my pants in both hands and ran for the dugout I laughed about it when I got to the shelter but if you could see the poor guys here running like that you would feel sorry for them."[34]

Intense bombardment continued through the end of May and into the first week of June, with the French and Germans exchanging fire with equal force: "We are," Paul asserted with undisguised pride, "sending some real stuff over to those bastard Germans so that they won't be able to advance." That being said, the "bastard Germans" were replying in kind. In the midst of a massive French barrage, the scale of which prompted Paul to observe, "It is impossible that previous or future generations could have seen or will ever see such things," the Germans unleashed a counterbarrage on 31 May that came pretty close to killing Paul and his companions. "At 5 A.M. I went up to the battery with four comrades I was carrying a pot of soup their shells were falling to our left so instead of continuing up to the battery we took shelter behind an embankment those bastards lengthened their range and demolished a house right in front of us we lay down flat on the ground to let them fire a bit longer when they let up we left in a hurry . . . You can imag-

ine how soaked my shirt was, but what of it it was nothing I
hope that we will be taken out of here pretty soon and you can
be sure that until then I will be careful . . . I noticed that your
letter was scented thank you for your thoughtfulness to me."[35]

Paul was not alone in wondering when the battery would
be relieved. Whereas infantry companies (or what was left of
them after ten days' exposure to the guns of Verdun) rotated
in and out of the line, in a system known as the noria that
Pétain would make famous, artillery regiments, somewhat less
exposed than the poor infantrymen and by their very nature
much less mobile, stayed in position for long stretches. It made
good tactical sense to keep men in position long enough to become familiar with the terrain and their targets.[36] Troops in
the line and women waiting anxiously at home, however, found
this extended service at Verdun insufferable. By early June,
wives and mothers in Limoges and Angoulême were actively demanding that their men, having served almost two
full months at Verdun, be taken out of the line. Almost seven
months pregnant and far from either town, Marie was in no position to take to the streets in protest, but her anxiety was no
less acute: "Tell me my dear Paul," she wrote on 1 June, "aren't
they talking about relieving you any time soon what are they
saying about that tell me." Paul, whose intelligence on this
score was no more reliable than Marie's, could offer little in the
way of satisfying assurances: "As for our situation, a month ago
they talked about relieving us and we are still here." Even when
the bombardment let up momentarily, as it did for a few hours
on 4 June, after aerial observers successfully pinpointed the opposing batteries, the cumulative effect of two months in the
line was intensely wearing. On 5 June, as the battery marked its
second full month of service at Verdun with no sign of respite,
leave, or quick victory, Paul found it hard not to succumb to

despair: "How I find the time weighs on me with this damned war when will this terrible nightmare be over I can hardly believe that one day it will be finished I can't ever imagine coming back to our little nest in our little paradise where we were so happy. On days like this when you have the time to think about these things it is even more annoying, you get depressed, oh well, you have to try to chase away these ideas in order to conserve enough courage to meet all these trials. So courage and confidence and all will be well."[37]

Finally, on 20 June the battery was relieved: "We are now out of that hell we now can hear the cannon only in the distance and without any danger we can now wash, eat, sleep, rest in complete safety how good that feels after such an ordeal." Paul would witness other ordeals before the war was over. At one point in 1918, when his battery was under fire from enemy guns and desperately seeking a breakthrough in northern Italy, he would consider the situation "worse than Verdun."[38] But something about Verdun defied description. The Artois had been grim, but Verdun was, as so many soldiers testified, unlike anything that could be imagined. Knowing that language was ultimately inadequate to the task of describing a battle that left more-educated men struggling for words, Paul nonetheless did what he could to bear witness to what he saw and to share his experience with his young wife.

He did not always describe the most gruesome effects of battle. Thus, when he wrote of gas attacks, he did not linger over the details. Under heavy bombardment on 28 May, he described how the entire hillside trembled under the impact of massive shells exploding around the dugout. When one especially brave (or foolhardy) comrade went outside to collect the glowing shards of the exploded shells—the stuff from which souvenir jewelry was made—tear gas seeped into the shelter.

Paul, who had to interrupt his letter, noted only, "We are going to have to put our masks on because my eyes are beginning to water." Tear gas was a nuisance, but poison gas was a more terrifying prospect, as Marie already knew. Two months earlier, she had described how her brother-in-law, Louis Chaboussie, had been assigned to a special training course where soldiers were subjected to a series of tests against poison-gas attacks.[39] Whether the trials were testing the new gas mask that would be distributed in the months to come or, more ominously, testing the effects of gases not yet deployed in the field is unclear. Either is possible. French gas masks were notoriously ill designed: loath to copy the British, whose gas masks were ugly but effective, the French tinkered with designs that were elegant and comfortable but not always up to the task.[40] At the same time, however, the French army was engaged in the secret development of new poison gases. Having argued in spring 1915 that the Germans, who used gas for the first time in modern warfare at Ypres, were truly barbarians, the French could not very well advertise their own efforts to develop disabling or lethal chemical weapons. Thus, throughout 1916 the army's censorship office rigorously excised any reference in the public press to French testing of poison gas.

State secrecy did not, however, stop Louis Chaboussie from telling his wife and sister-in-law that the French had poison gas and were testing it (for whatever purposes) on their own soldiers. Relaying to Paul what she had just learned of her brother-in-law's experience, Marie wrote of how the men, enclosed in a sealed room into which a pipe spewed poison gas, had to stay there for an hour or more wearing their gas masks. Because the masks were ill-fitting, one man had died and others left the room spitting blood. On the last day of the training session, twenty men were placed in a tunnel and exposed to a gas attack: "Three died and all the rest were spitting blood there were several, he said, who were in really bad shape and who weren't able to leave [for the front]."[41] Knowing this, Marie must have learned of Paul's exposure to a gas attack with real trepidation.

If there were things that Paul left unsaid because Marie already knew what needed to be known, there were other things of which he could hardly write at all. Thus on 27 May he described how two horses had been destroyed in front of the battery; given that one had had its "nose split open up to the left eye and the right shoulder torn away," Paul could not help wondering "what became of its rider."[42] If, as is probably the case, he knew full well what had happened to the hapless horseman, he did not dare tell Marie. Witnessing the suffering of animals—perhaps, indeed, animals that he had cared for, fed, and groomed—was grim enough; but what man could bring himself to tell his pregnant wife what happens to human flesh when hit full force by an exploding shell?

Sensitive to Marie's condition and far from callous, Paul nonetheless ended up telling her more than he perhaps initially intended. When Marie, a keen reader of the regional newspaper, noted that 2 June, the height of the German attack on Fort Vaux, was supposed to have been a particularly horrendous day, Paul responded, "Every day is terrible but there are days when it is worse here than in other places and other days that are especially bloody and terrible elsewhere we don't get very much while on other days they unleash everything on us. But the 1st of June was terrible *for us* I can't tell you about it I will explain it to you when I have the good fortune to come home and be close to you." In fact, however, he did not wait until he was home on leave, but described his closest brush with death in a letter written in late June from the safety of his rest camp behind the lines. Any infantry attack, such as the one the Germans had directed at Fort Vaux in the first week of June, was inevitably preceded by concentrated fire directed at the enemy's heavy guns. This "counterbattery" fire made life a real misery for men in the heavy artillery. The German guns having targeted his battery for destruction (if possible) or neutralization at the very least, Paul barely survived the first day of June 1916. "I've already told you that I'll remember 1 June 1916 for a long time to come. On that day there was a terrible bombardment one could not go out of the shelter shells were falling everywhere I ate my soup cold in the shelter a mate brought it to me, running all the way. I stepped back to make room for him at that very moment a shell fell in the corner of the shelter and shattered his jaw four splinters in the leg, three in the arm . . . If it were not for him I would have been the one to catch it and because he was a bit taller than I am and the splinter hit him in the jaw it would have got me in the temple and you wouldn't have had your little guy any more . . . The guys of the Eleventh Battery who replaced us saw a shell explode in their very midst . . . Another one fell in the middle of them and killed four guys, one of whom was cut in two . . . and that happened pretty close to my head. I tell you this because I came out of it alive."[43]

Perseverance in the face of such unparalleled adversity was by no means easy. Food was scarce, misery abundant, and danger inescapable. Confronted with this inhospitable reality, Paul— like so many others in the same circumstances—developed strategies that, if all went well, would help him overcome hunger, come to terms with suffering and danger, and contain, if not wholly conquer, fear. Reliant on his family, confident in the love of his wife, and inclined for the most part to believe that he would live to enjoy the fruits of victory, Paul drew strength from his conviction that France would triumph at Verdun. At times he feared that he would not live to see the day he so ardently longed for; and he occasionally succumbed to moments of deep, almost debilitating depression. In the final analysis, however, he held fast because he believed that France could not fail. Defeat—and the devastation that he believed would accompany it—was not to be contemplated.

Victory would be possible, however, only if the troops were fed. Given the difficulties and dangers of venturing out through glutinous mud, pouring rain, and persistent shell fire, provisioning the troops was always difficult, and often impossible. When the army could not guarantee the food supply, men in the line looked instead to their families. Food from home, Paul had to admit, was essential to their very survival: "I assure you that I wouldn't ask for it if I didn't have to have it." He begged Marie and his mother to send him a food package once a week. His previous concern that they were working themselves to the bone to indulge him with luxuries now disappeared: all that mattered was that he and his companions receive enough parcels to keep them fed. "It is noon," he wrote in mid-May, "and we have not eaten our soup I have been snacking on the preserves that my mother sent me it is likely that we will not be able to heat our soup and we will have to eat it cold you can see what our situation is like and why I ask all of you for packages." The next day he repeated his plea: "I beg of you as well as my parents to continue to send me parcels because it has been several days now when we can't eat our soup until noon or one in the afternoon and if we have something to snack on we can use it there were three days when we couldn't eat at all because they couldn't heat up the soup."[44]

Thus it came about that Marie joined forces with Charlotte

and her mother-in-law to guarantee that Paul would be well provided for, come what might. They made sausages and cherry jam, sent bottles of wine, brandy, and *crème de menthe*, and prided themselves on the varied abundance of their parcels. Rabbits, chickens, and ham, cherries and apples, cauliflowers and artichokes, chocolate and honey made their way to the front, reminders of the rich bounty of rural France and the affection of those who remained at home. Spoilage was inevitable, given the disruptions in postal delivery that infuriated civilians and soldiers alike in the spring of 1916: one package that Marie sent in April took so long to arrive that the apples had rotted; also, as the weather warmed up, recently slaughtered, unrefrigerated chickens and rabbits came to be a risky proposition. Anything that had spoiled was abandoned; that which could be salvaged was invariably shared.[45] In late April 1916, Paul wrote that his battery had received two packages a day for four days in a row. He happily reported, "Everyone has lived like princes . . . but we needed that to keep our morale up." By mid-May, parcels from home were often the only sustenance they could count on. When one of Marie's many packages arrived, Paul noted that without it they would have had nothing to eat but cold coffee and canned meat (which the French troops spoke of disparagingly as *singe*—monkey meat). As Paul readily admitted, parcels from home did much more than fill the stomachs of men staring into the face of hell. "I thank you with all my heart my poor beloved wife it is so pleasant to see one's lot improved by those one loves especially when one finds oneself in need." Having endured the atrocious day of 1 June, he was delighted to receive yet another package two days later: "I thank you my dearest this package in the situation that I find myself in is worth more to me than all the others and will do me more good." Tangible proof that the men who fought were remembered and loved, packages from home gave frontline troops both the capacity to fight and a reason for doing so.[46]

Feeling reassured that he was loved, Paul was better able to confront the danger of life under fire and the fear that was its constant companion. Some soldiers no doubt relished the danger and welcomed it as the ultimate test of manhood; others did what they could to evade it. But for most frontline troops, unnecessary valiance was incomprehensible and cowardice was not an option. Taking refuge in a dugout or a makeshift shelter, a real part of everyday life at Verdun, was not always possible, as Paul knew firsthand. Unlike the military police, whom he disparaged in one letter as "cowards who hide themselves away in their holes and call that waging war," soldiers had to venture out of doors. From day to day there were tasks to be performed: food had to be distributed, horses cared for, mail delivered, guns fired. Some of these tasks were not inherently dangerous—civilians, after all, delivered letters, cooked meals, and groomed horses at little risk to life and limb. Most of these duties were not in themselves heroic, but all were necessary, and more times than not they had to be carried out in the face of danger. As Paul remarked, "If we were to hide away every time we heard the shells how would we get our food and look after our horses it's all a question of getting used to it." Experience also suggested that evasion offered little real insurance against death. When shells regularly fell short of their mark, far from their target, and anywhere in between, when a shelter might collapse under the weight of a direct hit or a battery might withstand relentless assault, little was to be gained by skulking in dugouts. In the final analysis, Paul told himself, "A coward runs as great a risk as a foolhardy fellow."[47]

Resigned, therefore, to the inevitability of living in immediate danger and close proximity to death, Paul tempered his realistic recognition that he might not survive with an optimism that he would defy the odds. There was, he often asserted, no shell with his name on it. At times, to be sure, the fighting was so intense and the prospects of survival so remote that his confidence wavered. On 27 May, for example, when the battery was under constant bombardment, he confessed: "I am very much afraid my dear Marie that we will not have the happiness of seeing each other again, but in any case neither courage nor prudence is lacking and you can be sure that I am not a coward." Recognizing as he did that death could come for him at any moment, he nonetheless took refuge in a belief that he would somehow be spared. When Marie had written earlier in the month to say that a man from a neighboring village had been killed by an exploding shell, Paul, fearing that he too would be killed, articulated his simple psychological strategy for survival: trust in fate, and hope for the best. "You were telling me about the death of poor old Barraud it is very sad but what can you say it's what awaits all of us these days it's him yesterday someone else tomorrow you just have to give yourself up entirely to fate and in spite of that always have confidence in the future and the ineptitude of the Boches . . . There is nothing to be done but let things happen and not think about it."[48] Because Paul did not share the religious faith that sustained many French soldiers during the First World War, he found no solace in prayer, the prospect of heavenly salvation, or the promise of divine intercession. Born into a socialist home, he scorned the Catholic Church, mocked what he took to be its superstitions, and despised its priests. Nor was his assurance based entirely on rational calculation, for the evidence in front of him suggested that he had no better chance than the next guy of getting out of Verdun alive.

Yet Paul's trust in a benign fate was neither entirely unfounded nor absurdly irrational. Death was everywhere at Verdun,
but it was both arbitrary in its choice and unpredictable in its
timing. Without doubt, some were destined to die, but experience suggested with equal persuasiveness that others seemed
destined to live. How else could one explain the fact that two
men running from shell hole to shell hole could survive a direct
attack? Once safely behind the lines, Paul described one very
near miss that made his fatalistic optimism seem justified. Several days earlier he and a companion had set out in search of
firewood. As Paul was about to venture back to the battery,
his companion, who was somewhat overweight, easily winded,
and now out of breath, urged him to sit and rest awhile. Just as
they sat down, a shell fell in front of them, shattering the logs
they were about to collect. Paul remarked, "If my buddy hadn't
been tired, we too would have been hit."[49] When a single shell
could scrape one man's jaw and shatter another man's skull;
when an overweight man, panting for breath, could save one's
life, it was not too unreasonable to "give oneself over to fate."
And like religious faith, this psychological mechanism was, in
the grim context of Verdun, of real practical value. It allowed
Paul to face the day's tasks, offer some much-needed reassurance to his ever anxious wife, and steel himself against adversity.

Had Paul lacked this perhaps unrealistic belief that there
was no shell with his name on it, he could easily have succumbed to despair. He certainly knew some who did. When he
met a young man from Nanteuil who was very "discouraged
and had given up hope of ever returning home," Paul remarked:
"It is true that the situation is critical but we must not despair
like that however bad things are." Despair would, he feared,
lead only to defeat: "If we were to think about the danger if we

were to abandon ourselves to discouragement pretty soon we would be shaking, quivering wrecks . . . And the Germans would quickly have the better of us this is precisely what must not happen because right now demoralization is getting the better of them and it's the beginning of the final round." He knew neither how long the "final round" would be nor how bitterly contested, but he did believe that France would emerge from it victorious. And so it was that from early April through the end of June, Pétain's charge to his troops, "On les aura," became Paul's mantra. In mid-April, when circumstances made it difficult to wash, shave, or even find clean water, when the mire and mud left him filthy beyond recognition and repulsive, he feared, to human touch, he wrote quite simply: "You must see in the papers that it's pretty rough here these days. But as Pétain said: 'On les aura.'" This was neither patriotic palaver repeated to make the folks at home feel better nor the innocent utterance of a man not yet embittered by the horrors of Verdun; it was an essential article of faith. On 25 April, once again reflecting on the wretched discomfort of daily life under fire, he was astonished by his own resilience: "I didn't even catch a cold or toothache it's this that makes me say that we will get them however crafty they are . . . We will have to get them [Il faudra les avoir]." Finally, when the Germans were bearing down on Fort Vaux, making their most significant territorial gains of the battle, Paul reassured Marie (and himself) that the French line would hold, the enemy would be pushed back, and victory would be secured: "They must have advanced a little toward V[aux], but they must be taking something with all these attacks that don't lead to anything because they won't take V[erdun] it can't happen it will be defended to the very end . . . Don't worry they won't take it they will exhaust all of their reserves without any result . . . so patience, and we will get them [*nous les aurons*]."⁵⁰ No other outcome could be contemplated.

Paul never spoke of the war in grand patriotic terms. The word "France" does not figure in his discussions of why he believed the war was worth fighting and the suffering worth enduring (although it becomes clear later in the war that he harbored a profound love for his homeland); nor indeed did he speak often of *la patrie*. Unlike many more-educated soldiers who believed fervently that France represented the cause of justice, liberty, and civilization, and unlike others, who saw in the war the opportunity for a religious revival—thanks to which the authority of the Catholic Church, under siege in the defiantly secular Third Republic, would be reasserted—Paul Pireaud was neither a well-educated nor a devout man. As an avowed socialist, he had little patience with the strident nationalism of the French Right. He certainly had no fondness for Germany, but recapturing Alsace and Lorraine, avenging the loss of 1871, and asserting French power on the Continent were not causes for which he ever expressed a willingness to die. He recognized other, equally compelling reasons to hold the line, however. Victory, he was convinced, would bring with it a better future. Like Henri Barbusse, who imagined in his novel *Under Fire* (published to much acclaim in 1916) a new world emerging from the agony of war, death, and unremitting suffering, a world forever immunized against militarism and committed to the principle of perpetual peace, Paul believed that victory would bring with it the wisdom "to know better how to avoid a storm [like this] in the future if it should arise."⁵¹

Following the birth of his son, this would seem reason enough to fight. Paul would suffer on the battlefield so that little Serge would never have to. But in the short term, he looked forward to the more immediate sensual domestic pleasures that victory would bring. However horrible the circumstances of the moment, Paul and Marie both took comfort in thinking that adversity reinforced their love for and emotional reliance on each other. In mid-May, Paul reflected on his dreams for the future: "It seems to me that after this trial things will be better than ever and that our happiness will be even more lasting than before because we will understand the value of it better by the sacrifice that was imposed on us . . . Some fellows say that we are spending the best years of our youth here and that when we get home we will be old and disgusted by the pleasures of the flesh that used to make us so happy. I don't say anything but it seems to me that to the extent that we will be together and united by a love as sincere and as powerful as ours, well, it seems that we will always be young even twenty or thirty years from now it seems to me that the noble flame of our love that joins us together will never die. What do you think of my ideas perhaps you find them a bit baroque but you know very well how much I love you I think only of you and of our future happiness." Far from thinking these ideas "a bit baroque," Marie admitted that she, too, dreamed of a day when her husband would be safe, her anxiety alleviated, and their desires satisfied. She assured him that her love and passion would not abate: "Ah yes, as you say they could separate us for twenty years and we would love each other as much as on the very first day it seems to me that I will love you as much as at the beginning when people say that there will come a time when we will no longer enjoy each other's caresses As for me, I believe that that will never happen not even a baby will prevent us from caressing each other as we did before How I would love to see you again."[52]

If victory could be expected to bring with it domestic tranquillity and sensual pleasure, defeat would unleash unthinkable devastation. That the Germans would ravage the land and rape the women of France was, in Paul's mind, indisputable. Tales of such atrocities were dismissed after the war as exaggerated, unwarranted wartime propaganda, but there was more than a grain of truth in many of the stories that circulated during the war, both at the front and behind the lines. As the German army advanced through Belgium and into northern France in August 1914, some of its troops, afraid of being set upon by civilian insurgents, did shoot civilians, take hostages, and rape women.[53] Stories that women had been brutalized in northern France strengthened Paul's resolve to fight on. He had no doubt that the Germans would violate French women, or that some of the women being protected from such atrocities were unworthy of the sacrifices made on their behalf. In March 1915, when he was still far behind the lines and had plenty of opportunity to watch the sexual shenanigans of his comrades and their occasional partners, he expressed his disgust at unfaithful women who indulged in affairs while "their poor husbands are in the trenches enduring the worst miseries putting their own lives on the line to prevent the Prussians from coming to defile and slit the throats of these women." A year later, and only weeks before being transferred to Verdun, he reiterated his contempt for women who were living a life of ease, while "we are having our faces bashed in to stop the Boches from coming to rape them."[54]

Though convinced that some women were unworthy, Paul was confident that his wife was not of their number. Marie had proved herself to be a faithful companion, constant in her correspondence, diligent in her duties, and unwavering in her affection. Pregnant with his child, she repeatedly reassured him of her love, fed him when he needed it most, and supported him in his moments of anguish. When he feared that no one would want to touch him because he was so disgustingly dirty, Marie reassured him: "You tell me that if you were to come home on leave in that state that no one would want to touch you. You are greatly mistaken because I assure you that dirt would not stop me from embracing you. Oh how I wish that you could come home like that because at least it would be soon and how happy I would be to see you again." When he was depressed and battling despair, she comforted him: "I see that you are completely despondent that you don't have much hope. I beg you, take heart, don't despair, even if you should be wounded by this ordeal you will get better and we will be happy in any event."[55]

However comforting these words of reassurance were, Paul was in his darkest moments wracked by doubt and tormented by fears that the domestic dream that sustained him would never come true. He never explicitly doubted Marie's faithfulness, but he did fear that she might nonetheless forsake him. In mid-May he described a dream that had, he said, unsettled him the previous night: seriously wounded and taken prisoner by the Germans, he had been forced to stay in convalescent hospitals in Germany long after the war was over. When he slowly made his way home, he found that Marie, believing that Paul had been killed in action, had remarried. Unwilling to disturb the happiness that his wife and young child now enjoyed, Paul left for America, where he made his fortune. Heartsick and all alone, he took consolation only in the thought that he would be able to leave his wealth to the son he had never known. It is possible that Paul had no such dream, for his recounting of it resembles in many particulars Balzac's story of Colonel Chabert, which was frequently retold—with appropriate updates to suit the circumstances of the early twentieth century—during the Great War. Perhaps Paul invented the dream in order to share with Marie anxieties to which he could not otherwise admit. Whatever the truth of it, he closed his account of the dream with a plea for reassurance: "Tell me to console me about this dream that you will never belong to another even if before and after my death someone else could give you more than I. I wonder so often if it is possible to be loved more than I love you I don't believe it is."[56]

Marie immediately gave Paul the assurance he craved: "This is a dream that will never come about oh yes I can swear to you that I will never be with anyone else first loving you as I do I would never be able to forget you and would not be able to be happy with another and second the little one we are going to have would never be happy [either] and so be assured on this subject that you have nothing to fear have confidence in me as I have confidence that if I were to die you would not take another wife who would certainly make our little one unhappy one can never replace the affection of a father or a mother it would be better to have no one." Thus reassured, Paul reciprocated: under incoming shellfire he gave his "pledge in the face of death" that he would never remarry. His sentence was marred by a scribble caused, he explained, by the shock of an exploding shell.[57]

Letters of this sort both tormented and reassured those who wrote and read them. How could Marie not be distressed by physical evidence that her husband was coming under direct fire? How could Paul, when surrounded by death, not fear for the future? At the same time, it was only contact with home that made the hell of Verdun endurable. When Marie offered Paul essential words of encouragement interspersed with promises of sexual pleasure, he drew sustenance from her unwavering constancy, gratification from her unabashed sensuality, and moral strength from her words of solace. However much he savored her most intimate confessions, he also appreciated her simple words of encouragement: "As for courage," he wrote in the aftermath of a ferocious attack, "thank you for having the strength of character to revive my morale I have all the courage I could need to see me through all possible trials."[58] Knowing that he was loved, reassured that he would not be forgotten, Paul confronted the terrors of life under fire resolute in the belief that if he and his companions-in-arms held fast, victory would be theirs and his future happiness would be secured.

My Paul how happy I am that you are not here because from five o'clock in the evening on the 11th till four o'clock on the 13th, oh how I suffered. It was the midwife from Verteillac who was here she looked after me well and she still hasn't left me. She took good care of me and I needed it because I was in a pretty state. She told me that I was lucky to push right then because being so weak I could have been put to bed much quicker I don't have a drop of blood left it was a dry birth and it will be three weeks before I will be able to lift my head up, so delay your leave until I am better. Don't worry about it the hardest part is over now and this morning I feel very well. We have a big hungry boy Marthe is nursing him for me until my milk comes in I will have to breast-feed him during these three or four hot months, for his sake and for mine. I can tell you that your father and mine and everyone are happy to have a boy in my last letter on Wednesday the pain had let up a little I did not believe what it was but then it came back this terrible pain. Oh how I suffered my poor Paul. And as they say it's too much work but for you I didn't feel weak . . .

Marie to Paul, 15 July 1916

THREE

Oh, How I Suffered, My Poor Paul

*O*n the day that Paul's battery left Verdun, Marie was three weeks away from giving birth. Like many expectant parents, the young couple spent much of their time in the months leading up to their baby's birth discussing the proper care for a pregnant woman: What should Marie eat? How much should she work? Should she consult a doctor, and if so when? Would a midwife suffice at the birth? Knowing that it was unlikely that Paul would be present to assist at the delivery (as was the custom in rural French society before the war), they also anticipated—with some justifiable anxiety—the moment of childbirth and hoped that all the care and precautions they had taken in the preceding months would guarantee a safe, uncomplicated delivery. Following the baby's birth on 13 July 1916, they turned their attention to the difficult and often emotionally wearing task of long-distance parenting. Serge Pireaud was a sickly baby who fell prey to many of the most dangerous infant maladies of the day and came close to death at least twice. But Marie was a stubborn, determined, and very modern mother, who would not, if she could help it, allow her newborn son to suffer from the serious illnesses of infancy, or for that matter the sniffles, without recourse to medical care. Convinced that medicine and the scientifically grounded procedures propounded in child-care manuals offered the best defense against her baby's illness, she braved the occasional opposition of parents and in-laws not yet convinced of the necessity or efficacy of newfangled methods. Buttressed by Paul's oft-repeated belief that no price was too high, no effort too excessive if their son could be saved, she consulted doctors when she could, paid willingly for expensive prescriptions when she had to, and sought out the most advanced advice available in her village community.

The Pireaud correspondence reveals how profoundly the war, far from being only a military venture played out on the battlefields of the western front, left its imprint on processes and practices of life that we think of as essentially and exclusively domestic. Mobilization made it almost impossible for fathers to help their pregnant wives, assist at childbirth, or contribute directly to the daily tasks of child-rearing. For millions of young mothers in all the belligerent nations, single-parenting became the temporary norm; for those whose husbands died at the front, it became a permanent reality. But insofar as the war diminished food supplies, increased women's workloads, and reduced civilian access to medical care, it also made it more difficult for a pregnant woman to eat well, to rest during the final stages of pregnancy, or to secure medical help in the event of an emergency. In rural France the requisitioning of cattle meant that milk was in short supply by the spring of 1916 and the military mobilization made it imperative that all women work in the fields, especially during the harvest months. Since many country doctors were serving as army medics, professional medical care was difficult to find and expensive when available. Nor could expectant women and young mothers easily observe professional advice that they avoid stress and anxiety. When their husbands were under fire, their infants colicky, and their lives punctuated by unexplained but inevitably nerve-wracking lapses in correspondence, a worry-free life was beyond their ken.

The letters that Paul and Marie exchanged throughout 1916

and into 1917 remind us how difficult—and dangerous—pregnancy, childbirth, and infancy could be in the early years of the twentieth century. The letters also reveal how profoundly this young peasant couple believed in the benefits to be gained from seeking medical assistance and embracing scientific principles of child care. Indeed, the war appears to have accelerated a fundamental cultural transformation in rural French society, one only dimly evident in the decades preceding 1914. For many centuries French peasant society had confronted the mysteries, anxieties, and dangers of childbirth and infant care by developing and depending upon an extensive body of traditional lore and practice. By 1916, however, those time-honored ways were susceptible to challenge, buffeted by scientific developments and demographic anxieties that demonized the old ways as superstitious, irrational, and inadequate and called upon peasants to turn their back on tradition, cultural lore, and practices that had been passed from generation to generation. The Pasteurian revolution of the late nineteenth century, with its emphasis on the lethal effects of microbes, demonstrated that illness caused by contamination could be prevented through sterilization. Because infant diarrhea brought about by the ingestion of unsterilized milk was the most pervasive and pernicious killer of children under the age of two, Pasteur's insights—if applied systematically—held out the promise of saving thousands of infants every year. Pediatricians inspired by these new ideas and appalled by the high rates of infant mortality that continued to plague France in the early years of the twentieth century (when 15 percent of all newborns died before their first birthday) produced child-care manuals that preached the moral necessity of applying Pasteurian principles in every nursery in the nation. Only by saving its infants from an untimely and now avoidable death, could France, the nation with the lowest birthrate in Europe, hope to defend itself in the future. The crusade against infant mortality thus became a battle for the future of France itself.

Insofar as doom-laden arguments of this sort—constituent elements of a national campaign against depopulation that dated back to the 1890s—were plentiful in the years leading up to the First World War, it is possible that improvements in infant health and a noticeable decline in infant mortality might have taken place in France with or without the advent of war. War, however, infused these arguments with a new, unprecedented urgency. Because the war simultaneously increased the death rate of young men (and potential fathers) and decreased even further an already anemic birthrate, it exacerbated long-standing fears that France was on the road to demographic annihilation. By the early 1920s, essays with alarmist titles that asked, "Will There Still Be a France in Thirty Years?" were by no means unusual. But the war did more than ratchet up the rhetoric in the national debate. It also compelled individual men (and the women they loved) to confront both the real possibility and the unwelcome implications of early death. Coming to terms with their own mortality, soldiers (and their wives at home) had to accept the possibility that a child born before or during the war might be their only heir. This meant that infants born during the war were in a very real sense potentially irreplaceable and thus uniquely valuable. When it was very possible that a child might be a couple's only offspring—the visible reminder of a man now lost, solace and support to a grieving widow—that child acquired a value that justified, as never before, all efforts to keep him (or her) alive and healthy. Members of a generation that was both blessed by the gift of literacy and cursed by the circumstances of war, Paul and Marie confronted the challenges of pregnancy, childbirth, and infant care with the neophyte's faith in science and the condemned man's determination to resist obliteration. Literacy gave them access to scientific ideas unknown to their parents' generation; intimations of mortality made them realize that if Paul were to die, Serge would be his mother's only comfort, his father's most poignant memorial.

From the earliest months of their marriage Paul and Marie hoped that she would soon conceive. In this regard they seem to have accepted the traditional belief that a young peasant wife was not fully a woman until she conceived and gave birth to a child. Pregnancy, perhaps more than marriage, remained the essential rite of passage conferring full adult status upon young women in rural France.[1] On each occasion when Marie ventured to join Paul behind the lines, she went home hoping that she was pregnant. These hopes were disappointed in late 1914, when it seems possible (but by no means certain) that Marie suffered a miscarriage; she certainly spoke of being ill before her period arrived to dash whatever hopes she might have entertained of pregnancy in January 1915. Several months later, in September 1915, there were other promising signs, for Paul wrote, "You tell me that you are sick could this not be a sign of pregnancy?" If so, Marie was to look after herself, for Paul ardently desired it to be "an heir that we produced there." When by mid-October it was evident that there was still no heir in the making, Paul wrote, with obvious disappointment, "I greatly regret that our work didn't lead to anything but I'm not giving up hope." Although Marie was not pregnant in October 1915, she certainly was by January 1916, when Paul worried that she might be "often inconvenienced" by feelings of illness.[2] This suggests that the baby was conceived in mid-November 1915, during Marie's last and longest visit to Paul's billet. Born in mid-July, Serge was, according to the midwife's best estimate, born two weeks early—but in rural French society, where only babies with gestation periods of less than seven months were considered premature, he was a baby who entered the world close to full-term.[3]

Although Marie was apparently eager to become pregnant, she contemplated childbirth with considerable trepidation. More than once, she expressed her relief at not being pregnant, for she was tormented by the fear that she would die in childbirth. Thus, in August 1915, when Paul had wondered whether she might be pregnant, she confessed that she was glad that she was not, for she "feared dying without seeing [her husband] again."[4] That Marie should have harbored such fears was neither unusual nor irrational. Fear of death in childbirth—expressed in such popular proverbs as "Pregnancy, one foot in the grave, and the other outside it"—persisted into the early twentieth century.[5] Maternal death rates for the war years reveal that the grim wisdom of this proverb was grounded in stark reality: in 1916 almost two thousand women died of complications relating to pregnancy and delivery. This maternal mortality rate of 1 death for every 175 full-term deliveries—a rate now replicated only in the world's most underdeveloped nations—gave young pregnant women like Marie real reason to fear for their own survival.[6]

Even if Marie knew nothing of the statistics, she certainly knew from local experience that a prolonged labor or complicated delivery could threaten the lives of mother and baby alike. In April 1915 the death of a local woman and child in childbirth prompted Marie to speculate that the mother had been unable to survive the knowledge that her husband had recently been killed at the front. This distressing incident, so emotionally wrenching for a young woman whose own husband was also at war, perhaps shaped Marie's anxieties more profoundly than any statistical evidence could have done, for "the memory of a woman who had suffered horribly and died without bringing her child to birth would long remain etched on the memory of the villagers or local townspeople."⁷ Thus, the unease that Marie confided to Paul before she became pregnant was by no means unfounded. It was only after she had safely—albeit painfully—given birth, that she could dismiss such fears as so much nonsense. In December 1916, she noted that a young woman of her acquaintance wanted to have a baby but was afraid that she would die in childbirth. Marie now had no time for such qualms: "As long as she thinks like that she will never have [a baby], as for me I never thought about that." But then she let slip a confession of abiding apprehension: "If I were pregnant now I would be more afraid."⁸

Until February 1916 Marie mentioned her pregnancy to no one but Paul. Not yet showing, she could still evade the prying eyes and unsolicited advice of curious neighbors and well-intentioned friends. But in early February, when her sister, having remarked that she was looking unusually full in the bust and rear, asked—perhaps in feigned innocence—what this could possibly mean, Marie realized that her condition would soon be public knowledge.⁹ Her sister, it seemed, had a well-known fondness for gossip. Neither Marie nor Paul looked upon this prospect with much enthusiasm, perhaps because their own ideas about how to care for a pregnant woman were in many respects at odds with much of the received wisdom that still circulated in the village.

At the beginning of the twentieth century few facets of French rural life remained more deeply influenced by traditional practices and revered ritual than pregnancy, childbirth, and infant care. Centuries-old customs were still prevalent in many parts of peasant France, including the Dordogne, and hygienists who urged pregnant women to reject well-established ways and embrace modernity instead—by seeking medical advice early in their pregnancy, resting during their final trimester, and eating a balanced diet—were often frustrated by the

persistence of customs that in their judgment were both irrational and injurious to mother and child alike.[10] One modern pe-
diatrician was appalled that new mothers, moved more by sentiment than by rigorous science, wrapped the stump of their
newborn's umbilical cord in the handkerchief they had carried
on their wedding day. And he was outraged that farm animals
often had the run of peasants' homes: "It has often happened,"
he lamented, "that pigs have eaten the hands of unfortunate babies, or have even devoured them entirely."[11] But tradition persisted, Dr. Pinard's efforts notwithstanding. In the farmhouses
of rural France, medical doctors' advice sometimes seemed im-
practical or hard to implement. Peasants were often not yet
convinced that modern medical precepts were any more effective than traditional practices in ensuring a healthy pregnancy
and a robust infant. For generations, women had placed their
hopes in the reassuring conventions of religious intercession
and in symbolic practices that called to mind the beneficial
outcome being sought—an expectant mother should, for example, eat carrots if she hoped to have a boy, onions for a girl;
to protect against fetal strangulation she should never wear
jewelry around her neck—and these customary practices did
not succumb quickly to the onslaught of science.[12]

Marie was not entirely unfamiliar with beliefs and practices of this sort. By early March, when her bouts with morning
sickness were behind her, she was eating well and seemed in
good health. She did, however, suffer from toothaches. She explained it to Paul, "Blood is going up to my head." Pregnancy
often resulted in decalcification, which could easily lead to
toothaches, especially at a time when regular dental care was
the exception rather than the rule. Unfamiliar with this scientific fact, peasants relied instead on a symbolic explanation for
a pregnant woman's dental ailments: as the body filled out, so
did the mouth. Marie thus perceived in the swelling of her

mouth a reflection of her swelling, pregnant body.[13] She saw her swollen mouth as a sign, not a treatable symptom, of her condition.

Paul, however, seemed to have very different ideas. Early in March 1916, when Marie was still in the first trimester of her pregnancy, he asked whether she had consulted a doctor yet and, as the weeks went by, insisted with increasing intensity that she drink milk on a daily basis. A pregnant woman's diet was not ordinarily subjected to close scrutiny, and dietary practices now taken for granted were often ignored or outright rejected. It was by no means the norm for pregnant women to consume milk every day, and here medical opinion sometimes reinforced popular practice. Although some doctors recommended that pregnant women drink milk as part of a balanced diet, others offered the very opposite advice: because calcium built strong fetal bones, a diet rich in dairy products would, they feared, make for a difficult delivery.[14] In the absence of any scientific consensus at the beginning of the century calling for women to drink milk during pregnancy, it is unclear why Paul was so adamant that Marie do so. Perhaps he thought that a more balanced diet, rich in protein, vitamins, and calcium, would help her combat the anemia that had in the past left her frail and easily tired and that might endanger her life during delivery by increasing the risk of hemorrhage.[15] Marie was attentive to but not obsessed by his admonitions. She assured him that she was drinking milk when she could get it, and she promised that her father, who was temporarily under the weather, would purchase her a milk cow when he felt well enough. As for consulting a doctor, she saw no point in doing so: "They can't do anything for me yet, I'll have to wait . . . In a few months we'll see if everything is where it should be."[16]

This was not good enough for Paul. From late March, when his battery was temporarily behind the lines, through the end of April, when he was consistently under fire at Verdun, he wrote repeatedly about the importance of buying a milk cow. On 28 March he put his case very plainly: "I have other more serious things to tell you and I am even going to lose my temper. Do you have milk? Has anyone bought you a cow because you should have been drinking milk for a long time already if your father doesn't want to do it then my father is there tell him straight out when it's such a serious matter of life . . . I want you to take care of yourself and that you do whatever is necessary. Do it for me. Think about the situation I find myself in if by your imprudence I were to remain here on this earth all alone with a baby to look after what will become of me what will my life be like? I beg of you, listen to me take care of yourself, stay strong so that everything will turn out all right and that we will be able to be happy together one day." On the following day, having learned that no one had yet taken the initiative to buy the dairy cow, he resolved to write his parents directly to impress upon them the urgency of the enterprise: "When it comes to a thing as important as this I cannot understand that they are not taking this more seriously."[17]

Marie, who seemed to live in quiet fear of her father-in-law, was reluctant to ask that he buy her a cow. "Your parents know that I want one they have not offered [to purchase one] and as for me I would never dare to tell them this because according to them it is not worthwhile and because I do not want to press the subject, I will wait." In spring 1916 not one of the family farms to which Marie had regular access—her own, that of her parents, or that of her in-laws—had a cow whose milk an expectant mother could have used. The farms had not lost their cattle, in spite of government requisitioning that continued to threaten every farm. In 1915, when Marie had worried that requisitioning would take half their cattle, Paul had reassured her that animals deemed "necessary for the exploitation of a farm" were not in danger of being confiscated. Thus, the farm still had access in spring 1915 to four cows, two of which soon calved. The arrival of the calves created new problems, however, as Marie subsequently explained. Because lactating cows, whose caloric consumption is high, could not simultaneously feed their young and be put to work in the fields, the farm was seriously short of draft animals: "The worst thing is that we are badly off for animals. We have one that has her calf, and Barotte had a superb calf yesterday morning. Now my father says that he wants to keep the new one because she's much bigger than the other one . . . We can't raise both of them in this season they won't have enough milk." The smaller of the two calves thus went to market in late July 1915, and Marie happily reported having realized the handsome price of 80 centimes per livre (for a total of 180 francs) from the sale. A year later, even if the farm still had the full complement of cattle from 1915, none was available for milk, either because the cows were pregnant once again and not yet lactating, or because they had weaned the calves born the previous spring and were no longer producing milk.[18]

Reluctant to press her case with her father-in-law, Marie looked to her father instead to find a milk cow. But he remained in poor health in spring 1916 and could not make the daylong journey to Angoulême that such a purchase now required. As draft animals of all kinds became increasingly hard to find, cattle that could once have been purchased at the local fair were now sold only in the big market towns, and at considerable expense. Indeed, scarcity, brought on by the requisitioning of more than a million dairy cows since August 1914, had caused the price of cattle to double in the first two years of the war.[19] And a new regulation introduced in October 1915 to prohibit the slaughter of calves only exacerbated the problem. This ban had been drawn up to protect the future cattle stock: if too many calves were slaughtered, soon no mature cattle would be available to meet the nation's ever growing needs. Well intentioned though it clearly was, this regulation weighed heavily on the peasantry, for it reduced the stock of milk for human consumption and imposed on farm families the additional expense of raising cattle that might otherwise have been sold or slaughtered.[20] Many peasant households, convinced that a calf was a luxury a wartime farm could no longer afford, were loath to observe the regulation: the sooner the calf was weaned, the sooner its mother could be put back to work in the fields or her milk sold for profit. At a time when milk supplies were dropping precipitately—from 51.2 million hectoliters in 1914 to 38.1 million two years later—for want of adequate fodder, this was no minor consideration. Although milk shortages would assume critical proportions only in 1917, when scarcity afflicted various parts of the nation and when lack of fodder compelled farmers to slaughter their mature animals, the outlines of the crisis were evident in 1916.[21]

If all these factors combined to make Paul's parents reluctant to buy a dairy cow for their pregnant daughter-in-law, their resistance was not driven by economic considerations alone. They were, Marie remarked, not convinced that it was "worthwhile." Truth to tell, it is not clear that Marie believed it was worth making much of a fuss about, either. When pressed by Paul for the reassurance that she drank milk daily, she responded that she did so when she could get it, but since this required that she walk into the village, a few kilometers away, sometimes she preferred to stay at home. She assured Paul, "Don't worry about it milk isn't going to save me or kill me especially when I only have to go and look for it in order to have some." There is no evidence in Marie's correspondence that she or her in-laws were indifferent to the health of her unborn child. Indeed, Paul's mother was clearly delighted by the prospect of becoming a grandmother—confident that the baby would be a boy, she rejoiced during these saddest of days at the thought of an heir—and reported in April 1916 that Marie looked wonderful: she was getting fat everywhere and had a "beautiful bust." And Marie took steps to consult with doctors and midwives relatively early in her pregnancy, in order to prepare herself adequately for childbirth. Thus, we can only conclude that neither she nor those around her believed that it was necessary for pregnant (or anemic) women to drink milk on a regular basis. Paul, nonetheless, had his way. In a nation that so revered its valiant poilus, how could Marie, her parents, and her in-laws have resisted the wishes of a man facing death at Verdun? Whether the cow would do Marie any good or not, it would be bought. And so in late April, more than a month after Paul had first raised the issue, Marie confirmed that her father and father-in-law had at last purchased the milk cow. Paul was greatly relieved: living under daily bombardment, he took comfort in the knowledge that his wife, at least, would be well looked after.[22]

Paul then turned his attention to two other aspects of prenatal care: was Marie receiving adequate and appropriate medical care? And was she staying out of the fields, where the heavy labor of summer farming was, he feared, bound to place her health and that of their unborn child in jeopardy? In both regards, his opinions—firmly held, frequently asserted—were at odds with conventional opinion. It certainly was not customary for rural women to consult a doctor in the early stages of pregnancy, however much Paul insisted on it. In early April 1916, Marie reported that she had just had a visit from one of the local midwives, who had impressed upon her the need to take good care of herself. Because Marie was not of the most robust health, the midwife advised that she consume a fortified diet, which seemed to comprise nothing more than some medicinal drops in her milk, and bathe regularly one month before delivery. Marie's frailty notwithstanding, the midwife held out hope that the baby would be healthy: "Often the mother is weak and the baby is strong." This assessment did not fully reassure Marie, who wondered whether she should follow the midwife's counsel or that of the local doctor, who recommended no special precautions until a few weeks before delivery. Marie seemed inclined to favor the doctor, for rumor had it that the midwife from Verteillac killed her patients, but she wanted to be directed by Paul's preference: "Tell me what to do if you prefer that I follow the doctor's advice or the midwife's tell me frankly your opinion as for me I have no preferences it's all the same to me." She did however recount that the midwife had attended at eight deliveries—and had successfully delivered nine babies, including one set of twins—in the first four months of the year.[23]

When Paul responded four days later, he confessed, "I am so afraid for you that I dare not talk about these things." Nonetheless, he would try to make arrangements for a local doctor to visit Marie and hoped that she would then be in a better position to decide. As for the doctor and midwife she had already consulted, Paul had nothing but contempt: "I have almost no confidence in either the one or the other . . . I tell you again, I cannot give you advice look at my situation if something bad were to happen you will understand. Consult other doctors and midwives if you wish and you will see then which ones are in agreement." Two months later, he returned to this theme, urging her to consult either a doctor or a midwife if she was feeling unwell. He thought that the baby might come earlier than expected and that it would be better to be well cared for in advance of the delivery.[24]

However much Paul might have wanted Marie to seek a doctor's opinion and have a doctor attend at the delivery, the prospects that this would happen were very slim. Half the doctors and pharmacists who had practiced in the Dordogne before August 1914 were mobilized and serving either at the front or in military hospitals behind the lines, and their absence left the civilian population of Dordogne seriously underserved for the duration of the war. In the region comprising Nanteuil-de-Bourzac, the doctor from Verteillac and the medical officer (*officier de santé*) from Saint-Martial-Viveyrol were both mobilized; only Aline Faudout, the midwife from Verteillac who had trained in Paris and had received her diploma in 1889, remained on call in the immediately surrounding region.[25] Nor was the situation significantly better in the nearby villages of the Charente. Ordinarily, Salles-Lavalette had access to two doctors, but both were in uniform, and villagers now had to go at least ten kilometers to find a doctor or a pharmacist. Overworked and newly responsible for keeping up practices that extended far from their home base, the doctors who remained in the region did not hesitate to raise their fees: before the war the established rate for a house call in Salles-Lavalette was eight francs; by 1916 it had risen to fifteen francs.[26] Other village reports tell much the same story: either the regular doctor had been mobilized, or if a doctor was still to be found, his services were expensive and only intermittently available. A doctor in the small community of Saint-Paul-Lizonne, only a few kilometers from Nanteuil, continued to practice, but he was overworked and "did not visit his patients as regularly as he should." When a doctor could be found, the inflated price of medical care created "great difficulties," in the judgment of one local observer, "for those who were seriously ill."[27]

To guarantee that their baby would be healthy, Paul also continued to urge Marie to stop working in the fields: "You have to understand that you are being very imprudent to go and work with the carts in your condition promise me not to

take this up again or I will write to your parents to have them
forbid your doing this and I will be very angry with them for
letting you do so." He then went on to warn her of the dire
consequences of her foolhardiness: if he were to die and she
were to deliver a stillborn child, she would have nothing but a
memory of him and no one to look after her in the future. If
that did not cool her desire to work in the fields, nothing
would. And as if to make his point more emphatic still, he observed in the very next paragraph that he was going to have to
don his gas mask, for his eyes were starting to water and a gas
attack seemed imminent. Paul's anxiety persisted, and in mid-
June he urged Marie once again not to work in the fields: "I beg
you take care of yourself don't work promise me to be sensible
so that everything will turn out well and promise me especially
even though everything is going well to hire a doctor along
with the midwife."[28]

In his insistence that Marie abandon her agricultural labors,
Paul sounded for all the world like the early twentieth-century
doctors who warned in apocalyptic terms of the dangers
women courted by working during the final trimester of their
pregnancy. Without doubt many of the professional men who
urged young couples to do what they could to improve the
birthrate and save France from demographic decline had a very
conservative political agenda: they believed that the nation
would be best served if women were to abandon paid employ-
ment (especially in factories) and devote themselves exclusively to their maternal responsibilities. But even those who
recognized that some women had to work counseled that for
the sake of the child they refrain from doing so in the last
trimester of pregnancy. Women who worked at strenuous jobs
through the end of their pregnancy delivered babies that
weighed approximately .35 kilograms (12 ounces) less than ba-

bies born to women who did not work at all during their last three months. The deficit was even more apparent among rural women who worked in the fields up through delivery: their babies weighed, on average, four hundred grams less than babies born to peasant women who rested during the final trimester. Such indisputable data prompted one doctor to argue that women should be under a doctor's supervision for the first six months of pregnancy and should be required by law not to work during the final three months.[29]

Advice of this sort, which seemed heedless of the economic realities of rural life, especially in wartime, also ran counter to received opinion in rural society. Popular wisdom occasionally recommended that a pregnant woman reduce her workload, "but these recommendations were rare." Indeed, many believed that a pregnant woman benefited from sustained agricultural labor: by strengthening her, it helped prepare her for the hard work of childbirth and thus reduced the time spent in labor.[30] Such attitudes remained evident in the southwest of France in the early years of the twentieth century, where peasant women rarely had the luxury of resting during pregnancy. Indeed, in one village not far from Nanteuil-de-Bourzac, a local woman continued to work in the fields until labor pains forced her to stop.[31] Perhaps she was an exception in the last years before the war—would an entire village take note of something that was considered ordinary behavior?—but probably not during the war itself. Certainly there were fewer pregnant women in wartime France, when the birthrate dropped by 40 percent, but peasant women who did conceive during the war often had little choice but to work in the fields.[32] With so many men away at war, the luxury of rest was unthinkable. The risks of continued labor remained, however: during the war years women who bore the burdens of farmwork through the last months of their pregnancy seemed more liable than ever before to still-births and premature deliveries.[33]

Although it was not advisable for Marie to work through the last months of her pregnancy, it is not surprising that she did so. Necessity compelled her to ignore advice she knew to be good. Her mother, fearing Paul's wrath, worried that she was, in fact, doing too much, and Marie in retrospect conceded as much. She certainly went into labor earlier than she or the midwife had anticipated. Writing on the morning of 13 July—less than twelve hours before her son was born—Marie confessed to Paul that she had begun to experience what she thought might be her first labor pains. "I can tell you that I'm beginning to suffer a lot and yesterday evening I would have sent for someone I said nothing and this morning I'm suffering a little less All morning long my mother has been fretting, saying that I worked too much these past days. I know that it's true." Perhaps, however, this was only false labor: "I saw in the book that 12 to 13 days before a first delivery one suffers prelabor pains." Within hours of writing this letter, Marie gave birth to her son, Serge. As her letter to Paul announcing the birth and an undated fragment written shortly thereafter make plain, labor and delivery were unusually difficult, and the recovery of mother and child were fraught with problems.

The very existence of these letters is remarkable. Marie belonged to the first generation of peasant women who had both the ability and the need to describe in writing the experience of giving birth. Women of previous generations had probably not been sufficiently literate for the task, but the need had not presented itself, either. Their husbands would have been close at hand, at most no farther than an adjacent room, and in many instances would have assisted with the delivery itself. In the southwest of France, where women customarily delivered standing up while gripping a bar placed above the hearth, their husbands would often hold them up to lend them strength. During the war, however, men were rarely present for the birth of their children, and thus it became necessary to set down in writing events that previous generations of new fathers had observed directly.[34]

However much Marie missed her husband and longed for his safe return, she confessed that she was happy that he had not been home to attend the birth, for he would have seen "how much she suffered" from five o'clock in the evening of 11 July through four in the afternoon on the thirteenth. In the end, it was the midwife from Verteillac who assisted at the birth, and she had been, Marie averred, a model of compassion and useful assistance: "She took very good care of me and I needed it because I was not in a pretty state." The birth had been "dry"—in all likelihood, the amniotic sac had ruptured in advance of delivery—and had thus increased the risk of maternal and infant infection. Nonetheless Marie had displayed a courage that had astonished the midwife, who observed that many stronger women just let themselves go when confronted with the difficulties of labor. Whatever fears she had once harbored, Marie did not think once of the possibility that she might die in delivery. At least, she did not confess such thoughts to Paul: "I thought of you and the joy I was going to give you the joy that I would be able to let you experience." Positive thinking did not, however, ease the pain entirely: shortly before the baby was delivered Marie fainted, coming to only when revived with coffee laced with brandy. She must have been unconscious for more than a fleeting moment, for the midwife and Paul's mother were both convinced that Marie had died, and the baby with her. Once revived, she followed the midwife's final instructions and with "one last spasm of suffering" delivered the baby. Seeking reassurance that he had no injuries or physical handicaps, Marie immediately inquired about his health. And then her suffering continued, for she had to be "delivered by force" of the after-birth. Experience suggested—and custom asserted—that "until the placenta had emerged, 'nothing was finished yet': the mother still had 'one foot in the grave.'"[35] Marie certainly did. She lost significant quantities of blood (as was often the case when women suffered from anemia), suffered a vaginal tear that required stitches "to be put back together again," and was confined to bed for at least three weeks. Marie's experience was almost too much for all who witnessed it: her mother became physically sick, her father-in-law had to hide himself away, in order not to hear her screams, and her father wept. Nor could Marie rid herself of the memory of an agonizing labor: she lamented, "Oh, how I suffered, my poor Paul."[36]

Sustained through her travails by thoughts of "our son, your return, and our complete happiness," Marie hesitated to ask Paul to come home immediately. The birth of his son certainly gave him legitimate grounds to request compassionate leave, but neither he nor Marie wanted him to "waste" a leave while she remained confined to bed. Thus Marie advised Paul more than once that he should postpone his leave until she was "completely healed." Having made the point initially in the letter written on 15 July, Marie returned to it the following day, when she assured Paul that she was slowly recovering. She promised that she would take no risks with her health, for she had to think about "the pretty little one" who needed her. Nonetheless the prognosis for her recovery remained unchanged: "After such suffering, I will have to stay in bed for three weeks, and then would only be allowed up for a few hours at most for an additional week." For this reason, she wrote, "it will be at least a month before I can be with you." She did not forbid Paul to request the leave that would bring him home earlier but explained, "I would like it much more to be up on my feet again especially so that I can be with you." After seven months of enforced separation, the agony of childbirth, and the anguish of Verdun, Paul and Marie were, not surprisingly, eager for each other's sexual company. But as the midwife made very clear to Marie, that would have to wait until she was fully recovered, and even then the couple would have to take precautions. Marie could not risk becoming pregnant again.[37]

She remained in fragile health for several weeks after the birth, unable to get out of bed and subject to dizzy spells. She learned the hard way that she was not one of those women who could be up within a week of delivery, because when her father had carried her from one bed to another (to change the linens), she all but passed out. Her fainting spells persisted into late July. On a day when the rest of the family was occupied with the harvest, Marie, impatient to retrieve the mail that had been dropped inside the front door, pulled herself out of bed. She barely made it across the room before her legs buckled under her. Determined nonetheless, she made her way to the front door, holding on to the wall as she went. Once safely back in bed, she admitted that she had acted imprudently: she could have fainted when no one was on hand to revive her. Although she remained swollen and had, she confessed, "the pallor of death," she hoped that she would be fully recovered by the time Paul arrived home in mid-August.[38]

Whatever her own trials, they paled in comparison with those of a local woman whose husband was one of Paul's boyhood friends. In mid-October Marie wrote about Jean Nadal's wife, who had recently been delivered of a stillborn baby. The midwife, recognizing immediately that this would be a complicated delivery, had called for a doctor. By the time he arrived, however, Nadal's poor wife had been in labor for the better part of twenty-four hours and it was too late to save the baby, who

Le 16 juillet 1916

16/7/16

Mon Paul C. est toujours de tel comme
le pense que si t. écris. J'ai épuiser
le crayon il faut que j'écrive à l'encre
et se ne va pas enfin maintenant
avec beaucoup de soin et pas d'imprudence
on ce sortira de la. Et je t. assure
que avec un si j'ai petit que nous
avons j'en ferais pas. Je recois chaque
jour tes lettres dans celle du 9
ou tu parles d'une depeche tu ferais
comme moi tu ne le croyais pas
encore la. Si c'est du 23 tu fait

Letter from Marie to Paul Pireaud, 16 July 1916. Service historique
de la défense, France.

10 jours d'avance La sage femme dit
elle que j'ai avancer de 15 jours
Enfin c'est fait c'est le principal
et j'espere que se te fera rien et
que tu ne m'en voudras pas

Pour ta permission voila il me
faut apes de telles souffrances 3
semaines de lit huit jours de chambre
et passer que 2 ou 3 heures dehors alors
tu vois autant dire un mois pour
que je puisse etre un peu avec toi
Maintenant fait comme tu voudras
je serais toujours contente mais j'
aimerai mieu etre retablit surtout
pour etre a toi il me faut bien ce
temps j'ai de rude dechirure qu'on
a etait obliger de me mettre des
machins en argent pour le faire recoler je
ne sois pas le temps qu'on l'y laissera
jusqu'a tant que je me trouvrai bien

was asphyxiated at birth. Marie believed that the baby might have lived if the doctor had been able to get there sooner, but he was of the opinion that nothing could have been done. Had he been consulted earlier in the pregnancy, he might have been able to reposition the baby, so that the delivery would have been straightforward, but by the time labor set in, there was, he insisted, nothing to be done. When Nadal received a telegram calling him home, there was no word that the baby had died. Thus, when he discovered the truth, he was overwhelmed by grief and inclined to blame the midwife. Many in the community probably agreed, for the woman who had attended at the birth was, Marie reported, widely believed to be lazy and incompetent. By contrast, Mlle Aline was, in Marie's estimation, rather fearsome but intelligent and experienced. The Nadal family's experience only confirmed Marie's confidence in obstetrical expertise: if one called "either an intelligent midwife or a doctor one would have a little baby."[39]

Paul learned of his son's birth on 17 July, the day he rejoiced at being able to claim the "sweet name of daddy" and wrote: "To have a son, that makes me mad with joy it is what I have always dreamed of. Oh yes, I wanted a son very much." Although neither had said as much in the previous months, a son would guarantee not only the survival of the family farm but also, something perhaps more important in the circumstances of 1916, the continuation of the family name. Paul's joy was, however, tinged with regret at not having been present to alleviate Marie's suffering. He could not help weeping when he read her description, in her own trembling hand, of her difficult labor. "How you must have suffered my dear such a Calvary with us separated must be engraved on your memory What a sad life but let us hope something tells me that we will have happy days again especially with such a sweet baby who will be our joy our hope for the future and always our happiness." He begged her to take care of herself and not do anything that might endanger her health, for the sooner she was fully recovered, the sooner they could be together again. "When I think that I now have another person to love and cherish I am completely overcome by emotion how long the days are going to seem to me now."[40]

Marie was convinced that her baby was beautiful. With his chestnut brown hair, blue-gray eyes, and face as round as an apple, he was, in her considered judgment, certainly lovelier than their cousin's baby at the same age, "but, as they say, the one you love is always beautiful." She expected that at six months he would be "a pretty little cherub." The sad truth was that little Serge was anything but lovely at birth. Long and thin, with too little of the baby fat that doctors deemed proof of an abundant prenatal diet, he would be sickly, gaunt, and susceptible to life-threatening illness. Marie believed that he was thin because she had been "all swollen" in the last months before delivery, perhaps a sign that she suffered from toxemia or prenatal diabetes. But in rural France, it was customary to look askance at a pregnant woman who appeared to gain too much weight, not because she was placing her own health in jeopardy, but because every ounce that a mother gained was supposedly one that she took from her unborn child.[41] If Marie subscribed to this belief, and she certainly believed in retrospect that she should have seen the swelling she experienced in pregnancy as an ominous sign, then perhaps she considered Serge's undernourished frame the unfortunate consequence of her own "swollen" form.

If Marie had not experienced real difficulties with breast-feeding, Serge might have quickly made up for any nutritional deficiencies evident at birth. He certainly took to Marthe, the wet nurse Marie hired until her own milk came in. The situation became serious, however, when on the fourth day he still had trouble nursing at his mother's breast. On 18 July Marie wrote for the first time to Paul of the difficulties mother and child (as yet unnamed) were having with nursing. On the previous day, the midwife had recommended that he be put to Marie's breast, but to no effect. Convinced that if he were hungry enough he would suckle properly, they had let him cry the whole day long. Beside herself with anger, Marie finally abandoned hope of nursing her son, and handed him back to Marthe. A week after delivery, the situation was no better: although Marie tried to nurse her son every morning, he quickly grew impatient at her inadequate milk supply and howled until given to the wet nurse.[42] Marie's troubles with breast-feeding were no doubt caused in part by the trauma of an exceptionally difficult delivery and the meagerness of her prenatal and postnatal diet. Everyone seemed convinced that all would be well once she starting eating solid food again, for she consumed nothing more substantial than broth for a week or more after the delivery. Marie was not entirely sure, however: "Perhaps solid food will make my milk come in if not I will have to nurse him with cow's milk but I am hopeful that it [breast milk] will come because I will be much happier and my little one will do much better." Anxiety, ever present for wartime wives, may also have reduced her milk supply. After the war, a doctor who specialized in neonatal and infant care observed that many young mothers, distraught by the mobilization of their husbands and the unease that necessarily accompanied it, had been unable to produce adequate quantities of milk.[43] Marie might well have been one of these unfortunate women: she labored in the fields until days before the delivery, did not consume the extra calories needed for nursing, worried constantly about her husband, under fire at Verdun, and endured a difficult delivery. It was hardly surprising that she could not nurse her infant son.

Marie was definitely grateful for Marthe's assistance: "I assure you that Marthe has done us a good turn for which we will never be able to be sufficiently grateful you will see when you get home what I mean yes you will be happy you will see that it took someone patient, intelligent, and devoted to save your little son."[44] In closing, she sought to reassure her husband, who until that moment had no idea that his son was in need of saving, that all was well: both she and the baby were, she affirmed, on the road to recovery. This remained true for as long as Marthe was available to help. She was a suitable wet nurse: she lived nearby, agreed to stay with Marie and the new baby for the first week, and had ample milk. She seems to have been unconcerned that her services were illegal. The Roussel law, passed in the 1870s to regulate a wet-nursing industry that placed many nurslings with women who could not provide for them sufficiently, prohibited women from acting as wet nurses if their own babies were younger than seven months.[45] Still, Marthe had no interest in staying at Lescure for the long term. She had her own daughter to care for and a farm that needed her attention. Thus, when Marthe returned home in the last week of July, Marie had to find some alternate source of nourishment for her son. There was, as she had already indicated, only one real option: cow's milk. This was, however, an imperfect solution. She told Paul that she would prefer to nurse their son until autumn came. Whatever reservations she had, though, the couple agreed that she was in no condition to nurse the baby. Paul, in fact, was so worried that she was going to wear herself out to no good effect that he readily seconded her decision to put Serge on a bottle.[46]

For a child born in midsummer, few things were more dangerous than a baby bottle. Milk soured quickly in the summer heat, and farmhouses, lacking electricity, running water, and surfaces that could be kept sanitized, rarely had the facilities needed to sterilize or safely store bottles, nipples, and milk sup-

ply. Babies fed from unsterilized bottles almost always got diarrhea and often died of it. The malady had accounted for at least
a third of all infant deaths in prewar France.[47] The dangers were
greatest in large cities, where working women were more likely
than peasant women to abandon breast-feeding shortly after
giving birth and where the sterilizing of bottles was rare. Children born in the countryside were considerably better off: the
infant mortality rate for the Dordogne was less than half that
of Paris.[48] Nonetheless, the summer months were especially
treacherous because babies were often put on a bottle while
their mothers worked to bring in the harvest.

Marie certainly knew that babies were most susceptible to
life-threatening illness in midsummer. No doubt she had heard
as much from her mother and other women in the village,
whose collective experience would have acquainted them with
sad stories of babies laid low by summertime infections, but it is
also likely that she had read in a child-care manual that she frequently consulted of the danger of bottle-feeding in the heat of
summer. We do not know which book she kept by her bedside
or how she came to possess it. It is probable, however, that she
owned some version of Adolphe Pinard's *L'Enfant de sa naissance à
la fin de la première enfance*. This manual, aimed at young parents
who had the opportunity, in the age of Pasteur, to protect their
newborns from the ravages of bacterial infection, was part of an
extensive prescriptive literature that emerged in France in the
years before the First World War. An active contributor to the
depopulation debates, Pinard, the Dr. Spock of early twentieth-
century France, believed emphatically that the population crisis could be addressed by increasing the life expectancy of
newborns: "The weakness, infirmity, and illnesses of infancy
are," he insisted, "avoidable." His infant and child-care manual
(originally used in elementary school classes) was reissued in
1914 for the use of adults "who are strangers to medicine."

For Pinard the key to infant well-being was sterilization: everything from the scissors used to cut the umbilical cord to the baby's cradle to the food supply, of course, had to be completely germ-free. To this end he championed breast-feeding and insisted that nearly all new mothers could successfully nurse their babies. Only 2 percent of mothers were, in his judgment, physically incapable of doing so. But many new mothers (Marie among them) who had difficulty producing enough milk in the early days to satisfy their babies' hunger abandoned the enterprise entirely. Whereas some doctors believed that infant formula was an acceptable alternative to mother's milk (but only in cases where the mother could not nurse), Pinard was of the emphatic opinion that "any kind of food other than milk is poison" for a baby. If a mother had to choose something other than human milk, cow's milk was acceptable, but only if it was fully sterilized and properly stored. Unsterilized milk would lead to "illness almost always, death sometimes." This, sadly, was especially true in the summer months—"the killing season" in Pinard's unambiguous phrase—when it was most difficult to protect milk from contamination.[49]

When Marie, against her better judgment, put Serge on a bottle, at first all seemed fine. An infatuated mother who could not bear to hear her baby cry, she gave him his bottle whenever he whimpered. More experienced mothers, convinced that he would soon be running her a merry chase, warned that she was going to regret her soft-hearted ways. "They tell me that I will probably not have seen the end of [such behavior]," she reported, but admitted that she didn't care: "I cannot bear it when he cries every cry tears at my heart so I'm ready to do anything for him." She did worry, however, that perhaps he liked his bottle too much, for he slept with it and she feared that he would "take it too much and that would make him sick." Nonetheless, for the moment all was wonderful: "I am seated on my bed, and he is lying across me; he's holding his empty bottle in his two hands and is looking up at me with his big eyes and making not a sound my mother is preparing his milk and he is about to fall off to sleep I would give a great deal for you to be able to see him right now he is so cute his skin is fine and so white he is starting to develop a double chin."[50]

Within days, however, it was evident that the baby had colic, not in itself a life-threatening condition, but nerve-wracking enough; he cried constantly unless she picked him up and carried him in her arms. Marie assured Paul (and reassured herself) that there was nothing to worry about, but she could not ignore his cries. Desperate for a little peace and quiet, she experimented with a new ploy, much touted by the Belgian refugee families in the area and guaranteed to calm a crying baby: a soother, made by wrapping a piece of bread in cotton and soaked in sugar, would, it was said, quickly calm a cranky baby. Marie was not convinced. Although her baby had taken to it immediately, he lost interest once he had sucked the sugar dry. And in any case, too much sugar was not, in her judgment, good for newborns. All of which suggested, to Marie at least, that "without doubt the Belgians are stupider than the French."[51] Disappointed by home remedies that did not work and distraught that her baby continued to cry, Marie walked back and forth with him in her arms until he settled down.

In the following weeks Marie worried that her son was not yet gaining weight at an appropriate rate. Suspecting that Paul would expect to find a plump baby when he arrived home in late August, Marie warned him that Serge remained thin and seemed to her inexperienced eye to be gaining weight slowly. To allay her own anxieties she arranged to have him weighed when he was three weeks old. Traditional rural practice held that babies should not be weighed at birth or in the weeks immediately following. Pinard believed that this was yet another example of rural ignorance, and people's increasing willingness in recent years to weigh their babies at birth gave him hope for the future.[52] The practice was not yet commonplace in Nanteuil-de-Bourzac. Little Serge, at least, was not weighed when he was born, and thus Marie had only a very rough idea of how much weight he might have gained in his first weeks. "Yesterday I weighed him to see if he's gaining weight he weighs 6 livres 3 if they had let me weigh him at birth I could be more precise I saw in the books that they are supposed to weigh about 5 livres [2.5 kilograms] and that in the first week they lose weight and that by the 15th day they are at the same weight as when they were born so you see that he's just about right now he should gain between 20 and 30 grams a day." Although the birth-weight figure Marie cited here was low when compared with some data of that era—one expert wrote that a full-term baby should weigh about 3.2 kilograms—the growth rate corresponded almost exactly to Pinard's statistics: a healthy baby, having lost weight in the first week, should gain between fifteen and thirty grams per day in the first month, and between twenty and thirty-five grams in the second month.[53]

If Serge was indeed gaining weight at the rate Marie suggested, he was probably not seriously ill in the weeks immediately after being weaned. His crying would have been a normal manifestation of infant colic. Nonetheless, he seemed less than robust when his father saw him for the first time in late August. Upon returning to active duty, Paul confessed how astonished he had been to find the baby so small and fragile: "I must open my heart to you completely since my leave you must know that I had never seen such a small baby . . . I had no idea how he would look I imagined him in my mind as looking like Valentine's baby and when I saw how small he was especially when he was naked I was surprised but I quickly realized that I had been mistaken to imagine him as if he were already one year old and from that first day onward to tell you how much more I loved him poor little fellow that he is." Paul's reaction was natural enough—who has not been surprised by the fragility of a newborn baby? Yet Serge was now on the brink of life-threatening illness. Although the colic that had troubled him in the first month was undoubtedly uncomfortable, the ailment that tormented him in early September, sometimes referred to as convulsive colic or *cholera infantum* (for its grim similarity to cholera), was dire indeed. Marie's letters tell of successive days and nights occupied with walking and holding her screaming baby until he settled down. On one occasion it took three hours and two bottles before he fell asleep. A syrup that she was administering seemed to calm him somewhat, and Marie noted that she would soon have to get a second bottle from the pharmacy. By this point Marie, only barely recovered from labor and delivery, was suffering the effects of single parenthood: having spent the days and evenings walking the baby till he fell asleep, she herself was feeling ill and had a persistent cough. On one evening, the baby slept for only a few hours before awakening in real distress and then kept his mother up until 3 A.M. Marie's mother spelled her at that point, but the baby remained restless all day long and would not sleep until 8 P.M. Marie noted with some alarm: "This is not ordinary colic."[54]

As Marie wrote her daily letter on 14 September, the baby, now two months old, was sitting on her lap, crying for all he was worth. Two days later, she feared that he was on the brink of death. He was gaining no weight, crying day and night, and Marie thought she would have to consult the doctor again. This she did within the next day or so, because by 19 September he was doing much better, thanks to a remedy that the doctor had recommended. Although the medicine was expensive, Marie was indifferent to the cost: "Nothing is too expensive for

our little one and we started the new treatment yesterday evening and this morning he is laughing as much as you would
like." By 23 September he was noticeably better and was putting on weight. The crisis had passed, but, as Marie warily admitted, he had had them all worried for a while, crying as he
did for a week straight.[55]

Only at the end of September did she divulge the whole
story. Having inquired about the babies of other men in Paul's
battery, and whether they were being breast-fed or bottle-fed,
she opined that breast-feeding was much the better option because many babies could not digest cow's milk. This had obviously been true of Serge: when she had put him on cow's milk
he had had violent gastrointestinal distress, with diarrhea and
vividly discolored bowel movements. These were danger signs
of the first order. Pinard alerted young mothers to be attentive
to any kind of bowel irregularity: too many bowel movements
or too few should give equal cause for alarm. If a baby had
stools that were dark green or otherwise unusual, especially
during the dangerous summer months, the mother should call
for a doctor immediately.[56] Yet when Marie expressed her concerns to her mother and other neighborhood women, they all
assured her that there was nothing to worry about. This lasted
for a week. By Saturday the baby was gaunt and pale, and by
Sunday morning he was "nothing but a cadaver, yellow, pale,
and with dark rings around his eyes." Overwhelmed with worry
and no longer willing to be placated by her mother's reassurances, Marie ran to the neighboring farm and asked Charlotte's
husband, who was home on leave, to fetch the doctor. Delayed
at a childbirth, Dr. Gaillard could not come until the next day.
While waiting for him to arrive, Marie desperately tried to get
Serge to take a bottle, but whatever he took—which was little
enough—he promptly threw up. Her cousin Alice, the mother
of a four-year-old, came by and mentioned that her son had

had exactly the same problem, which she attributed to unsterilized milk. Marie thus took it upon herself to call for Marthe,
begging her to come and nurse the baby once more. When the
doctor finally arrived, he seconded Alice's judgment: under no
condition should Serge be kept on cow's milk. Marie immediately rehired Marthe as a live-in wet nurse, and although Serge
benefited from the new regimen very little at first, clear improvement was evident by the second week.[57]

Serge was luckier than an infant Marie told Paul about in
October 1916. A woman from a nearby village had delivered her
third child a few weeks after Serge had been born. Like Marie,
the new mother found that her breast milk was insufficient and
so put her baby first on a combination of breast milk and cow's
milk and then exclusively on cow's milk. Within a week the
child, only three months old, was dead. The baby's father, who
was recovering from shell shock, relapsed into madness.[58] This
story is especially heart-rending, but illness and early death
were all too common among infants. A survey conducted in 1917
revealed that although Nanteuil-de-Bourzac had suffered no infant deaths in the previous year, in nearby communes four of
twelve children born in 1916 died in infancy, and of those diarrhea had claimed two.[59] These stark statistics suggest that infant diarrhea remained a real danger. Clearly, Pinard's insistence
that young mothers sterilize milk, bottles, and artificial nipples
was not yet sufficiently heeded. Yet his advice was not falling
entirely on deaf ears. It seems clear that neither the milk that
Serge consumed nor his bottle had been sterilized. Perhaps
Lescure lacked the amenities to do so easily; perhaps Marie
could not persuade her mother, who prepared at least some of
the baby's bottles, of the need. But even though Marie could not,
for whatever reasons, guarantee the sterility of her son's bottles,
she was by no means unresponsive to all of Pinard's advice. She
did insist that a doctor be called in for a baby in distress.

This determination to seek medical attention for a small infant raised the hackles of many of the older women in the village, including Marie's mother and mother-in-law. When Marie apologized to Paul for not telling him immediately that his son was desperately ill, she noted that she had had to contend with the skepticism of more than one critic who upbraided her for her excessive alarm and her willingness to spend money unnecessarily. Some thought she overreacted when she hired Marthe, and Marie felt vindicated that her hunch had been well-founded. Only when it became evident that Serge, who had remained so sickly when nourished with cow's milk, was thriving on mother's milk, did these critics concede that she had done the right thing. The doctor, by contrast, had reassured her immediately that she had acted wisely; in his judgment the baby would not have lived more than a day or two longer without medical intervention.[60]

Those who found fault with Marie's actions were by no means hard-hearted women unmoved by the sight of a sickly infant. Serge's grandmothers were, in all other regards, doting admirers. But as members of a generation that had given birth in the days before the Pasteurian revolution, they probably found Pinard's obsession with germs strange, his contemptuous disdain for traditional ways insulting, and his advocacy of modern medicine suspicious. Although rural residents had been impressed in 1885 by Pasteur's widely reported and dramatically successful efforts to save a young boy from rabies and had embraced new techniques that could save children from diphtheria, they were not entirely convinced that all modern scientific methods were equally effective.[61] And to a certain extent their skepticism was grounded in bitter experience. For most of the nineteenth century doctors had been unable to do much to improve the life chances of newborns and infants—whose survival was threatened by diarrhea, congenital deformities, and viral infections—and some of their proposed cures seemed only to inflict suffering with no positive effect. Thus parents of previous generations were understandably loath to call upon a doctor when prior experience had taught them that he could not do much good. The real value of medical intervention and, more generally, the advantages to be gained by adopting Pasteurian practices emerged only at the very end of the nineteenth century.[62] Women like Marie, who were schooled during the last decades of the nineteenth century and who were accustomed to seeking advice in books, were more receptive than their mothers or grandmothers to the promises of science and the novel idea that a microbe so small as to be invisible to the human eye could cause illness and death.

Marie's struggles against old ways and older women began early. A few days after his birth, Serge had developed conjunctivitis, and although the midwife reassured Marie that there was no cause for alarm, she was not easily persuaded. When she consulted the midwife's manual, she read that if left untreated, neonatal conjunctivitis could lead to blindness. Thus, she called for the doctor, who prescribed medicated eyedrops, to be administered every two hours. Since Marie was still in frail health, it fell to Marthe to bandage the baby's eyes and give him the "injections"; this was, Marie admitted, "delicate work" that required the almost undivided attention of someone with good eyes. She was immensely grateful that Marthe had been willing to take on the task, even though her own baby could have caught the infection herself. It was, Marie judged, only thanks to Marthe's careful ministrations that the baby's eyes had been saved.[63] When Paul, having heard nothing earlier of the eye infection, read Marie's letter in which she nonchalantly noted that the baby's eyes were "almost healed there is no more danger," he was understandably distraught. He had had no inkling that the baby's sight had ever been imperiled.

As she looked back on the days when she feared for her baby's eyesight, Marie expressed her anger at those who had told her not to worry: "That they had dared to tell me that it was nothing that it would go away on its own that not everyone who has a sick baby called the doctor or the midwife, I assure you that I didn't tell them what I was thinking even though a few times I let a few words slip out I don't want to think about that I will look after him as seems best to me and those who aren't happy about it can take a walk for when they told me that there's nothing to be done, no use in having a doctor that it is nothing. I wonder what they would have wanted me to do let him become an invalid probably but I didn't listen to anyone." Convinced that she had done the right thing in spite of the expense, she asserted: "If it pleases me to call the doctor again I will do so and I bet that you will not blame me on the contrary." After all, the story of a local boy, now five years old, showed how much benefit was to be gained by seeking medical care. This little fellow had also suffered from conjunctivitis shortly after birth, and his parents had waited a full week before consulting a doctor. The doctor had immediately prescribed silver nitrate drops, which had saved his vision. Marie was happy to report that the boy now enjoyed perfect eyesight.[64]

Serge, too, responded well to medical ministrations and motherly attention. At the end of October, with the worst crises behind them, Marie observed, "How lucky we are because when he was born everyone thought he was not going to make it but what a joy it is to have such a beautiful baby." When measured in early November, he was fifty-eight centimeters long, only five centimeters shorter than Marthe's baby, who was six weeks older. At four months, he was showing signs of teething (though it is not likely that he would have actually cut his first tooth at such an early age), and he was often cranky as a result.

All in all, however, he was perfectly delightful, at least in the eyes of his mother. He was certainly as adorable as any baby of their acquaintance, and probably more advanced than most. It seemed incredible to Marie that cousin Valentine's baby (whom Paul had made the mistake of admiring on earlier occasions) should be so slow to walk and talk. Serge, she was convinced, would certainly be more precocious than that. He was already as chubby as Valentine's little one, and "as cute as the babies on postcards." He was also full of delightful (and not so delightful) tricks: when he tugged on his grandfather's mustache, it made everyone laugh; even his urinating on them elicited a chuckle or two.[65]

The grandparents continued to look askance, however, at Marie's insistence on calling for the doctor at every sign of illness. In the bitterly cold winter of 1916–17, when Serge and Marthe came down with coughs severe enough to make Marie worry, she lamented that Dr. Gaillard, of whom she otherwise thought highly, was making his rounds only selectively. Although he stopped in when Marie first called for him—and confirmed her fear that the baby's rasping cough might be a sign of croup—he failed to make a follow-up visit as promptly as she would have liked. Paul's mother thought it was ridiculous to call a doctor to check a baby's cough, but Marie remained adamant: "A lot of people in my place wouldn't call the doctor, you know me and when it comes to my son I consult only my own mind so I had to call the doctor your mother came by yesterday I told her that I had called the doctor she told me that I was crazy with such a big baby like that . . . Anyway, to each her own." Rosa Pireaud's judgment was, in this case at least, well founded: Serge recovered on his own. Noting, "The doctor didn't come and probably won't come," Marie reported with relief that Serge seemed over the worst of his cold. Nonetheless, she remained exasperated with the doctor: "If it had been dangerous you can see that he can't be counted on he's like that with everyone if it had been urgent I would have found another but I think we can do without him." This seemed true enough, for two weeks after the onset of the cold the baby's "cough [was] almost completely gone" and Marie was awaiting the return of milder weather, so that she could take him out in the baby carriage his grandparents had recently purchased.[66]

By spring 1917, Serge was old enough to sit on his mother's knee and help "write" the daily letter to his father, even though he seemed to think that tearing the paper would make things go better. By eight months, he could say "Papa" and "Mama," was learning to play peek-a-boo, and could laugh out loud. The brown hair he had had at birth had fallen out and was now replaced with golden blond hair as fine as silk. When Paul proudly showed his colleagues a photograph of Serge at a year old, he was the envy of the men in the company: "If you could only know how cute my comrades find our little son, they think he is like a plaster angel because they can't believe that a baby could be so beautiful."[67]

This angelic child was, however, going to be raised in a defiantly secular household. When the baby's fragile health had prompted Marie to seek Paul's advice on whether he should be baptized, Paul had rejected the idea of religious intercession. Of all the established traditions in rural French society that marked the early months of a child's life, none was more deeply rooted than baptism. A religious ritual that marked the child's entry into a state of grace, baptism was also important as a social rite of passage that marked his entry into the village community. Indeed, a child who died without benefit of baptism was considered a child who had not really lived at all. Presented at the church by his godparents (who were by tradition the people who chose his name and were the first people al-

lowed to embrace him), the baptized baby belonged henceforth not just to his parents but to the village as a whole. Custom held that a newborn child was neither to be fed mother's
milk until after baptism nor hugged or embraced between birth
and the ceremony. It was at baptism that the newborn was
officially named.[68] Such practices meant, of course, that a baby
would have to be baptized within a day or two of birth, a practice reinforced by church dogma. In the centuries-long era
of high infant mortality the Catholic Church insisted on the
prompt baptism of newborns to ensure that they would live—
and die—in a state of grace. Thus, to deny a child baptism was
to deny him or her the prospect of eternal salvation and full entry into the life of the temporal community.

Paul and Marie were almost entirely indifferent to these
well-established practices. They waited six weeks before giving
their child a name and two months, rather than two days, before even broaching the question of baptism. These delays suggest an insouciant disregard of customary ways, a lukewarm
faith on the part of the young parents, and a lingering, suspicious fear on the part of Marie. Established customs were certainly more difficult to observe in village society disrupted by
war. With so many young men in uniform, godfathers would
have been as hard-pressed as fathers themselves to fulfill their
traditional responsibilities to the newborn child. It is not surprising, then, that Paul and Marie never discussed who the
baby's godparents should be and certainly did not assume that
anyone but the parents themselves would choose the baby's
name. At the end of May, Paul had asked what Marie thought
of the recent practice of calling babies Verdun. Marie rejected
it as a name out of hand: "If you should come out of there alive I
wouldn't want ever to be reminded of these terrible days this
would be too sad a memory." Paul, in turn, wanted to reject the
name Paulette, in the event that the baby was a girl. Following

a controversy shortly after the baby's birth over what to call him, Paul conceded that Marie should choose whatever name she preferred. He was happy just to have a healthy wife and son. Marie was reluctant to take such a step on her own, though, and so the baby remained unnamed for at least two weeks. At the end of July she registered his name as Auguste but confessed to having no great fondness for the name and hoped they would find something that was a "little younger." Although Marie would have been happy to have Paul choose a name to his liking (as long as it wasn't Verdun), he preferred that they select a name together when he was home on leave.[69] They decided on Serge, an interesting choice in itself, in that it was not a name familiar in the village. There were no men or boys called Serge in either the 1891 or 1901 census. But as is often the case, the couple preferred a pet name and for the next three years nearly always spoke of their son as Nenette.

If choosing a name that honored neither grandfather was unusual, refusing to baptize the baby was truly exceptional. The letter in which Marie must first have raised the issue of baptism no longer exists, but it is clear from Paul's response that she saw in the sacramental rite some supernatural protection for the infant against illness. Paul had no patience with such thinking. In an impassioned letter, dated 28 September 1916, he made his opinions unambiguously clear: "You must know my ideas there is nothing there that will prevent him from getting sick. I ask of you only one thing that is do not have him baptized as long as I am alive. If I should pass into the other world then you can do as you like. In any case if when he comes of age he counts himself among the ranks of the believers then there will be time enough then for him to be baptized. The poor little one might be as sick as you can imagine you must know that this will not heal him of anything it is nothing but stupidity, a fraud in a word a pure comedy do you believe that he has already been able to commit a crime or a sin such that he needs to be pardoned . . . No I do not believe it so leave him as he is don't disturb him and make him cry perhaps he could catch a cold for such a stupid thing."[70]

Even in the anticlerical atmosphere of the Dordogne, where hostility to priests was commonplace, these were unusually strong opinions. By the beginning of the twentieth century most men in the Dordogne did not receive Easter communion (without which one could not be considered a practicing Catholic), but piety and social custom were sufficiently strong among the women to ensure that infant baptism remained the norm until the middle of the century. Nonetheless, a practice that most citizens deemed indispensable before the First World War waned in importance thereafter: by 1947, a survey of religious practice in France noted that most residents of the region surrounding Nanteuil no longer practiced their faith, and that more than 20 percent of children had not been baptized.[71] However unusual at the time, Paul's rejection of baptism was, therefore, a portent of things to come.

Having scorned the power of religion to protect his infant son, Paul preferred to place his hopes in the curative powers of medicine. Whenever Marie asked whether she should call for a doctor and whenever she told Paul after the fact that she had done so, he consented wholeheartedly. Believing that medical science could protect infants from ailments and preserve them from premature death, the young couple willingly braved the opposition of parents, paid for the services of doctors, and purchased prescriptions that promised recovery from life-threatening illness. In late September, after Serge had survived his bout with infantile cholera, Marie admitted that she had wanted so desperately to save his life that she had not given a second thought to the expense: "I would have done anything, whatever the price." There was, she averred, "nothing too expensive for our little one." On another occasion, when Serge needed a pricey prescription, she did not hesitate to send her father-in-law in search of the medication, while justifying her actions on these grounds: "That won't be expensive if it cures our little one." And time and time again, Paul concurred. He was indignant that local women should have thought her extravagant for hiring Marthe as a live-in wet nurse when Serge was so desperately ill. Far from thinking that Marie was wasting money that should have been saved, he urged her to pay whatever she could afford—and Marthe's fees were, Marie noted, uncommonly high—in recognition and gratitude for what she had done to save their baby: "Take good care of her it is a great sacrifice that she has made for us compensate her to the best of our ability. I will always think that it is she who by her devotion and her self-sacrifice saved my baby from certain death." As for the critical neighbors, Marie should ignore them "listen to no one, do what you think best, and above all take care of Marthe." Even lesser ailments, like the winter cold that so worried Marie in February 1917, merited medical attention and justified extraordinary expenditures: "As for the cost it is nothing just as long as he is cured that is the only thing."[72]

Yet the costs were far from negligible. In early October, when Marie provided Paul with an accounting of their recent medical expenses, she noted that the midwife's bill was eighty-two francs; medication for the baby had cost fifty-two francs; and two doctors were owed twenty-four francs and fourteen francs, respectively. In light of Marie's difficult delivery and the extra time Mlle Aline had spent caring for her after the baby was born, it is perhaps not surprising that she charged so much, but it is nonetheless noteworthy, given that a decade earlier the average fee charged by a midwife attending a delivery had been only twenty francs.[73] When it became evident that Serge needed a wet nurse, Marthe asked for forty francs a month, even though the customary rate for nursing a baby and doing his laundry was, Marie believed, between twenty-five and thirty francs a month. In no position to bargain, Marie accepted Marthe's price. She insisted, however (and Paul applauded her for this) that Marthe live in, in spite of her quite understandable preference to take the baby home. Perhaps Marie recalled, as Pinard's infant care manual pointed out, that babies shipped out to live with wet nurses were often poorly fed and subject to neglect. Perhaps she feared that Serge would grow too fond of Marthe. Whatever the case, she insisted, as only an affluent mother could once have insisted, that Marthe live with them at Lescure.[74]

To a certain extent, the advent of a cash economy made it possible for young parents like Paul and Marie to embrace ways that had once been the preserve of the affluent and the urban. The military allowance that Marie received with the full approval of Paul and his father either when she became pregnant or after the baby's birth meant that services once too expensive for most family budgets were now within reach, in spite of the inflation that was evident by 1916 in many sectors of the consumer economy. But if ready access to cash made it easier for farm families to pay for medical services when they needed to, the expansion of a cash economy into the villages of rural France does not in and of itself explain Paul and Marie's confident faith in the benefits of medicine. A cultural receptivity to new ways—made possible by advances in literacy, exposure to novel ideas, and a heightened appreciation of the fragility of life—was equally important.

Compulsory education and mandatory military service, both introduced in the 1880s, were two of the most important transformative forces in rural France.[75] Marie's careful reading of her child-care book—and of course her ability to write about her experiences as a young mother—prove the point.

And military service, before and during the war, exposed Paul and others of his generation to ideas and cultural practices once unknown in their local community. It is doubtful, however, that many of the young conscripts who had traveled far from home to fulfill their mandatory service before the war had spent their idle hours exchanging ideas and insights on pregnancy, care of infants, and the perils of bottle feeding. In a nation where men usually did not marry until their mid- to late twenties, these young men would have had no appreciable interest in such topics. When the war came, however, military service mingled raw recruits with thousands of family men—at least 40 percent of the Frenchmen killed between 1914 and 1918 were married—whose interests and experiences would have been more domestic than those of younger men. By 1916 Paul was serving in a regiment that brought together men with whom he had grown up and total strangers. Although his closest confidant remained a local man, he also spent much of his time in the company of men who lived far from the farms of Nanteuil. Many of these erstwhile strangers were, like Paul himself, fathers of young children, and they often compared notes with one another on what constituted appropriate child-rearing practices. On one occasion, for example, Paul advised Marie not to allow Serge to sleep in her bed. He had been chatting with his good friend, a cook in the battery, who had a five-year-old at home. It was the cook's considered opinion that it was dangerous to take a small baby into one's bed because "something unfortunate could happen so quickly."[76] Conjuring up as it does the unexpected image of frontline soldiers engaged in serious conversation about care of infants, this anecdote also suggests that wartime service introduced fathers (and subsequently young mothers) to ideas about domestic life theretofore unknown or rarely observed in their own local community.

More than anything else, however, the war made Paul

acutely aware of his own mortality. However much he trusted in fate and the inaccuracy of German artillery, he could not deny the fundamental truth that he might not live to see the next morning, let alone the end of the war. This realization made his pregnant wife and only son infinitely precious. The child that Marie carried, bore, and tended so lovingly in 1916 and 1917 was, Paul had to see, potentially irreplaceable. If Paul were to die, there would be no more children conceived, no siblings to carry on the family name, and—as he noted while under fire at Verdun—no one to care for Marie in her old age. The future of the Pireaud family was embodied in little Serge. In the weeks after his birth, when mother and baby were struggling to survive, Paul's letters interspersed explicit allusions to his own mortality with entreaties to Marie that she do all she could to look after herself and the baby: "In the event that I should die please do whatever you can so that you will be there to look after him . . . It's very sad for a father to watch such a drama from so far away and so incapable of doing anything it casts a shadow over all his happiness when I think of the danger that I have witnessed I judge myself very lucky to still have people who keep me so attached to life."[77]

Confronting as he did the reality that he might not survive the war, Paul derived from his identity as a father an unexpected strength in the face of death. In early October, he observed, "You fear death less when you know that you leave an heir behind and you still have hope that after this damned butchery is over you will have a life filled with delight, how beautiful and good that will be if we have the good luck to survive and how we will be able to appreciate our happiness after seeing such terrible things and [enduring] such a Calvary."[78] The promise of happiness to come combined with the stark realization that pregnancy was a minefield of a different sort prompted Paul to insist that Marie not run the risks of a second pregnancy. When he learned how difficult her labor had been and how fraught with danger the delivery, he feared that she might have had second thoughts about becoming pregnant: "All my love will never be powerful enough to make up to you for the suffering that you endured to give me a son If I didn't know that you too are happy to have a child I would regret ever having done it. Tell me in your suffering did you ever regret it?" Marie assured him that she had no regrets, but she acknowledged that a second pregnancy was, in the short term at least, out of the question. The midwife had told her in no uncertain terms that when Paul came home on leave the young couple would have to take precautions. Paul understood as much before being told: "I realize that you are very weak that you must have suffered greatly I am sorry to think of you in such a state you can rest assured I am very happy to have a son but this will definitely be the last one." Reassured that her husband would do what was necessary to prevent another pregnancy, Marie nonetheless passed several anxious days in early September when her period was later than she had expected. On 3 September, she wrote in real anguish: "I've still seen nothing, I tell myself that there is no danger and yet I'm very worried about this, I'm afraid, if you were here to console me and to tell me again that there is no danger but all by myself worrying with no one to tell little secrets to how sad it is to be crying all the time and suffering in silence with no one to comfort me." Two days later, Marie's fears were allayed: "Rest assured my dear Paul this time you are not going to be a father for a second time." Paul, understanding the "trial she had recently endured" and anxious not to subject her to such a trial again, was relieved to learn that her anxieties had been for naught.[79]

Serge Pireaud thus became an adored only child. His mother, aunt, and grandparents doted on him—buying him a baby buggy so that Marie could present the baby proudly to admiring neighbors; dressing him in lace-trimmed bonnets and lovingly made garments; conveying him to the nearest town, where a professional photographer could take his picture—and his father rejoiced from afar at his son's development. Convinced that her son was so clever that he would "soon know his letters," Marie taught him as a toddler to add his name and a few words to letters sent to his father.[80] This young boy, whose earliest years were marked by his father's absence, was shaped by the Great War in yet another, and very significant, way. He was a child of the "hollow years." Born in 1916, he would be one of only 313,000 French children to possess a birth certificate inscribed with the year of Verdun.[81] As he grew up, he would discover that fewer children were in his classes than in all other classes, and later fewer conscripts in his military cohort than France had ever known. In fact, so few children were born in the middle years of the Great War that fears arose for the future: twenty years hence, when the boys born in 1916 and 1917 came of military age, would France be able, should the need arise, to field an army large enough to defend itself?

If Serge Pireaud's very existence was exceptional when taken in the national context, Paul and Marie were, in their determination to keep their young son alive, in their embrace of modern child-care methods, and in their intellectual and economic investment in professional medical advice, neither exceptional nor out of step with broader national developments. Local and national statistics show that many other parents did battle with serious infant illness, and many were also lucky enough to win the battle. Indeed, from 1915 on, France showed a marked improvement in the rates of infant mortality that was caused by diarrhea. Whereas diarrhea had accounted for a third (or more) of all infant deaths in the years immediately preceding the war, it claimed a fourth of all infants who died in wartime France.

Improvement was particularly evident for the "killing months" of summer, during which the wartime rate of infant deaths dropped noticeably.[82] A nightmare for parents and babies alike, infant diarrhea was a scourge that young families were slowly conquering. Because diarrhea (unlike the other major causes of infant death—congenital deformity and viral infection) could be combated through the vigilant efforts of informed parents alone, this marked improvement suggests that many infants benefited during the war years from the conscientious efforts of mothers like Marie who were receptive to new ideas and new approaches.

The life story of Serge Pireaud suggests that the low birthrate and the improved survival rate of infants born during the war were not entirely unrelated. When fewer children were being conceived, more had to be done to protect those who were born. In the case of Paul and Marie at least, the war directly affected how they thought about reproduction, family size, and the irreplaceability of a child. Recognizing that they might have only one child, they invested everything they could to secure his well-being. Medical care, once dismissed as a luxury at best and a futile investment at worst, thus became a necessity. And all the resources that might once have been divided among three or four children would now be concentrated on one or two. Paul and Marie certainly thought of their infant son as someone who would grow up to look after his mother, in the event of his father's death, saving her from the penury and hardship that often made life miserable for rural widows who had no children. Grandparental reservations about the newfangled ways embraced by the young parents went unheeded, for in the eyes of his doting and battle-scarred parents Serge Pireaud was a child too precious to be neglected. The very precariousness of life, so bitterly evident every day at the front, made this sickly infant a prize worthy of preservation at any cost.

I received your letter from the 3rd where you say that I seem to be happy. Listen my dear if I didn't cherish in my heart the love of my wife and my child and my parents if I were all alone on this earth then yes I could count myself happy because when the weather is warm as it has been lately and I have everything that I need I cannot really say that I am unhappy especially since the Boches don't ever fire on us. I am not happy because no one is happy in war I miss my home and those who are dear to me I also miss my freedom but in comparing my life to that of all my comrades then in comparison to them I really am happy.

Paul to Marie, 7 July 1917

FOUR

No One Is Happy in War

$\mathcal{I}$n April 1917 the French army's disastrous Chemin des Dames offensive created a crisis of unprecedented severity in the ranks, giving rise to mutinies that affected well over half of all infantry divisions. At the same time, chronic shortages of food and fuel threatened to destabilize the home front. Material conditions, adequate during the first two years of the war, had deteriorated to such a point that the well-being of families was (or at least seemed to be) in real jeopardy. These two crises—of plummeting military morale and prospective civilian destitution—were distinct but not entirely unrelated. Men on the front lines were, as one postal censor observed, "calling for any kind of peace, to put an end to the butchery, to the food shortages which are getting worse and worse, and to the high cost of living."[1] Of the many factors that contributed to the mutinies of 1917, most concerned specifically military matters: soldiers who had endured both Verdun and the Somme in 1916 were bitterly disillusioned when the major battle of April 1917, which was supposed to bring both an end to the war and victory to France, failed to do either and succeeded only in slaughtering thousands. The failure of this offensive meant first and foremost that the war would not be won by the summer of 1917. Men who had hoped in April that they would be heading home for good by June had to acknowledge that they would remain in uniform for at least another year. This dismal truth, demoralizing for all combatants, was doubly dispiriting for peasant soldiers, who contemplated, in addition to the prospect of further combat with uncertain results, the possibility that their families—unassisted, overworked, and exhausted in their agricultural labors—would be unable to keep enough land under cultivation to guarantee their food supply for the coming year.

By the spring of 1917 it was distressingly obvious that peasant labor could no longer produce enough food to meet the combined needs of rural and urban citizens alike. The cumulative effects of military mobilization, which continued to take men away from the land, when combined with an uncommonly cold winter, seriously delayed and impeded work in the fields. After thirty months of war France confronted, for the first time since the 1840s, the unsettling specter of dearth and, more ominously still, the imagined threat of famine. Although the fear of famine was exaggerated—food shortages in France were not nearly as severe as in Russia (where they contributed directly to the fall of the tsar in March 1917) or in Germany (where the infamous "turnip winter" of 1916–17 pushed the endurance of civilians to the limit)—it was a fear widely held, psychologically unnerving, and militarily disruptive. The mutinies were not driven only, or indeed predominantly, by apprehensions about hunger on the home front. It was anger at military mismanagement that pushed troops into outright revolt in May and June. But central to their demands—and to the laments of soldiers like Paul who were not demoralized enough to participate in outright rebellion—was a call for real improvements in the leave schedule. The longing for leave was fueled both by an understandable war-weariness and by the desire of predominantly peasant soldiers to return home, if only temporarily, to work the land.

For the first two years of the war, the constancy and compassion of civilians far from the front lines had offered soldiers

solace in the face of suffering and had reinforced bonds of affection that linked men in uniform with those at home. Letters
and food packages, assembled with real effort and at considerable cost, reminded husbands, sons, and brothers that the families for whom they were fighting remained constant in their devotion and kindness. When avaricious strangers close to the
front lines were all too ready to charge extortionate amounts
for goods of indifferent quality, when insouciant strangers eating pastries in cafés and drinking aperitifs in boulevard bistros
seemed oblivious to the suffering of fighting men, a package
from home assured frontline soldiers that the civilians who
mattered most remained loyal, selfless, and loving. And now in
the spring of 1917 these compassionate compatriots, once well
provided for, confronted hardships of their own. For peasant
soldiers who were convinced that their families were facing deprivation and who were unsettled by evidence that their once
productive land was lying fallow, victory acquired a new urgency. If the war could be won quickly, as French commanders
so confidently predicted, then, soldiers believed, they would
be able to go home to work the land, harvest the crops, and
save their families from hunger. But if victory were to elude
the French forces yet again and men already uneasy about the
well-being of their families were compelled to remain in arms
for another agricultural season, then morale would surely suffer.
Fear of famine, throughout the first half of 1917, thus exacerbated soldiers' melancholy, intensified their desire for leave,
and sharpened their appetite for victory.

Paul spent the six months immediately preceding the Chemin
des Dames Battle on the Somme, where the French and British
had been waging ferocious warfare against deeply entrenched
enemy forces since July. From early October, when his battery
established its position on the Somme battlefront, through

mid-November, the guns of the 112th Regiment battered German installations in the second great military confrontation of 1916. After the fighting at Verdun—mitigated only by four months of quiet service in Champagne—this was an unenviable duty. Although several batteries of the 112th Heavy Artillery Regiment had been assigned to the Somme since early August, it was only in October that Paul's captain had given his men notice that they too would soon be sent into the "great battle." Addressing battle-hardened survivors of Verdun, he warned that this was "going to be more difficult than ever." He predicted, "Many of you will not come back and will leave behind you widows and orphans." Suitably chastened, men contributed one franc each to a national loan campaign to help war widows and orphans. Paul grudgingly gave his twenty sous, hoping that Marie and Serge would not be beneficiaries of his and his comrades' forced generosity. Thoughts of what awaited him on the Somme left him in a somber mood: "Poor Marie if you could only know how much I am suffering and how much I love you you, my life my treasure my only thought you for whom I have suffered so much for the past few years. Oh how often I curse our lot especially when I see myself obliged to imagine a future so full of worries. Whatever might happen my dearly beloved be persuaded and convinced that I love you with the strength of all my soul and that I will love you to my very last breath if that is my fate. In the hope, in spite of all that, that we will still have happy days ahead of us I embrace you most tenderly."[2]

Paul's discouragement was well founded. The Battle of the Somme, having commenced four months earlier, was in its final, still fearsome throes when the First Battery of the 112th Heavy Artillery Regiment took up its position in mid-October 1916. The Battle of the Somme will remain forever infamous for the losses on its first day, when the British suffered more than fifty thousand casualties (including almost twenty thousand deaths). The battle was a joint Anglo-French undertaking intended, initially at least, to break through the German lines and bring the war to a victorious close. Because the French army was fully occupied at Verdun, however, the Somme became a predominantly British enterprise. By the time the battle petered out in late November, having brought some territorial gains but no decisive victory, two-thirds of all Allied casualties in this ferocious battle affected men who had fought under British command. If the French contribution at the Somme was less weighty—and certainly has been less well remembered—it was by no means insignificant. General Foch commanded an army corps that included the French Sixth and Tenth Armies. It held a sector thirteen kilometers long, extending southeast from Bray-sur-Somme toward Péronne. More than six hundred thousand French troops saw action here, and the French suffered almost two hundred thousand casualties. Lt. Marcel Etévé, who died on the Somme in July 1916, observed the first day of battle in fine spirits, buoyed by the beautiful weather and confident in victory. Two weeks later, on 18 July, he wrote (in words eerily reminiscent of Paul's description of Verdun), "There is not a square meter of land that hasn't been completely overturned. All the houses have disappeared. The German lines [are] completely leveled; shelters, even the deepest ones, crushed." Killed two days later, while trying to capture a trench still held by German troops, he wrote on the eve of his death that the "spectacle" that surrounded him—of villages destroyed and dead bodies still unburied—was an affront to the honor of mankind.[3]

At the Somme, as at Verdun, "the poor bloody infantry" bore the brunt of battle. Advancing at a measured pace into the merciless fire of enemy machine guns, men armed only with a rifle, a bayonet, and a few hand-grenades died by the thousands. This was especially true in the British sector, where an artillery barrage in which more than a million shells were spent in the week preceding the attack neither cut the German barbed wire nor disabled German gun emplacements. Moreover, a critical shortage of heavy guns left the British infantry inadequately protected.[4] On the French sector of the battlefront, more extensive heavy artillery provided the infantry with better cover, allowing at first for greater territorial advances at a lower—but by no means minimal—cost. If the French infantrymen fared somewhat better than their British comrades, the heavy artillery suffered more. Recognizing the efficacy of the French heavy artillery, the Germans aimed to disable the heavy guns arrayed almost five kilometers behind the front lines. The surviving logbooks of the 112th make it clear that they often did so to grisly effect.

The regiment had served on the Somme since at least August 1916, when the Twenty-seventh Battery took up positions on the very western edge of the French sector. Occupying a site that had marked Germany's front lines when the battle opened on 1 July, the battery received and returned fire from mid-August (when two men were mentioned in citations for their valor under fire) until early October. On 11 September at least a hundred large-caliber shells bombarded their position; one man was buried alive. This assault did not disable the battery, however, and on the following day it retaliated with such withering fire that the French infantry successfully advanced on the small town of Bouchavesnes. Two weeks later the 112th launched another massive barrage, firing approximately nine hundred shells in the course of a single day. This, the company log stated, made 25 September a "very active" day. Early October was just as intense: on one day 250 shells fell on the battery during a two-hour interval; one direct hit killed three men outright when their shelter collapsed on top of them. Three others were dug out alive. On 6 October, shortly before the Twenty-seventh Battery was relieved—possibly by Paul's battery—it endured five hours of bombardment, suffering another three deaths. Two men died instantly, but a third, who had his left arm blown off and suffered a direct hit to the chest, lingered for three hours, no doubt in excruciating pain, before succumbing to his wounds.[5]

When the First Battery arrived on the Somme in mid-October, the "great battle" of which Paul's captain had spoken was drawing to a close. For the preceding six weeks, the French had been bogged down in heavy fighting centered on the village of Sailly-Saillisel. In an undated letter that was probably written shortly after his arrival in the sector, Paul described a German barrage: "It's in a rather uncomfortable position that I'm writing you because for us the life of moles has started again Right now I'm in a corridor six meters deep lit only by a candle When you go outside boy if you could see the fireworks it's impossible to imagine especially since we are especially well placed for seeing it we can see everything that leaves and arrives in front of us behind to the right to the left . . . But for us there is nothing yet the Boches don't know where we are. If only they don't find out if you could see what is being sent over in their direction if this keeps up they will soon have to abandon Péronne you must have seen those who were captured at Sailly-Saillisel and Combles . . . Anyway, I hope that we will get them?"[6]

The question mark is noteworthy. The mantra of Verdun ("On les aura"), and the confidence it exuded, are now expressed more tentatively. As the Somme drew to an inconclusive close, those who witnessed its last moments were subject to disabling doubt: Would France indeed prevail? That even Paul Pireaud, who by this time had landed a plum position as messenger for the battery, should have harbored such doubts is surely significant, for they hint at the weakening of morale that would become endemic in the ranks of the French army by the spring of 1917.

Paul had long wanted to serve as the battery's messenger, and he had received his captain's assurance that the position was as good as his. He was furious, therefore, when a new arrival—a despicable *embusqué* only recently transferred from his job well behind the lines—landed the coveted appointment instead. When the new man, having overstayed a one-day leave, received a fifteen-day sentence, the captain made amends and moved Paul into the position. Given a cot in the captain's dugout (where the captain's orderly, the cook, and he slept in much greater comfort and security than did the gunners), Paul knew that he had done well for himself. His new responsibilities included securing the daily provisions for the officers, waiting on them at dinner, and running messages from the battery to the command post. There were things about his new position that rankled—Paul admitted that it was "not in [his] character to serve others, especially at table"—but he swallowed his pride and did what was asked of him: "When it's a question of saving your skin and coming home one day to your marquise and your son," then you do whatever is asked.[7]

Without doubt, messengers ran risks of their own—two assigned to the Twenty-seventh Battery had been killed by "friendly fire" in October—which gave Marie cause for concern. She feared that as Paul made his way alone between the command post and the battery, he might be hit and would be unable, for want of companions, to secure the medical treatment that would save him. Even less perilous assignments had their dangers. When Paul went to a nearby railway station to collect a message from his captain's wife, he ran afoul of the military police. Lacking a properly signed pass from his commanding officer, he was arrested as a deserter and interrogated by the regimental colonel. This must have been an unsettling experience. Desertion was a capital offense, and although few deserters were in fact executed, it was not an act to be taken lightly in the fall of 1916, when desertion rates were on the rise. An interview with a colonel—in all probability, Lt. Colonel Solonte, the commander of the 112th Heavy Artillery Regiment—would have unnerved many a simple soldier who had in the natural course of things little contact with officers of such elevated rank. In his own defense, Paul made the case that he had legitimate business in the town, secured his release, and returned under escort to his unit. His captain found the whole incident more amusing than alarming and provided Paul with a glowing testimonial to the effect that he was a fine and dependable soldier who had served the battery well at Verdun. Such misadventures aside, messengers enjoyed more protection than the men firing the guns. And Paul's new position, which allowed him to eat like a "real gent" (réel bourgeois), as he mentioned with some pride, was a good one; he assured Marie that he would do what he could to hold on to it.[8]

When properly provided with signed papers, a messenger in the heavy artillery could hope to enjoy a few moments of welcome respite. Unlike messengers closer to the front lines, who were ready targets for snipers, machine gunners, and exploding shells, those who served in the heavy artillery often circulated well beyond the range of the enemy's guns. Thus, Paul could relish two days he spent in Amiens, more than fifty kilometers from the front lines, in late November 1916. Sent to purchase provisions for the officers of his battery, he was struck by the rich variety of troops that congregated in and moved through this provincial city: "There are only Hindus, Vietnamese, Senegalese and especially English and Scots." His return to the battery on 25 November was much less agreeable: a well-aimed German barrage claimed four casualties in the adjacent regiment. Enemy guns continued to target the battery through early December, landing shells perilously close to Paul's new billet: one of the junior officers in his battery stepped out of the dugout, took no more than ten steps, and was hit by a shell fragment just above the eye.[9]

Technically, the Battle of the Somme ended on 18 November 1916, following weeks of rain that made the region's low-lying clay terrain impassable. The official end of pitched battle did not mean, however, that frontline troops on the Somme were immune to attack. Indeed, the winter of 1916–17 was marked, especially on the French lines, by an intensification of low-grade hostile action—trench raids and shelling, in particular—to which the Germans responded in kind. The lines remained dangerous well into the new year. In January 1917, when the Germans were testing new ordnance, Paul and his lieutenant spent one afternoon collecting and examining the unfamiliar fuses of shells sent their way. But shelling seemed almost the least of their concerns. The weather was beyond miserable, and prospects for the future far from reassuring. Because the battles of the previous year, hard fought and costly in execution, had proved indecisive, soldiers had to accept that they would be sent once more into battle. Germany had not prevailed at Verdun and thus had not forced France to withdraw from the war; but neither had the Entente powers broken Germany's tenacious hold on the Somme. Victory remained elusive and would be won only through further sacrifices. The bitter promise of the coming spring was, therefore, that the battle would be resumed, and soldiers who had survived this long would have to steel themselves for another round of intense hostilities. If the spring campaign could secure victory, then perhaps this would be the troops' last winter in the trenches. If not, the consequences were too grim to contemplate.

Such thoughts and calculations offered little comfort to men forced to live outdoors in the coldest winter on record. The relentless rains that had forced Allied commanders to call a halt to the Somme offensive in mid-November continued into the first week of January, with devastating effect. Mud made the roads impassable and even the shortest foray outside the trenches perilous. An artilleryman noted that however inconvenient the mire was for those who manned the guns, it was ghastly for the frontline infantry, which had to battle mud at least a meter deep in places. One hapless sergeant, he reported, had drowned in the mud, despite the best efforts of six men to pull him free. When the rains stopped, a bone-chilling cold set in. Canadian troops—no strangers to winter—froze to death in their trenches; and soldiers of all nationalities huddled in their dugouts, longing for the warmth and comfort of home. In the French Tenth Army, to which the 112th Heavy Artillery Regiment was assigned in the winter of 1916–17, everyone grumbled about the cold and the inconveniences that accompanied it. Food was difficult to prepare; wine froze in the canteens; morale plummeted. Men filled their letters with complaints about the weather, their longing for home, and in some cases at least a troublesome war-weariness: "The men are suffering from the cold and the snow," the postal censor reported; "they complain about it and sometimes show themselves to be a bit discouraged by the conditions, which, as one of them writes, makes them depressed." Two dozen soldiers in one regiment admitted outright that "they would be happy to return home promptly, with the war over." Even those who did not mention the weather directly were showing signs of demoralization and fatigue: at the beginning of January a majority of letters surveyed from one territorial regiment revealed a "very intense desire for peace and a return home."[10]

The men of the 112th did what they could to protect themselves from the harsh winter.[11] On the evening of 17 January, twenty-five centimeters (ten inches) of snow fell on Paul's battery, located at Maurepas to the northwest of Péronne. As he watched his mates toss snowballs at one another, he hoped that the snow would warm things up a bit. A week later, however, it was twelve degrees below zero Celsius (or about 10°F) and everything—bread, water, wine—was frozen solid. Marie fretted (as did many wives whose letters were intercepted by the censors) that the cold was making life at the front unendurable. She feared that Paul was inadequately outfitted and longed to provide him with warm woolens, blankets, a better overcoat. In a winter when even the Dordogne got at least twenty centimeters of snow and Marie bundled Serge in blankets and a hot water bottle to take the edge off the frosty chill inside their house, she knew that life on the western front was infinitely worse. Paul tried to assure her that he was safe and adequately outfitted. On a night when three shells exploded within a hundred meters of the battery's kitchen, he wrote: "Don't worry yourself I am not as unfortunate as you think it's really cold here but I have my galoshes my sheepskin my overcoat and my beret and I will be able to face whatever winter throws at me you can rest assured on this matter. Our little one must be suffering more from the winter than I am . . . How long it will be till I can go home and kiss him and his *maman* too how happy I will be on that day."[12]

In the long intervals from one leave to another, husbands and wives had to content themselves with the lesser consolation of letter writing. It was irksome, therefore, that the army at the end of 1916 introduced a more intrusive system of postal oversight. Unlike the limited system of censorship that had remained in place since the earliest days of the war—which held letters back in advance of major offensives and prohibited any mention of a soldier's location on the line—the new system would review a random sample of the letters generated by a handful of regiments each week. The French system, though it

was neither as comprehensive in scope nor as intrusive in practice as the British system, which compelled junior officers to
read nearly all the letters written by enlisted men in their unit,
was an unwelcome innovation, nonetheless. Soldiers and their
civilian correspondents complained bitterly that they could no
longer write to one another without fear of officious eavesdrop-
ping; they castigated the censors as voyeurs who invaded the
privacy of decent, patriotic citizens; and they scorned the manhood of *embusqué* officials who were too old to fight but not too
old to feel titillated by the sexual secrets of men and women
separated by a war that would not end.

Even the censors' most legitimate concerns provoked the
wrath of the soldiers. Many resented that the long-established
but oft-ignored regulation prohibiting any explicit mention of
where they found themselves at the front would now be more
rigorously enforced. Some, like the soldier who used invisible
ink to tell his wife where he was, went to considerable (in this
case unsuccessful) lengths to thwart the censors. Others simply
ignored the regulations, as they had done since the start of the
war. One soldier wrote in mid-January 1917: "It is prohibited
by the military authorities to say where we are, but as for me,
they can punish me, they are never going to prevent me from
telling my parents where I am, because if something were to
happen to me at least they would know where, and then it is
true that you prefer to know where we are, you are less worried
that way, I understand that."[13]

Although some troops were punished for violating the regulation, now that it was being enforced—in May 1917 two pharmacists were sentenced to a week's imprisonment for revealing
their location on the line—the threat of punishment certainly
did not silence Paul, who continued to give Marie information that he should by rights have kept to himself.[14] He wrote
explicitly of troop movements and the relocation of his regi-

ment. At the end of January his battery was "completely surrounded by English troops." He added, "There are three times
as many of them as of us . . . We certainly aren't going to
be staying here much longer. We are the only French [troops]
left here." Three weeks later, he traced the route the battery
took eastward into the Champagne region: having traveled
beyond Epernay, Châlons-sur-Marne, Suippes, Valmy, and
Sainte-Menehould (a site made famous in 1791 when an alert
postal employee foiled Louis XVI's attempt to flee France and
join forces with counterrevolutionary troops massed across the
border), the battery found itself in a still lovely, and to Paul's
eye surprisingly modern, part of the country—"the people are
very friendly and the houses are lit with electricity"—not far
from Vitry-le-François.[15]

More than anything, soldiers and their families were outraged that their much cherished privacy had come under assault. When inquisitive functionaries (who, everyone agreed,
should have been doing something useful for the war effort)
read letters exchanged between wives and husbands, parents
and sons, children and fathers, what strategic end was served
thereby? A soldier writing to his wife in Paris could not contain
his anger: "Really I don't understand the reason for this postal
censorship which seems to me to abuse my correspondence
which is being violated all the time . . . Poor France!!! It would
be laughable if the moment were not so serious; violating private correspondence, that's the work of these gentlemen! . . . If
they only knew how much the poilus detest them!"[16] And, he
might have added, many a wife or girlfriend at home felt the
same way. Indignant that strangers now had access to her most
private reflections, one woman wrote (in a letter directed as
much at the censors as at her husband): "You told me that you
received two of my letters that had been censored; it's really annoying because we can't say what we want to when we are writ-

ing without it being handed over to busybodies. If everyone was at home the government wouldn't have to pay men to control private correspondence. It's not in the letters that a wife sends to her husband that you are going to find spies."[17]

Perhaps there were no state secrets hiding in private correspondence, but there certainly were very intimate avowals of love and passion not meant for the censors' prying eyes. Many resented that the new censorship compromised their ability to write unabashedly of intimate secrets, romantic ardor, and erotic reveries. One soldier could not contain his indignation: "Those guys are just disgusting to disturb the intimacy of our letters with their curiosity. I no longer dare to speak lightly and with an open heart knowing that those old satyrs might have the pleasure of reading what I am writing, thinking, and feeling." A sailor on board a naval ship at harbor in Boulogne was even more forthright: "Yesterday's letter," he wrote to his wife, "was held back by the censors, I received it and it had been opened and it was your letter of the 20th so long, so sweet, and the guy who read this letter he got to see all our most intimate secrets, well at least it's some old *embusqué* who won't have to pay 40 sous to some woman after having read our letter, he found more about love than about military secrets [there], but it's unfortunate nonetheless that we can't speak openly about our private life without everyone gossiping about it."[18] However outrageous this intrusion into domestic intimacy appeared to be, some correspondents resolved to continue as they had before. One young woman asserted: "I believe that letters sent from this end are being opened. It is true that if they are old men then this will remind them of their youth. If they are young, like us, then they love [too]. In any event I will not be put out by it."[19]

This seemed to be Paul and Marie's response, too. Paul was certainly contemptuous of the censors, who applied themselves "with such zeal to controlling the kisses that we send to our wives," and believed the officials would have been better employed in the trenches, but neither he nor Marie was ever fully cowed by the intrusive presence of postal surveillance. Their letters took on a more cautious tone on occasion, but in the main they remained richly detailed, descriptive, and passionate. There were times when Paul begged Marie's indulgence for letters that seemed flat and uninformative; he would have written more but he had nothing "much to tell you only things that you wouldn't find interesting and which I am forbidden to talk about." When the postal authorities did read one of his letters (and then sent it on to Nanteuil), he was vaguely annoyed but, like many other soldiers who intentionally voiced their complaints in unambiguous terms in the hope that the high command would realize what life was like for the little guy on the front lines, he did not mind unduly: "I received the letter that had gone through the censor. I am happy that it was that one at least that way they were able to get some sense of what our situation is like." In the final analysis, however, postal censorship was for Paul and Marie more a psychological irritant than a genuine impediment to free and affectionate expression. The intimacy and honesty they had cultivated over more than two years of separation continued to flourish. In mid-March, when Paul was deeply despondent and heartsick, Marie did what she could to lighten his depression with this reminder: "You have a wife and a son who adore you and who will love you forever think that before long it won't be possible for this to last much longer with all the shortages of everything; we will be able to resume our sweet lives full of happiness while there will be many who won't be able to do so." Paul, in turn, wrote unabashedly of his love for Marie and little Serge. "Always love me," he implored; "I need that more than ever to put up with this life and always be assured my two loves my two treasures that I will love you forever with all the strength of my soul and all the love my heart is capable of . . . I live only for you while waiting to taste the happiness which is our due if that should be allowed us."[20]

The shortages of which Marie complained were widespread and worrisome to soldiers and civilians alike. By the spring of 1917 much of the nation's arable land was no longer in full production; the prolonged winter had delayed essential work in fields that had not yet been abandoned. As a consequence, a nation once agriculturally self-sufficient had to face the unpleasant truth that, even with the aid of imports, the available food might not suffice to satisfy the collective appetite of a nation at war. Grain and grapes, which supplied the staples of the French diet, were both in short supply. To some extent, this was due to the occupation and (in the early months of 1917) destruction of farmland located in the north of France: in its retreat toward the Hindenburg Line, the German army slashed, burned, and uprooted crops and orchards along its way. Elsewhere, the inevitable consequence of inadequate manpower was underproduction. The dire effects of conscription (compounded by persistent military requisitioning of cattle and fertilizer) that had made the harvest of 1915 so difficult grew more serious still in 1916. When the army called up young men in advance of their draft age, farms that might once have been able to hire boys in their late teens (as Marie's sister had done in 1915) were hard-pressed to do so. Chronic manpower shortages also substantially increased the cost of hired labor. In southwest France, for example, where families were small and surplus labor scarce, agricultural wages increased more than 60 percent between 1914 and 1916.[21] For those who could not afford the elevated wages—or even those who could, for it was not easy to find workers at any cost—it became more and more difficult to keep farms in full operation. In the labor-intensive

vineyards of Bordeaux, estate owners could not convince laborers to stay on the land when higher wages and better working
conditions were on offer in munitions factories.[22]

Unable to keep land under full production, many women
were forced to leave their fields fallow. In the village of Juignac,
only a few kilometers from Nanteuil, the schoolteacher noted
that the harvest of 1916 had yielded significantly less than
those of 1914 and 1915 and "a certain amount of the land usually under cultivation had been left fallow."[23] This expedient,
common throughout France by the spring of 1917, prompted
frequent criticism from urban commentators, many of whom
held peasant women solely responsible for the nation's food
crisis: indolence and self-indulgence were, some claimed, the
besetting vices of rural Frenchwomen. Peasant soldiers were
much less inclined to blame their wives or parents for failing to
keep land under full cultivation. In the north, where manpower
shortages caused by the disruptions of war and the displace-
ment of local populations were most grievous, men at the front
urged their wives to let lapse leases on land they could no
longer cultivate.[24] Elsewhere, men often encouraged wives or
parents not to overexert themselves for little real gain; it would
be better to allow fields to lie fallow. A few even urged their
loved ones to abandon their agricultural efforts entirely: agricultural productivity, once considered a patriotic virtue, amounted
by that time, in the judgment of the most disaffected poilus,
to a form of betrayal that only extended the war indefinitely.
Most, however, favored a more moderate course. Loath to see
their land overrun with weeds, they wanted to return home—
for good if possible, but at any rate for a week or two—to lend
wives and parents a much-needed hand. Peasant soldiers feared
that without their sturdy contributions, the next harvest would
be dangerously deficient. As one put it: "If the war does not end
this year, I wonder what there will be to eat next winter."[25]

The consequences of underproduction were evident throughout much of the nation, though more acute in some regions than in others. It is possible that in Brittany, where families were large and adolescent labor more plentiful, the economic crisis of 1917 barely registered. Very little land if any was left fallow in the last three years of the war, and although the people of Brittany certainly bore their share of misfortune, they suffered little economic deprivation. Indeed, by 1918 they seemed more prosperous than ever.[26] The same was not true elsewhere in France. In the Beaujolais region of southeast France, hardship had set in as early as 1916. Three successive years of bad weather had left proprietors of small-scale vineyards in a sorry state. And in the agriculturally rich departments of southwest France, where self-sufficiency had been the norm in 1916, the new year brought bleak prospects. Some basic commodities were hard to come by, as Marie reported in March; other civilians in the region echoed her complaint. Sugar (needed to preserve the summer fruit harvest) was scarce throughout the region, and bread was difficult to procure in some areas. The mayor of Montpon, a town in the same arrondissement as Nanteuil, noting in May 1917 that wheat and flour were both in short supply, spoke of the "need to cut back on the consumption of bread." Scarcity was not unique to Montpon: flour supplies had been running low for more than a month in several parts of the Dordogne, and some bakers had to close their shops at least one day a week.[27]

The government was by no means indifferent to the looming food crisis. Scarcely a politician in all of France would have been unaware of the revolutionary consequences of hunger. As the Revolution of 1789 had made abundantly clear, hunger, in conjunction with wide-ranging political discontent, could depose kings, undermine the authority of elected officials, and spark mayhem in the streets. The months from March through

July, when harvest surpluses from the previous year were running low and the young crops were not yet ripe, gave cause
for particular concern. Recent events in Russia, France's most
tenuous ally, only reinforced this history lesson. When women
whose husbands were away at war marched in the streets of
Petrograd in March 1917, to express outrage at the inability of the tsarist government to provide civilians and soldiers
with the food they needed, they had precipitated the revolution that overthrew Nicholas II.[28] Though conditions in France
were not as dire as those in Russia, they were certainly unsettling. Without bread, France could not wage war, feed its urban
population, or sustain the peasantry, on whose daily labors the
nation depended. Much discussion was thus given over to the
merits of regulating the grain trade, requisitioning existing supplies, and, if all else failed, rationing bread. Before resorting to
rationing, however, the authorities took steps to increase the
agricultural labor supply (without unduly compromising the
efficacy of the armed forces). As of January 1917, men conscripted from the classes of 1892 and earlier (who had been at
least forty-two years old when the war started) were entitled to
twenty days of agricultural leave to help their family bring in
the harvest.[29] Because younger men received no such special
consideration, this policy did little to increase agricultural productivity, and it embittered those—soldiers and their families
alike—who did not benefit from the provisions.

The state also took steps to safeguard the diminished food
supply. Millers had been accustomed to milling grain in such a
way that only 70 to 80 percent of the wheat found its way into
the flour. This process produced a very fine flour (and tasty
bread) but significant wastage. Starting in May 1917, millers
were required by law to incorporate into the flour much of the
dross usually discarded in the milling process (and previously
used only as fodder for cattle); bakers and peasants made their

bread from the rough flour that the millers sold; and consumers had little choice but to eat the heavy, unrefined bread
made from this coarse flour. Those who had to chew their way
through the leaden loaves that emerged from bakers' ovens in
spring 1917 were not impressed: "It's not good; perhaps once
we are used to it, it will seem better, but really it's not very
appetizing at all."[30] Nor was it easy, in fact, to get millers to
comply with these regulations. In small communities in the
Dordogne, for example, they still customarily discarded up to
25 percent of the wheat milled, because their equipment was
not sophisticated enough to accommodate the more exacting
specifications. Mindful of their customers' tastes, millers who
catered to urban appetites consistently produced flour of a finer
quality than the law mandated.[31]

Peasants who took their grain to be milled were rarely satisfied with the flour their millers returned to them. Their real anger, however, was directed at government officials who threatened to tax bread, requisition supplies, and forcibly limit the
bread available for consumption. The peasants, who produced
the grain that would be requisitioned and who depended on
bread as the staple of their diet, were outraged.[32] So were men
at the front who stayed in contact with their families in rural
France. Although soldiers in the trenches had nothing but contempt for civilians who continued to live well while all others
suffered, they always exempted their own parents, wives, and
children from the blanket condemnation.[33] When it became
apparent to soldiers in spring 1917 that their families were suffering the effects of food shortages—and that greater hardships
loomed ahead—men in the trenches were furious. For those
who accepted their own suffering as the price to be paid for
protecting their families, the knowledge that their wives, children, and parents were suffering too was bitter. Peasant soldiers
were outraged when they learned of government plans to req-

uisition grain and maybe even introduce bread rationing. One soldier from the Gironde, who had heard from men in his regiment about plans afoot to ration bread to half a kilogram per person per day, feared that his wife and children would be unable to feed themselves adequately. Others worried that their families would have their remaining grain stocks requisitioned by government agents ignorant of, or indifferent to, the real needs of an agricultural population. Like their ancestors during the Revolution who had resented similar government initiatives (also designed first and foremost to pacify rebellious city folk), the peasantry perceived rank injustice in the wartime requisitioning and regulation of grain. Soldiers whose families still had grain reserves had no compunctions about advising them to hide them when the government agents came to call: "Keep enough wheat [for yourself] you will be able to have enough to eat and those idlers in the city who don't do a damn thing will only have to go and work the land that has been left fallow." Or as this soldier from the Charente recommended: "I've heard that they are going to come by and collect the grain that you have, and that bread is going to be taxed. Try to put to one side several sacks that they won't be able to find—I think that will be useful, we are on the road to real misery."[34]

Although such advice made good sense to those who produced the grain and hoped to guarantee their food (and seed) supply through the next harvest, placing grain outside the reach of requisitioning agents—a practice denounced as "hoarding" by city dwellers in danger of going hungry—did little to improve the bread supply. And city residents were not the only ones to suffer the negative effects of such initiatives. Peasants who had no grain reserves to hide, either because their 1916 harvest was already depleted or because they did not grow grain in the first place, were in a particularly sorry state. Villagers in Montignac-le-Coq, a community within walking distance of Nanteuil, did not meet their grain quota for 1917, but it is impossible to know whether they were actively hiding grain from government agents or, as the village schoolteacher preferred to believe, simply lacked supplies sufficient to meet the quotas.[35] Somewhat farther afield, small-scale wine producers in the Gironde worried that the meager grain supplies would not be adequate to see them through lean summer months that preceded the wheat harvest.[36] Wine producers, whose land was given over entirely to vines, were dependent on others for their daily bread.

Aware since early March of the growing food crisis, angry that their wives and children were forced to eat unpalatable bread, outraged that the government wanted to confiscate the hard-earned fruits of their labors, peasant soldiers longed for victory, which would allow them to go home for good, reclaim their land, and preserve their families from the prospect of famine. But if victory could not be secured, then at the very least soldiers wanted—indeed, demanded—leave, not just as a well-earned respite from the horrors of war, but also as a chance to go home and work their fields.

The Chemin des Dames offensive, launched on 16 April 1917, was—like the Second Battle of Champagne more than eighteen months earlier—supposed to win the war. The plan, confidently proclaimed by Robert Nivelle, the newly appointed commander in chief of the French army, promised to succeed where every previous Allied offensive had failed: troops would pierce the German lines decisively enough to break the enemy's hold on northern France once and for all. The key to this grand plan was a tactical innovation that Nivelle had introduced in autumn 1916 and then employed to excellent effect when French troops had retaken Fort Douaumont at Verdun: a closely coordinated rolling artillery barrage that made it impossible for the enemy to man the machine guns gave the advancing infantry essential protection as it crossed No Man's Land and approached the German front lines. Nivelle was convinced that the same principle could be applied with equal success along a much larger front. In winter 1916–17, he had devised a plan of attack that would bring the full brunt of British and French forces to bear on the weakest points of the German front. He originally envisaged a two-part flanking attack on what was, until February 1917, a massive German salient that traced an arc deep into French territory from Arras to Reims. British and Dominion troops would breach the German salient north of Arras, while the French would attack farther south, near the fabled but now much battered city of Reims. Once the Germans began their strategic retreat in February 1917 to the Hindenburg Line (thus eliminating in one fell swoop the salient that they had held since September 1914), Nivelle's original plan was invalidated. But Robert Nivelle was not a man easily thwarted: skeptics and naysayers on the general staff and the French government notwithstanding, he remained convinced that his rolling barrage would give the French forces an unprecedented advantage in the field. He chose to adapt rather than abandon his grand plan for a spring offensive. Absent a German salient, the French would launch a frontal attack along an eighty-kilometer front running from Soissons in the west, along the Aisne River, eastward past Reims into the heart of the Champagne region.

Central to this plan was the determination to capture the Chemin des Dames. This elevated ridge, located in the department of the Aisne and running west to east from Soissons to Craonne, had been held by the Germans since September 1914. Once a route favored by eighteenth-century princesses and their ladies-in-waiting, the Chemin des Dames had been transformed in the first three years of the war into a powerfully fortified German stronghold. Occupying the high ground north of the river Aisne, the Chemin did not lend itself easily to a frontal assault. And after months of snow, sleet, and rain that continued well into the first days of spring—Paul reported twenty centimeters of snow and driving winds as late as 3 April—the conditions that confronted French troops in mid-April were far from ideal. They gave pause to many on Nivelle's staff, who expressed grave reservations about his ambitious (or some said foolhardy) plan.

Few complaints, however, came from the rank and file, who knew weeks in advance of the opening salvo that a huge battle would soon unfold. As the postal censors observed in early April, soldiers and civilians alike had been talking unrestrainedly about "the imminence, now closer than ever, of a huge offensive." Desperate to believe that the end of the war was within sight, men destined to storm the high ground enthusiastically embraced Nivelle's faith that this battle would break the deadlock, rout the enemy, and restore the territorial integrity of France. The censors noted appreciatively the powerful pulse of optimistic anticipation in the French ranks. "Almost oblivious of the danger" ahead of them, soldiers massing along the Aisne River revealed in their letters home "an admirable enthusiasm."[37] This was certainly how Paul contemplated the forthcoming offensive from his position on the right flank of the battlefield. Three days before the battle began, he wrote to warn Marie that the battery was leaving the following day for "an unknown destination." He confronted the prospect of renewed hostilities with admirable equanimity: "The essential thing is that I am healthy and that I will face this new test with courage and most especially with confidence." He urged Marie "not to worry" if she went for several days without word from him. It was impossible to say, he warned, "when I will be able to write you." On the following day, he announced that the battery, still well behind the lines, would soon move into "position for the famous pursuit." This knowledge—and the intimations of mortality that inevitably accompanied it—did not weaken his resolve, but it did reinforce his desire to protect his infant son: "I see that our little one is quite sick. I don't have to remind you any more to do whatever is necessary to look after him because I know very well that you will do everything possible."[38]

On 16 April Paul surveyed the combat scene unfolding in front of him; from his vantage point in the Champagne, the battle was by no means an unmitigated disaster. The weather was foul, with a cold rain that chilled men who were forced to "sleep outdoors under a tent sheet that doesn't keep the water out," but the French guns were firing with fierce determination: "I can tell you that the Boches are taking it in the neck right now it's really terrible. Anyway, everything is going well and kiss our little one for me."[39] Farther westward, however, the offensive quickly ran into difficulty on inhospitable terrain. Called upon to advance uphill in driving rain chilled by sleet, the unfortunate infantry made slight progress in the first days of the battle, while suffering massive casualties. In three weeks, an attacking army that had numbered 1,200,000 million men (almost exactly as many men as had died in the French ranks since August 1914) suffered almost 150,000 total casualties. Thirty thousand men died in the last weeks of April, trying against the odds to capture territory that resisted almost all advances.

Notwithstanding the setbacks, Nivelle remained resolute. Confident that his plan would work—and quickly—he had promised the skeptics on his staff and in the government that he would call off the attack forty-eight hours after it began if he had not attained his objectives. This, however, he was in no position to do. Although the offensive had accomplished none of its strategic objectives, it had made some local gains. Those could either be consolidated by ongoing offensive action, or abandoned in a full-scale retreat. Neither option was without cost. To suspend the offensive would have exposed the harried infantrymen in the most forward positions to the merciless counterbarrage of still solidly emplaced German guns; to continue it would mean more casualties. Moreover, any substantial reduction of activity on the French front would have allowed the Germans to reinforce their positions north of Arras and Vimy, where the British and Canadians were making significant gains. Even though winning the battle was by the end of April clearly impossible, abandoning the fight was no alternative. Thus, the battle continued through the end of the month, to be suspended officially on the ninth of May.[40]

Not surprisingly, the "admirable enthusiasm" that had animated troops in advance of the battle quickly gave way to profound dismay. Although some survivors continued to hope that the French would prevail, many did not hesitate to "emphasize the heavy losses suffered and the limited gains achieved."[41] Surrounded by the mayhem, uncertainty, and bitter disappointment of late April; appalled by indisputable evidence of horrendous losses—Paul wrote more than once of the "cemeteries that are being improvised here every day"[42]—many among the French troops gave voice to bitter recrimination. The much-vaunted rolling barrage had failed to provide the infantryman with effective cover; indeed, the artillery had (according to some estimations) done as much damage to their own men as to the enemy. One eyewitness claimed that French artillery fire had killed or wounded fourteen hundred men out of two thousand; another observed caustically that "after 13 days [of combat] it seems to me that they could have learned to adjust their fire."[43] As they buried their friends in makeshift graves, tended the wounded, and considered their own prospects for the future, hundreds of thousands of demoralized survivors had to confront the unpalatable truth that victory, so ardently desired, had eluded them yet again.

It is customary to speak of this botched offensive as the Battle of the Chemin des Dames, and without doubt much of the most brutal fighting occurred there. But the battlefront was not confined to this forty-kilometer sector alone; it extended eastward beyond Reims, into territory that had been fiercely contested eighteen months earlier. The Champagne offensive of September 1915, in which upwards of 30,000 French troops had died, now seemed a distant memory, but the soldiers called upon in spring 1917 to fight for that ground stained by the blood of so many of their countrymen must have felt disheartened at the prospect. Ferocious French efforts notwithstanding, the Germans still held (as they did on the Chemin des Dames) the most strategically important ground. In particular, they held a ridge of hills approximately two hundred meters in elevation that lay due east of Reims and offered a commanding view over the Châlons plain spread out below. Regaining these strategically important hills—Mont Cornillet, Haut Mont, and the two much more evocatively named hills of Casque (helmet) and Téton (which only the most polite soldier would translate as "breast")—was the objective of the Battle of Moronvilliers, which raged for several weeks after the suspension of the Chemin des Dames offensive. It was here, facing Mont Cornillet, that the First Battery of the 112th, now serving with the French Fourth Army, installed their guns.

Eyewitnesses agree that fighting in this sector was often intense, especially in late May when the Fourth Army launched a full-scale assault on Mont Cornillet, in mid-June during a hard-fought assault and German counterassault, and in mid-July when pitched battle inflicted severe casualties on many units, including Paul's battery. As was true everywhere on the western front, even quiet days, unmarked by massive assaults or mind-numbing casualties, bore mournful witness to the awesome power of heavy artillery. After a week of fierce combat at the beginning of the campaign, a lull set in on 25 April, yet it was while out on an errand on one of these almost tranquil days that Paul came across a "very sad spectacle." Half an hour earlier, a German shell had, he reported, "killed 15 soldiers and wounded 25." Paul arrived "just in time to see the bodies." He reflected ruefully that this "would be a beautiful country to make love with one's beloved but instead of that you see nothing but soldiers and instruments of death there isn't a civilian to be seen for at least 25 kilometers."[44]

Days later, the battle resumed in earnest. On 30 April the Nineteenth Infantry Division launched a concentrated assault on Mont Blond and Mont Cornillet. To clear the way, the artillery unleashed a "cannonade more terrible than anything [Paul had] ever seen even at Verdun." Indeed the barrage was so formidable that he wondered how the Germans could survive it; they certainly weren't returning fire. "I think that with everything that we are sending over to them they hardly have the time" to retaliate. Yet the infantry made little progress, gaining only five hundred meters of ground and suffering heavy losses. On 1 May, Fernand Maret, a young poilu who would receive the Croix de Guerre for valorous conduct in the battle for Mont Cornillet, observed in a letter to his parents that he was not even going to think any more about the end of the war, for it filled him with disgust to see how dim the prospect now was: "It is shameful," he judged, "to see how we are being led; I believe that they have no thought of finishing the war until every man is dead."[45]

Maret was not the only French soldier in May 1917 to condemn high-ranking commanders who had compelled the troops to fight a battle they could not win. Discontent, sometimes manifested in acts of collective indiscipline, was now rife in the French ranks, and much of the anger was directed (appropriately enough) at Robert Nivelle. Thoroughly discredited in the eyes of politicians, peers, and poilus alike, the commander in chief of the French army was dismissed on 15 May 1917, to be replaced by Philippe Pétain, another hero of Verdun and a noted critic of Nivelle's hubristic plan. The change in leadership prompted Paul to speculate, "This will all end sooner than we think." It is difficult to know precisely whether he shared his comrades' contempt for the man responsible for the spring offensive, for he wrote somewhat enigmatically: "The majority of the guys are pleased to see the fall of Nivelle. I don't know why. Anyway? . . ."[46] Perhaps Paul realized that Pétain, like Nivelle before him, could not win the war without continuing the offensive, but he could not continue the offensive without undermining—perhaps fatally—the morale of his men. What is certain is that Paul's hope for a speedy end to the war was doomed to be disappointed. Nivelle's dismissal did not bring his much-maligned offensive to a close, as the Fourth Army that was massed in front of Mont Cornillet learned to its considerable cost a week later.

If Fernand Maret and Paul Pireaud, two farm boys forced by unhappy circumstance to travel far from their familiar fields, had had occasion a month after the fall of Nivelle to compare notes (or even to read each other's letters), they would have agreed that appalling though the conditions of late April had been, much worse was yet to come. May 1917 would be marked both by a new French assault on Mont Cornillet and by German endeavors to repel this merciless attack and avenge the fallen. This choreography of assault and counterassault, which threatened the ranks of infantry and artillery alike, gave frontline poilus and rearguard gunners radically different perspectives on the unfolding battle and its manifold dangers. Maret (and his younger brother) served in infantry regiments destined to charge the hills in front of the French lines; they witnessed close-up the grisly spectacle of machine guns strafing the advancing infantry with impunity. Paul, by contrast, remained well behind the range of machine-guns and the enemy's field artillery. This vantage point allowed him on occasion to watch, at little danger to life and limb, much of the savage action unfolding in front of him. Inured by war to the suffering of those he did not know, he described in the tones of a disinterested observer a German bombardment directed at two field artillery batteries a kilometer in front of his position: recognizing that the "formidable explosions" that tore up the landscape were making life a misery for the gunners manning the 75's ahead of him, he admitted, "For the time being since it's not for us we hardly worry about it." But soon the German artillery adjusted its aim so that the shots landed farther back, in order to disable the heavy French guns that were inflicting damage of an unprecedented scale on the German lines in late May. Life in the First Battery of the 112th became unbearable.

The Fourth Army planned to unleash a frontal assault on Mont Cornillet on 20 May 1917. The goal was to capture the hill and dislodge the two battalions of German infantry garrisoned in a tunnel deep beneath it. As was customary in preparation for any offensive action, the attacking army's heavy artillery targeted the opposing batteries, in hopes of disabling guns that if left untouched would destroy any prospect for a real infantry advance. But the preliminary barrage inevitably alerted the enemy to the imminence of an impending attack and at the same time left the batteries of the heavy artillery exposed to counterattack, as the 112th knew all too well. In the week preceding the French attack, Paul's battery came under heavy fire on both the fifteenth and the nineteenth of May. The latter attack was especially fearsome: incoming shells left craters "four or five meters deep" in the very middle of the battery, destroyed Paul's bicycle, and to a large degree obliterated the company canteen. It was, Paul averred, just like Verdun. The "bastard" Germans were giving the men of the battery plenty of work, as they tried desperately to restore order to their site. And venturing beyond the confines of the battery, as the messenger had to do, was nerve-wracking in the extreme. Writing on the twenty-first, Paul described his plight: "I spent the night [of May 19–20] white with fear carrying orders all the telephone lines having been cut and the next day (yesterday) to get back to my battery I had to leave on a different bike with mine on my back so that I could exchange it 15 kilometers away." Upon his safe return from that harrowing adventure, he sought solace in alcohol-induced oblivion, by drinking five liters of cheap, watered-down wine: "I was so mad at those dirty Boches that I drank as much as I could to pull myself together and I can tell you that I can really drink now you can tell your father and mother that they should plant some vines for when I get home. I have really got used to this 'plonk.'"[47]

As the French assault on Mont Cornillet unfolded in the late afternoon of 20 May—under a brilliant sun that effaced recent memories of snow and sleet—the First Battery of the 112th looked out on the attack with evident enjoyment. Now that it was clear that the French were attacking with ruthless ferocity positions the Germans had held for more than two years, Paul could laugh at the memory of his recent "adventure" under fire. The Germans were, he opined, being given a hearty dose of their own medicine. He had little idea how bitter that dose really was, however. To capture the hill and force the evacuation of the troops quartered in the garrison dug beneath it, the heaviest French guns bombarded the entry to the tunnel with poison-gas shells. A direct hit collapsed the underground galleries, blocked all exit paths, and asphyxiated the helpless troops caught inside. When the French infantry penetrated the tunnel, a grotesque sight confronted them: four hundred men had suffocated in the labyrinthine tunnels. The bodies of the dead, their features contorted with pain, were piled one on top of the other: men desperate for air had hurled themselves in vain against the obstructions that sealed the escape routes. It was, the witnesses concurred, "one of the worst spectacles of the war, a nameless horror."[48] The tunnel, so quickly transformed into a tomb for the men of the 476th Württemberg Infantry, would remain closed until 1975.[49]

Losses on this scale could not go unanswered. In the last week of May, the German guns retaliated, firing relentlessly into and behind the French front lines. In a rest camp when the battle for Mont Cornillet opened on 20 May, Fernand Maret's regiment soon moved into position, and what he witnessed left him almost at a loss for words: "Today I am in the furnace; my God, what martyrdom, what suffering, you can't possibly imagine it. It's worse than ferocious the butchery that one sees [here]." He admitted: "If we have to stay here long, I believe we will go mad; there are moments when fear makes me break out in sweat over my whole body." Once back behind the lines at the end of the month, he described the battle he had just survived as "worse than Verdun."[50] Paul's ventures well beyond the forwardmost lines of the battlefield left him less traumatized than Maret, but appalled nonetheless. While scouring the supply depots in search of a replacement bicycle, he traipsed through several villages, one of which had come under direct attack only minutes earlier: "Four shells hit the bridge and one landed in the middle of the street." Paul tried not to make too much of this—"It's only a small detail"—lest Marie become even more anxious, but he gave other hints, in a succession of letters, that this phase of the battle was truly terrifying. On 31 May he described a village that had been recently reduced to rubble: "This morning I went out on a mission that I can't tell you about I went through a village bombed by the vandals and at the intersection of three roads a 380 mm shell had fallen . . . I went down into the hole and it was impossible to see me you can imagine what kind of a hole that was."[51]

The weeks that followed brought a few moments of real respite: the men in Paul's battery built themselves a makeshift shower that promised temporary relief from the blistering heat; the occasional foray into the towns behind the lines gave Paul a chance to bask in the sun, chatting with an amiable mailman and share a bottle of decent white wine with him (this was, after all, a noted wine-growing region); and in early July he delighted in telling Marie that he had recently acquired a dog (whom he named Cornillet). At home with an infant who continued to combat fevers and sniffles, at odds with her in-laws, anxious about the future, and generally out of sorts, Marie wondered in a glum moment if Paul was not in fact happy to be away at war. This, he assured her in no uncertain terms, was utter nonsense: "I received your letter of the 3rd where you say that I seem be happy. Listen my dear if I didn't cherish in my heart the love of my wife and my child and my parents if I were all alone on this earth then yes I could count myself happy because when the weather is warm as it has been lately and I have everything that I need I cannot really say that I am unhappy especially since the Boches don't ever fire on us. I am not happy because no one is happy in war I miss my home and those who are dear to me I also miss my freedom but in comparing my life to that of all my comrades then in comparison to them I really am happy."[52] Life in the heavy artillery—often tedious, occasionally terrifying—was still better than in the frontline infantry.

Even so, the war and its dangers were always near at hand. Cornillet became his faithful "companion in misery" only because Paul had been "almost asphyxiated the other day and to figure out what had happened the doctor placed a big dog where [he] had been." When the animal survived its exposure to the poisonous fumes, Paul's captain assigned the dog to Paul's particular care: "The captain gave him to me to look after and to take with me wherever I go that's easy enough because he follows me everywhere and when he is really attached to me we will have to train him so that he can take my place as a messenger during bombardments." Attachment was all well and good, but in the final analysis it would be better for the dog rather than his master to take a direct hit. The danger from incoming shells—which in the evocative argot of the frontline soldier were known as prunes, for their ability to loosen one's bowels—in fact remained very real throughout the summer. In late May, while the Germans were bombarding the rear lines, Paul imagined how pleasant it would be in a few weeks' time to go strawberry-picking in the nearby woods. He would have to be careful: "If we are here when they are ripe we will take advantage of it, but only on condition that we don't put cotton in our ears when the prunes are whistling over head because if you let yourself be taken by surprise it's no fun at all."[53] Three weeks of relative tranquillity ended on 26 June 1917, when the battery once again came under direct attack. Shells rained down on the gun emplacements: "It was frightful there wasn't a shelter that could have withstood them they made holes that were 29 paces across and 4 to 5 meters deep it was beyond anything one could imagine. I left at the regular time and had to throw myself down flat on my stomach several times when I arrived [at the battery] I saw them falling all around . . . With every falling shell I threw my bike to the ground and threw myself flat out on the ground finally I made it to my destination but what a spectacle with all these shell holes everywhere there is an enormous one two meters from our canteen at the very spot where I usually put my bike." Fortunately, the soldiers in

Paul's battery escaped without injury, but two men in the adjacent battery were killed. The best that Paul could hope for was that the enemy guns would leave them in peace for the next two to three weeks, as was their usual practice after a heavy attack.[54]

The Germans did indeed hold their fire through mid-July, but only because they were engrossed in actions to reinforce their troop strength in the Moronvilliers sector. Having been a subsidiary sector in April and early May, this had become by mid-June a principal site of contention, and the Germans responded accordingly, moving a fourth division into a region that previously only three had manned. Anticipating a substantial German offensive, the French chose not to wait, preferring to initiate the attack. Thus, in the early evening of 14 July 1917 (a day marked in previous years by extra rations and the distribution of cheap champagne) the French stormed the German lines. True to form, the Germans counterattacked on the following two days, inflicting 1,500 casualties, including 350 deaths, on the French troops. Among those seriously wounded were the captain and one of the lieutenants of Paul's battery. Paul held his commanding officer in high esteem—after all, the captain had entrusted him with responsibilities not given to every simple private—and he was devastated by this turn of events. In the immediate aftermath of the bombardment, he had written a letter so suffused with anguish that he had torn it up. It was, he admitted, "too sad" to send home. On the following day, he conquered his emotions sufficiently to describe in two separate letters the events that had left him so distraught. His captain had been seriously wounded, had been evacuated to a hospital twenty kilometers behind the lines, and remained "in bad shape." Further details would have to wait: "I am too upset, I will tell you more in person." Within hours, though, he felt sufficiently composed to write a more descriptive letter: his captain had lost two fingers on his right hand and had taken a shell splinter in the head, another in the stomach, and a third in the right shoulder. "He will never, ever be coming back to our unit." Of the two lieutenants assigned to the battery, one had been wounded in the thigh and in the kidneys; the second had been on leave and had returned to the battery hours after the shells had hit.[55] Overwhelmed by grief and by a horror he could not put in words, Paul took some comfort in the fact that very soon he too would be headed home on leave. After three months in a sector that had been the focus of pitched battle intermittently since mid-April, after four months away from home, the prospect of leave was all that sustained him.

Leave was, by the late spring and early summer of 1917, one of the most contentious issues confronting the French army. A policy in effect since the previous September stipulated that troops would receive seven days of home leave every four months.[56] Everyone appreciated the predictability of the schedule, and spent any idle hours calculating almost to the day when he would next be headed home. Indeed, in early 1917, leave and all its attendant pleasures became "inexhaustible" topics of discussion in all letters home. Without doubt, leave was often a bittersweet experience, for the delight of going home was always marred by the knowledge that one would soon have to return to the front. After six or seven days of hot meals, a real bed, and the loving ministrations of an affectionate wife, readjusting to life in the trenches was rarely easy. Yet all longed for the respite that they would enjoy surrounded by family and the creature comforts of home. As Paul observed in January 1917, leave did one a world of good: "I felt so happy in your arms what a sweet joy to feel loved to feel close to you a gentle companion who shares your ideas your beliefs your pain and your pleasure who can give you comfort in difficult moments and a little baby like ours to encourage you."[57] Given the restorative powers of leave, any disruption in the leave schedule—however justified by military necessity—was distressing in the extreme. Even though every soldier knew that major battles invariably disrupted the leave schedule in unpleasant ways, it was cause for indignation when, in the weeks leading up to the spring offensive, the commanding officers ignored the leave roster, administered it unfairly, or even abandoned it altogether.[58] Some men went home before their turn; others waited impatiently for a leave that never came.

Paul was one of the lucky ones. Having spent the New Year's holiday at home, he could have expected that his next leave would fall in early May, if all went well. In fact, however, he headed home in early April, only three months after his last leave. His return to the front was, he confessed, "painful," haunted by images of the home he had just left behind: "I saw you at the table sadly looking at the empty spot and I saw myself replaced in our bed, next to you, by our beloved little guy. Oh yes I saw all that and how I suffered seeing myself all alone in the middle of this torment." Yet his plight was infinitely preferable to that of many who had expected to go home in late March or early April, only to discover that the leave roster in many regiments had been radically trimmed in anticipation of the impending battle. As if to illustrate anew the glaring inequalities that separated the infantry from the artillery, men serving in infantry regiments had their leave postponed until after the spring offensive. By contrast, artillerymen with leaves due in late April or early May were often granted leave in advance of battle. As Verdun had demonstrated, artillery batteries, once firmly in place, had to remain in position. If leave was to be granted, it would have to come before, rather than during, the battle. Justifiable or not, these inequities were galling to infantrymen whose plans for leave were thwarted by an impending offensive. Indeed, more equitable distribution of leave was one of the most persistent demands emanating from the ranks among the regiments that mutinied in May and June 1917.

In the aftermath of the Chemin des Dames offensive, upwards of thirty thousand troops, from sixty-eight different infantry divisions, challenged the authority of the high command by participating in individual or collective acts of military disobedience: some deserted; others jeered their commanding officers; many simply refused to move into frontline positions. The infantry, having suffered inordinately in one grisly battle after another, was the most rebellious; and units that had seen action on the Chemin des Dames were, not surprisingly, among the most bitterly disillusioned. As Leonard V. Smith has demonstrated, however, even infantry regiments that had not participated in the offensive were demoralized by its failure. Mutinous behavior in the Fifth Infantry Division, which had been well behind the lines for April and most of May, began when the division was ordered to take up position on the front lines at the end of May. It was not the experience of recent defeat but the prospect of imminent and essentially futile action that precipitated the acts of collective disobedience. In these and other regiments directly touched by the mutinies, soldiers simply refused to participate in any new offensive campaigns. The men claimed rightly enough that if recent experience was anything to go by, the price paid in such enterprises far exceeded the gains. Honoring their primary commitment to defend their homeland against enemy attack, soldiers already on the front lines did not abandon their posts; yet they refused to consent to new attacks conceived along old lines. The rank and file would take the offensive again only when the military high command could present them with a strategy for winning the war that would bring success more noteworthy than the sacrifices it demanded.[59]

Of all the sectors affected by the mutinies, only the wes-
ternmost flank of the Chemin des Dames (where the Sixth
Army was commanded by the formidable General Mangin)
generated more incidents of collective indiscipline than did the
Moronvilliers region, where regiments mutinied intermittently
from mid-April through at least mid-June. Maret, who served in
an infantry regiment that did not mutiny, described in two separate letters (one sent successfully through the regular chan-
nels, the second sent home surreptitiously, in the backpack of
another soldier going home on leave), the effects of mutiny in
this sector. In his second letter, dated 16 June, he wrote: "The
infantry regiments are completely fed up and a large number of
them are refusing to go to the front lines; it's for this reason that
Paul [his younger brother] is at Mont Haut, those who were
supposed to go there having refused to do so . . . I believe that
the war will end soon because the regiments are up in arms and
no longer want to march at all."[60] Yet even in this sector, some
regiments were more directly affected than others, and some
units, including the 112th Heavy Artillery Regiment, were entirely untouched. Paul's letters suggest that although daily life
in a heavy artillery regiment was undoubtedly difficult and depressing, the breaking point—the point beyond which troops
could not and would not continue to function—had not yet
been reached. It was, however, very close, unless fundamental adjustments could be made to the basic ground rules of
combat.

Paul shared with many soldiers on the front lines who did
rebel a scathing disdain for uniformed noncombatants and a
new-found appreciation for drink. When his bicycle was destroyed in the bombardment of 20 May (rendering it almost
impossible for him to fulfill his responsibilities as company
messenger), he quickly discovered that replacing it would be
no easy task. The quartermaster's staff was rife with cronyism.

Staff members saved the best equipment for their friends and fobbed second-rate gear off on strangers. When some officious desk clerk suggested that a small folding bicycle could serve as an adequate replacement for the one destroyed by German artillery fire, Paul was so outraged that he stood his ground until he was guaranteed a bicycle that met his specifications.[61] He took temporary consolation in drink. In the aftermath of the attack that destroyed his bicycle, he downed five liters of wine, much to Marie's consternation. She was convinced that he would come home an alcoholic. He reassured her that she had nothing to fear on that score, but did concede that he had "learned how to drink" since joining the army: "I really like to have something to drink with a meal you remember how I couldn't drink a liter with a meal and now I can easily drink two but if I have learned how to drink I have not learned how to become a drunk and you can rest assured that I will never learn that. And you must know well enough that even if I have acquired some bad habits with you I will abandon everything that you want me to."[62] Benign though it might have been, Paul's fondness for the bottle was revealing. By mid-1917, excessive consumption of alcohol and the attendant drunkenness and indiscipline were rife among the French ranks, contributing in many instances to their rebelliousness. Yet Paul and his regiment resisted the lure of mutiny. Exempt from the most onerous obligation of war—charging into enemy territory with little chance of success—gunners and messengers in the heavy artillery were spared some of the worst horrors of war. Depressed, embittered, and inclined to drink, they were, in the final analysis, melancholic but not yet mutinous.

The mutinies ended when French soldiers, determined as they were to rid their homeland of German troops, believed they had made their point: they would hold the line and would resume the offensive in the right circumstances, but they would not fight in ill-conceived campaigns that offered little prospect of success. Attentive to the men's legitimate complaints, Philippe Pétain exercised restraint in meting out punishment—only forty-seven soldiers were executed for taking part in the mutinies—and promised the vast majority that their grievances had been heard. Henceforth, men who had grumbled for months that the leave rotation was arbitrary, that the food on the front lines was inedible, and that their commanding officers expected them to die without complaint in offensives that rarely succeeded would benefit from an increase in pay, an improved leave roster, and a military strategy less wantonly wasteful of lives. Veteran soldiers who had received at the outset of the war the derisory sum of twenty-five centimes per day were to benefit from a pay raise. When Paul informed Marie at the end of May that he now earned one franc, forty-five centimes each day (of which he would receive eighty-five centimes in cash and the rest in savings stamps), he admitted that all his previous compunctions about accepting the government's money had disappeared. Two years earlier it had not seemed right to file a claim for the military allowance; now, as he joked about looking forward to a life of ease after the war ("We will be folks of independent means [petits rentiers] and fat bourgeois"), he had no qualms about profiting from the government's largesse. After all, in 1915 he had no idea that the "war would last this long."[63] Pétain also promised to liberalize the leave rota, to improve the quality of food on offer, and, most important, to engage his men only in offensives that were likely to succeed. The French army would dig in and "wait for the tanks and the Americans."

Clearly the mutinies were not just over leave. Leave nonetheless acquired a critical importance before and after the mutinies because home was both a refuge from and a reason for fighting. For one week every four months, it offered comfort and consolation to men weary, worn out, and spiritually wounded; at all other times, memories of home—made tangible in daily letters and packages of food and clean clothing—reinforced men's resolve: however horrible the war, they would have to persevere until France was safe, its frontiers restored, and its future secure. Leave acquired an added importance, as we have seen, in the summer of 1917, when men from rural communities all over France, beset by worries about the ability of their families to fend for themselves in a year of want and deprivation, yearned to go home to work the land. Pétain had promised that troops would be able to go home on leave more frequently and the leave roster would be administered more fairly. These concessions did not, however, fully address all complaints. One postal censor noted, "The fact that farmers are kept in uniform despite the fact that their presence, deemed indispensable, is required at home for the crops is the subject of many complaints." It was particularly irksome to see men with no knowledge of farming abuse the agricultural leave policy. Thus when one soldier complained about "guys leaving who have never worked the land . . . waiters in cafés and Apéri, that fat butcher, who owns land twenty kilometers from where he lives and which he rents out," he gave voice to the complaints of many others.[64] Women also complained when their husbands remained at the front, while so-called farmers took advantage of local connections to qualify for an agricultural leave: "I see that your request for leave was refused. Ah, yes, if you had been a notary, a schoolteacher, or something else and you had asked for agricultural leave, you wouldn't have been turned down; it's as if of all those who are on agricultural leave, none are farmers. If they had put all the farmers where they belong then we wouldn't soon be needing ration cards for bread."[65]

Paul, too, wanted to use his next leave to help with the harvest. Since he was in regular contact with Marie, he would have known how difficult circumstances were in his village, on his own land. Thus, he could not agree when she suggested that they would profit most from his next leave (which would fall due in late July or early August) if he came home after the heavy work of the harvest was finished. Enticing though the vision of a blissfully idle leave might be, he could not in fairness to his family contemplate doing nothing while on leave to secure their food supply for the coming year: "You told me to come home on leave after the harvest. On the contrary, if I can I would rather go now because it makes me heartsick to see that you are obliged to do everything." A family squabble—precipitated, it seems, by Charlotte's pregnancy and an inheritance dispute that pitted Paul's mother and Charlotte against Marie—had complicated matters at home and at the same time had increased Marie's obligations to her in-laws. Now that Charlotte was unable to work in the fields, Marie was expected to pick up the slack. Paul was outraged that his wife was being put upon by people who, in his judgment, "showed their gratitude in the manner of Judas." He advised Marie to contribute as little as possible to the collective labors of the extended family until he came home: "I advise you in fact I order you to do the least possible after all they will do what they can."[66]

In a subsequent letter (although undated, the contents clearly identify it as having been written in summer 1917) Paul reflected further on his desire to help his overburdened wife. Melancholy overtook him as he watched men in his battery go home on leave. Paul knew that his friend Bouthonnier (still mourning the death of a brother killed in the spring offensive) would soon be walking through the rolling hills of Nanteuil. "It is with a very heavy heart that I watched this evening as Bouthonnier and my cook left to think that he is going *there, there* to the countryside where he will go to see my wife my child my family. I remain completely lost in thought my heart heavy and with a depression that is impossible to shake. How I wanted to join them too. I know that my turn is coming but in spite of that it makes me angry. Oh when will this damned war end?" Without doubt, his moroseness owed much to war-weariness—exacerbated by the bombardments to which his battery had been so recently subjected—and to a persistent homesickness that had grown ever more intense following the birth of his son. But anger that his wife had to confront the burden of harvesting alone also pervaded his thoughts. It had been raining in Nanteuil and Paul acknowledged, "This won't make your labors any easier especially right now all of you are in the midst of reaping the countryside must be very sad right now with so much work to do and the shortage of workers. As you said, I would be very happy to spend a restful leave but I would be just as happy to help ease your burden a little with the heavy work in the fields . . . Give our son a big hug for me and for you, my tenderest caresses and my gentlest kisses."[67]

Paul's wish was granted. Almost four months to the day after his last leave, he went home in late July. His leave could not have been better timed. Indeed, it might well have saved his life, for when he returned to the front on 4 August he discovered that in his absence the battery had again come under direct fire and its best-loved lieutenant had been killed. Unaware of what was happening at the front, Paul had been fully occupied at home lending a hand in the fields—in late July, the wheat crop in the Dordogne was ripe for harvesting—and enjoying more than a few moments of sexual ecstasy. That they made the most of their time was evident in subsequent letters, in which Marie waited anxiously for reassurance that she was not pregnant.

Because no letters were written during the time when Paul was at home, it is impossible to know what he and Marie chatted about over the dinner table, while watching Serge crawl around their little stone cottage, or while snuggled in bed. No doubt they spoke about their ardent love, eager passion, and parental pride. Serge, having just celebrated his first birthday, was now the delightful little boy Paul's comrades were so quick to admire in the photographs he had proudly circulated at the front. But in the ongoing conversation from afar that Paul and Marie shared throughout the war, the intensely intimate always merged with the unavoidable reality of military life: babies and battles; ardor and artillery fire combined in run-on sentences that revealed how closely domestic concerns and military developments coexisted in their minds. It is therefore likely that while home on leave Paul also spoke of matters that he had only alluded to in recent letters. More than once he had indicated that he had things to tell Marie that could not safely be put down on paper. He had promised, though, that he would tell her all once he got home. It is likely, then, that in the intimacy of his home he undid the most significant silence of his letters and told Marie what he knew about the mutinies.

In the letters dispatched between April and July 1917, Paul wrote of poison-gas attacks, deadly bombardments, psychological depression, and the grievous injuries of men he held in high regard. He described faithfully and, to the extent that circumstances permitted, precisely the nature of combat as he witnessed it. Yet he said not a word about the mutinies. His silence seems curious and out of character, for ordinarily he had no great respect for the censors and was not easily intimidated by their injunctions or rules. Perhaps he was more cautious in late spring and early summer 1917 because the censors were unusually vigilant, but even increased scrutiny did not stop many other soldiers from writing quite explicitly about the mutinies. Some circumvented the censors by sending letters in the backpacks of men departing on leave; some simply took the gamble that their letters would not be intercepted. Others, like Maret, did both. Whatever strategy they chose, word was "getting out that certain units have refused to march and that the soldier 'has had enough.'"[68] Thus, Paul's decision not to write about the mutinies (a decision made by many other frontline troops, too) is intriguing. Perhaps his reticence owed something to his respect for his captain, who would have impressed upon his men the importance of silence on this genuine issue of military security. Whereas Paul was willing to brave the censors' wrath (and ignore their intrusiveness) on occasion, he always did so with a purpose: he defied the censors in order to tell Marie what in his judgment she needed to know. She had to know that he loved her, longed for her, and lamented their separation. She also had to know where he was and what conditions were like there, for such information could either reassure her that he was safe for the time being or brace her for knowledge that he was in immediate danger. To write in 1917 about circumstances that neither directly affected his fate nor touched on matters of essential family intimacy would in his eyes have been both unnecessary and irresponsible. Paul's first priority was to survive the war, but survival had to be accompanied by French victory. This calculus made him a hardheaded realist who could accept without evident remorse that French guns could and did inflict real damage on the enemy. But if he could accept even the grisliest aspects of war in the hope that they would advance the cause of victory, he could not bring himself to act in any way to compromise that cause. To describe the mutinies in a letter that might be intercepted by the enemy might have done just that. Although interception was unlikely, it was a risk not worth running. It was better to commit nothing to writing.

When home on leave, soldiers certainly talked about the mutinies, as observers in various parts of the country often noted. In southeast France, the prefect of the department of the Rhône remarked several months after the worst of the crisis was past: "Soldiers on leave, although reserved in the letters that they send home from the front, become very talkative once back on their home turf."[69] This was equally true in the tranquil heart of the Dordogne, where the subprefect for the arrondissement of Ribérac noted in June 1917 that civilians in his jurisdiction were hearing depressing stories from men home on leave: "These men, instead of bringing with them consoling words, instead of glorifying the admirable acts that they themselves have accomplished and see others accomplish every day, say at every turn that their leaders are betraying them, that entire regiments are refusing to march at the time of offensives and that they will do the same . . . that they have had enough of the war." In the neighboring department of the Gironde, the picture was no more encouraging. Taking refuge in bureaucratic vagueness, the police commissioner spoke in June 1917 of how "alarmist news coming from the front or brought back by soldiers on leave" was unsettling public opinion and prompting many to exaggerate the dire consequences of the failed offensive.[70]

Nor indeed is it likely that battle-hardened men would have held their tongues. By spring 1917, French soldiers were used to speaking their minds, thwarting the censors, and challenging established authority. Had they not been, there would not have been any mutinies to worry about. As Leonard V. Smith has persuasively demonstrated, the mutinies emerged from a collective sense within the rank and file that citizen-soldiers had the right to establish the limits of their obedience through negotiation with their commanding officers. Convinced that the fundamental goal of the war was worthwhile—France had to be defended, its territory liberated—they agreed to hold the line. To die in a campaign that might put France closer to victory was reasonable; to die for nothing, as so many men had done on the Chemin des Dames, was something else entirely. Citizen-soldiers who in the most extreme instances were ready to challenge the authority of their commanding officers through acts that could place them in front of a firing squad were not easily intimidated by orders not to talk about the mutinies. Even men who put nothing down in writing said a great deal once they were in the comforting confines of home.

Civil and military authorities tried in vain to control the flow of information between soldiers and civilians. Intimately connected to wives and parents by bonds of affection, daily correspondence, and precious private conversation, combatants shared with their closest civilian confidants the miseries of life in a war that would not end. Alarmed by signs that their families were suffering real material deprivation, outraged at inequities that seemed to favor those who lived in cities at the expense of the long-suffering peasantry, some rural soldiers rebelled outright; others only grumbled. All, however, reported back for duty when so required. The war was not yet won, their families not yet safe. By the fall of 1917, the crisis of morale that had provoked the mutinies was over, French troops were willing once again to take the offensive, and the prospect of military reinforcements from across the Atlantic revived the sagging morale of even the most war-weary. For many men from the Dordogne, however, the fall of 1917 marked a new and unsettling juncture in the history of the war. Having fought for three years on French soil to protect family and farm from invasion and enemy assault, they were now called to leave their homeland to defend a nation on the very brink of military collapse. Italy is a lovely place to visit, but not everyone was convinced of that in the last year of the Great War.

My beloved Marie,

I had a good letter yesterday and today the one from the 25th truly I am too fortunate to get such good letters every day from my Marquise I have never seen you so sweet so good so lovable and so confident just the way I have wanted so often without doubt you understood my dream and my desires you could not imagine how happy that makes me how happy you make me and how I love you like that there is no need for you to be afraid with hearts like ours nothing will ever tire them and nothing will break them our love will keep us forever young poor Marquise a love like the one I have for you will never die even on the threshold of old age for me you will still be the young girl who charmed me who made my heart beat hard and who brought me such feelings of happiness you will always be the one I love and that I will love forever with all my heart You are right to take my big Nenette to sleep with his grandpa that way when I have the good fortune to come home on leave we will be able as you say to practice our gentle caresses and other things that are even better without disturbing him how good that will be when I even think of it it makes me depressed, at night I have undreamable dreams that I cannot put down on paper.

Paul to Marie, 29 February 1918

FIVE

We Are Martyrs of the Century

When Paul learned in November 1917 that the 112th Heavy Artillery Regiment would soon be reassigned to the Italian front, he was anything but enthusiastic. He recognized that Italy was in desperate need of military reinforcements, but he felt only resentment that Italian incompetence, which had been tragically evident a few weeks earlier in the humiliating defeat at Caporetto, might extend the war well past 1918. In an offensive launched on 24 October 1917, Austro-Hungarian and German forces had routed the Italian enemy, had advanced a hundred kilometers, while taking more than a quarter of a million prisoners, and had watched as the Italian army—from which an additional three hundred thousand soldiers had deserted—fell into profound disarray.[1] From his vantage point in the Champagne, Paul expressed nothing but contempt for France's junior partner: "Don't you think it is unfortunate that having hoped that this damned war would end in 1918 the weakness of the Italians now makes it likely that it will last at least another 18 months?"[2] Many of his comrades-in-arms felt much the same way. However dismal life was on the western front, few French soldiers who served there through the fall of 1917 welcomed the news that they (or their compatriots) would soon be sent to restore the honor, fighting capacity, and devastated lines of an ally incapable (in their judgment) of defending itself. They would have preferred to stay in France, defending French soil and protecting French families.[3]

French commanders recognized, however, that the deployment of an Anglo-French expeditionary force to Italy was an unfortunate necessity. When Italy, a peacetime ally of Germany and Austria-Hungary, had entered the war in May 1915 on the side of Britain and France, Allied strategists had hoped that the newly created Italian front would force the Central Powers (already fighting a two-front war) to attenuate their fighting strength on the western front even further. If Austria-Hungary, the weaker of the two Central Powers, had to hold the line against Italy in the Alps, then Germany would have to divert more of its manpower to the campaign against Russia. Thus, Italy's participation in the war could force Germany to weaken its presence on the western front, to the obvious advantage of Britain and France. After Caporetto, however, this entire equation was reversed: once Allied troops were reassigned to Italy, Germany and Austria-Hungary stood to gain from Italy's participation in the war, and Britain and France only to lose. The Allies had no choice but to reinforce the vulnerable Italian line—if Italy were to collapse entirely and sue for a separate peace, the Central Powers would be able to redirect all their military strength to the western front—but they could do so only by diminishing their own strength on the western front. Faced with this unattractive prospect, the high command agreed to succor their Italian ally.[4]

The deployment of British and French troops to Italy would cause an erosion in Allied troop strength in northern France at a time when it could ill be afforded. In the aftermath of the mutinies, real progress had been made to restore discipline in the French ranks. Pétain revived soldiers' confidence in the high command by launching a series of small-scale but successful attacks in fall 1917 which demonstrated that the French were capable once more of taking the offensive; and he made real strides toward improving the material conditions of frontline

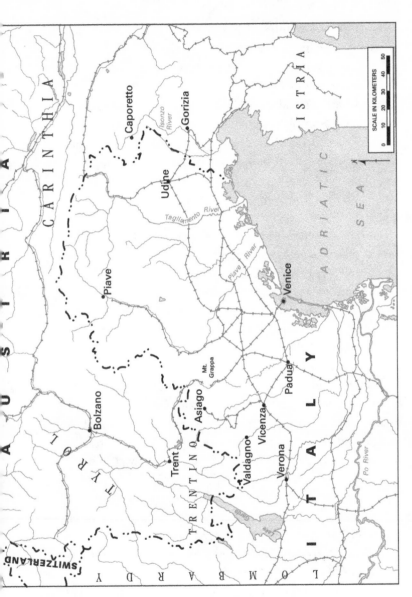

The Italian front. Map from Robert A. Doughty, *Pyrrhic Victory: French Strategy and Operations in the Great War* (Cambridge, Mass.: Harvard University Press, 2005), 396.

service.[5] Troops too often deprived of hot food, adequate rest, affordable supplies, and regular leave welcomed the improvements introduced in the fall of 1917: officers now supervised the distribution of palatable (and hot) food; military cooperatives sold such essential supplies as wine, warm socks, and stationery at reasonable prices; and a new leave roster held forth the prospect of ten days of leave every four months.[6] Such measures would, it was hoped, restore the French to full fighting form. But Pétain was as cautious as Nivelle had been intemperate. Not yet ready to commit to a full deployment of French forces, he preferred to bide his time. American troops, committed to the Entente cause since April 1917, would not be on hand in significant numbers until the summer of 1918. Meanwhile, the French and British would have to hold the line against an enemy able as never before to press its advantage on the western front. Fortuitously strengthened by the Bolshevik seizure of power, which meant that after November 1917 Russia was committed to withdrawing from the war, the Central Powers hoped to take advantage of the period between the Russian exit and full American deployment to bring the war to a victorious end. Recognizing that a major German offensive in France was imminent, yet fearing a complete collapse of the Italian front, French and British commanders agreed to reassign a small force of Allied troops from the western front to northern Italy.

Marshaling no more than two hundred thousand men, the expeditionary force to Italy constituted but a fraction of the entire French army. Consequently, very little attention has been paid to its efforts and very little is known about its adventures. Yet its postal censorship records, when read in conjunction with the letters Paul sent home to Marie, show that troops compelled to serve in a foreign land for the last year of the war felt uncomfortably distant from their families, separated from the essential work of war, and aggrieved by the material inconveniences of life in uniform. Even though combat in northern Italy was—everyone agreed—neither as trying nor, in the main, as dangerous as combat on the western front, expeditionary service wore on men's nerves. Fighting to hold the line for a hapless ally did not stir the blood as did fighting to defend home and hearth. To keep the enemy from the gates of Paris was one thing; to keep him from the banks of the Piave was something else entirely.

If service in Italy presented none of the immediate and obvious moral imperative of service in France, neither did it afford many of the amenities that after September 1917 made life on the western front somewhat less wretched and separation from loved ones slightly more endurable. In Italy the much-appreciated military cooperatives were few and far between; the leave roster was less generous and the postal service less efficient than in France; even stationery was hard to come by. These shortages and inconveniences were far from insignificant. Since 1914, French troops had devoted much of their energy and most of their spare hours to maintaining their connection with home, and their families had reciprocated in kind. Letters, parcels, and leave had kept families united, their affection alive. This effort was threatened by foreign service. Soldiers serving in Italy, and their families at home, felt sorely the relative absence of leave, the irregularity of mail delivery, and the scarcity of such simple commodities as stationery.

What was perhaps most dispiriting was that those deployed to Italy and those who cared about them in France wondered whether the Italian enterprise was worthwhile. Entering the fourth year of war, everyone longed for victory: to bring the men home, end the hardship of separation, and restore the viability of family farms too long deprived of male labor. In fact, in that year food and manpower shortages, which had first manifested themselves in spring 1917, only worsened, and war-weariness grew. The people of southwest France, whose husbands and sons were assigned in disproportionate numbers to the expeditionary force to Italy, were not easily convinced that the Italian campaign was doing anything to bring about a speedy and victorious end to the war. As long as the war continued, the economic and psychological stresses it created—over inadequate supplies and inflationary prices, loneliness and sexual frustration—intensified.

The French expeditionary force dispatched to Italy comprised four infantry divisions, seven squadrons, and seventeen artillery groups (including eleven groups of heavy artillery).[7] The heavy artillery had assumed an ever greater role in the war, as tactics, once focused almost exclusively on infantry charges, evolved. Because the Italians had been forced to abandon nearly all their heavy guns in the retreat from Caporetto, Allied artillery regiments were desperately needed to fill the gap. It was thus that the 112th Heavy Artillery Regiment found itself in late November en route to the Piave valley (where the Italian retreat had halted a month earlier). Still headquartered in the Champagne, where the regiment had enjoyed a few months of respite after the bitterly contested battles of the summer, the 112th received its marching orders on 12 November and left five days later. The journey was slow—Paul did not arrive in Italy until the first of December—and fraught with logistical difficulties. When men, horses, heavy guns, and all the supplies a regiment required had to be transferred from the plains of northern France across the Alps to northeast Italy; when railway stations all over the Rhône valley were thronged with troops, some heading home on leave, others making their way slowly to the Italian front, delays and unanticipated disruptions were unavoidable. It is hardly surprising, therefore, that when the 112th arrived in Lyon, Paul, sent into the heart of the city in search of essential provisions, became temporarily separated from his regiment. Having missed his connecting train, he (and the supplies) then followed the regiment's route eastward to Grenoble and from there (like Napoleon more than a century earlier) over the Alps into Italy.

Destined to take up positions 1,500 meters above sea level in the Dolomite mountains north of Venice, the 112th traveled eastward from Milan across the Lombardy plain and from there into the mountains. The region boasted some of the loveliest landscape and some of the best wine in a nation renowned for both. None of this was wasted on French troops, who were happy to drink the wine and to play at being tourists when the opportunity presented itself. Henry Guichard, a young peasant who served in Italy from October 1917 until his infantry regiment was reassigned to the western front in April 1918, noted appreciatively, "Everywhere we go we have been acclaimed by the local inhabitants, who have given us quite a bit of wine. In a railway station a group of young Italian girls was waiting for us with flowers. Everywhere everyone runs up to see the French passing by."[8] Paul made no mention in his letters of pretty girls flinging flowers at disembarking troops (Marie, one suspects, would not have looked kindly upon such news), but he did observe that the wine was excellent, "better even than at home." And the historic sites were well worth a visit. When the men of his battery arrived in Verona they found themselves in storied territory: within sight of their encampment were the two castles where, legend had it, Romeo and Juliet had been born. This was a popular spot for French troops making their way to or from the Piave front, and Guichard also wrote of his visit to the Montague castle. He was much taken by the underground passages that, he learned, had once afforded easy access to the Capulet castle nearby (and seemed to suggest that Shakespearean allegations of bitter enmity between the families may have been somewhat overblown).[9]

Visits to historic sites and bottles of good wine could not however overcome the inevitable ennui attendant on military service in an unfamiliar, impoverished, and only intermittently friendly land. In the winter of 1917–18, when alpine conditions made combat almost impossible, French troops assigned to the Italian front battled boredom and homesickness, chafed at the apparent ingratitude of their allies and the inefficiency of their own support staff, and in the absence of any immediate danger to distract them, fretted that their families were facing yet another year of hardship and hunger.

The palpable poverty of the Italian population unsettled many French soldiers who, like the Americans who would make their way across war-ravaged Europe in 1944, were often assailed by young children begging for food. Such scenes were no doubt especially distressing for men fearful that their own children would soon be in a similarly desperate situation, for the scarcity evident in Italy laid bare the material misery that war had wrought.[10] In Paul's judgment, however, much of the poverty that plagued Italy was due not to the disruptions of war but to the tyranny of an oppressive religion. "If you could see how fanatical the people are here the priest runs everything he is the mayor lawyer notary judge wholesale and retail grocer . . . Women have 12, 15, 18 children because the priest tells them that if they don't they will go to hell."[11] Traveling through a region dotted with roadside shrines dedicated to local saints, he was not the only newly arriving soldier unfavorably struck by the "superstitious" ways of many Italian peasants. Some French troops feared that an excess of piety prompted many Italians to look with a wary eye on their secular allies. Because France in the first decade of the twentieth century had introduced laws to curb the power and reduce the

political clout of the Catholic Church, the most religiously observant Italians, who derided France as atheistic and hostile to
the true faith, saw nothing to celebrate in the arrival of French
troops.[12]

Nor did Italians who had opposed the war from the outset
see any reason to acclaim the French presence. Paul observed
to Marie, "Some look at us sideways because Italy is divided
into three groups: those who want war with Germany, those
who want war with France, and those who don't want war at
any price."[13] Those who identified themselves as reluctant participants in a struggle that leaders had forced upon them for
territorial gain and nationalistic ambition feared that the arrival
of French troops would only prolong a war that many in Italy
had not wanted to enter at all. As one French soldier remarked:
"The Italian troops can't stand the sight of us; the civilians, just
barely. They say that we are the ones who are prolonging the
war. So I can tell you that it's not all a bed of roses." Another
observed, "On our arrival we were well received and looked
upon favorably, but where we are now, we are looked upon
very mistrustfully by all these dirty Italians who figure that we
have come here to prolong the war." Interallied relations were
strained by mutual antipathy, which resulted in violent alterca-
tions and at least one murderous brawl by March 1918.[14]

Paul shared with most of his comrades an undisguised disdain for the military capabilities of the Italian army. But his
animosity was temperate by comparison with that of many of
his comrades-in-arms, who complained that they were being
called on to bail out an inept ally that collapsed at the slightest
pressure from the enemy. Some suggested that most Italians
in uniform were shirkers who were happy to sit out the war on
the slightest pretext: "They have sent us here to Italy to get
smashed up, while the Italians are hanging around at the rear.
Those who have more than six teeth missing are declared unfit

for service . . ., while in our ranks there are fathers with four kids at home who are at the front and often in some of the worst spots."[15] Others berated the "bastard Italians," who seemed always to be in retreat and were incapable of defending their own border. As one soldier lamented: "You cannot know how much I suffer from being so far away and sacrificing myself for what? If you could see this Italian army!"[16] Perhaps Paul shared their opinions, but he reserved his most biting contempt for the Russians. Notwithstanding his socialist sympathies, he had no time for the Bolsheviks and their decision to pull Russia out of the war. In fact, he was so angry that he threatened idly to "sign up for an extra six-month stint at the end of the war to give the Russians a good thrashing."[17] In the short term, however, he had to do his bit in Italy, helping allies who only grudgingly expressed anything like gratitude to the French and British troops in their midst.[18]

Discouraged by international developments and by the "questionable friendship" of their Italian allies, French troops found their first months in Italy demoralizing. As one postal censor concluded in mid-December 1917, many were battling depression "caused perhaps by homesickness, by a desire to see the end of the war, by a certain disgust with the need to support allies who weren't able to defend themselves." More than anything else, though, "the desire for leave and the irregularity of the mail also [gave] rise to discouragement."[19] Troops accustomed to fighting in France felt their physical separation from families at home more intensely because mail delivery was more erratic and leave more infrequent in northern Italy than in France. Paul had feared as much as soon as he had heard that the battery was to be relocated, and in Italy his fears and those of his comrades were borne out. Indignation was almost universal when the leave schedule introduced in September 1917 was not extended also to men serving in Italy.[20] The Pétain schedule would have placed 13 percent of active-duty troops on leave at any given time. In Italy, however, only 4 percent were eligible for leave initially; this system stretched out the interval between leaves from four to six months. It infuriated soldiers who continued to think of leave as the most precious reward for frontline service. One soldier, already in a foul mood because his regiment was forced to subsist on a diet of rice and received clothing inadequate for the freezing temperatures, wrote with wilting sarcasm: "Apart from that, everything is fine, leave has been established at a rate that will allow everyone to get a turn every ten years. It's really cushy being sent to Italy."[21] Another, outraged by the leave roster, claimed perhaps not entirely honestly that he would rather be back on the western front: "We are beginning to have enough of Italy and would be happy to go back to France, even into a worse sector, because here leaves aren't operating at all."[22]

Paul did not share such intemperate opinions. Having listened to Marie's importunate pleas since the beginning of the war that he do whatever he could to stay out of danger, he was happy enough to find himself in a quiet sector: "I really believe that from the point of view of danger we will be better off here than in France because everyone believes that the Boches are going to unleash an offensive on the French front with the troops that have become available following the armistice with Russia."[23] But he, too, found the leave roster seriously inadequate and cause for justified complaint. When he read in the newspaper that the 13 percent rate was at last to be extended to Italy but with application only to men in support positions, he was beside himself with indignation: "Bunch of shirkers bunch of bastards it's high time that the Boches sent some bombs in their direction How is it possible to make such laws those who are chasing girls in Vicenza and Montbello and Verona will have leave every four months while those [of us] who are chasing the Austrians we only get to go home every six months The infantry troops who are going into the trenches these days, that's really going to raise their morale it's shameful nonetheless to think that they are trying to favor those who get to sleep in beds to the detriment of those who are bedded down in the snow and sleep only one night out of three. Anyway, I still love you very much but morale is really low."[24]

Only a letter from home could make a real difference. Family correspondence offered men on active duty the essential reassurance that they were still loved. In the tumult of war, obviously, regular correspondence was not always easy to maintain: military fiat sometimes disrupted delivery to and from the front, and insufficient supplies, which became ever more of a problem in the last two years of the war, made it difficult to write as often, or as extensively, as soldiers and their families would have liked. Masters of the famous "système D"—according to which people apply their ingenuity to overcome obstacles and make the most of a difficult situation—French troops (and their families) had learned the essential art of improvisation. Sometimes, when paper was scarce at the front, civilians would write on only one side of the page, leaving the other side blank for soldiers to send home their own news on the reverse side.[25] And if stationery was completely unavailable, regulation-issue postcards served as a somewhat unsatisfactory substitute. Marie was, under ordinary circumstances, no fan of postcards. In fall 1916, when Paul took to sending cards rather than the lengthy letters she had grown accustomed to, she made her displeasure known: "You seem to forget that I love long letters . . . Forgive me for saying this but there are moments when I am so upset by this sad and hard life that I impatiently await news from you and I would be so happy if they were long, very long." A bit put out by such reproaches, Paul recognized that Marie's testiness was caused more by the cumulative misery of life in wartime than by genuine ill will. Explaining in his own defense that the prepackaged postcards she found so offensive were more durable than ordinary writing paper and more impervious to the damp and jumble of a soldier's knapsack, he begged her indulgence.[26] He would send letters when he could, but Marie came to realize that sometimes postcards were all she was likely to get. A postcard might be inferior to a real letter, but it was infinitely better than nothing.

By the end of 1917, stationery was a necessity of wartime life; but in Italy it was almost impossible to come by. Whereas soldiers in northern France could count on finding it in the military cooperatives, men serving in Italy, where no more than a handful of co-ops were in operation, discovered that even the most rudimentary writing paper was a rare commodity. As a result, "all units [were] demanding stationery" by January 1918, and when soldiers could lay their hands on some, they filled the precious pages with laments about the inadequacy of the stationery supply.[27] By contrast, illustrated postcards were relatively easy to procure, and many a provisional tourist was tempted to send home photos of famous sites and the lush Italian landscape. On a day late in April 1918, when snow and hail still made life a misery in the mountains, Paul purchased postcards of Vicenza, resplendent in the sunshine more consistently seen on postcards than in daily life. These postcards did not, however, make it through the censorship sieve, for postal censors vigilantly intercepted any card that would either reveal soldiers' location at the front or show local landmarks that could serve as an artillery target for the enemy. The troops, once they realized that illustrated postcards were subject to interception, began to rely on government-issued stationery, when they could find it, or on paper sent by families back home.

In Italy not only was stationery hard to find, but mail delivery was infuriatingly erratic. Families were annoyed when they went for days without a letter from the Italian front, and the men fighting there, who had become accustomed to keeping track of which letters they had received and how long it had taken for them to arrive, were outraged that it could take a week or more for a letter from France to make its way to northern Italy. Used to receiving letters three days after they were sent, they found the delays infuriating and unacceptable. Even when they were unavoidable, as was the case when two trains derailed, killing hundreds of men and destroying thousands of letters and packages destined for or originating at the Italian front, the bleakness of life without letters was overwhelming. More often than not, however, nothing more serious than the laziness of postal clerks disrupted mail delivery, or so Paul was inclined to believe. He noted in late December that letters sent home were frequently lost or greatly delayed en route, just as were letters sent to the front: "I see that you, like me, are often without news. I wonder what is causing that lots [of us] are in the same situation." He suspected that the "bunch of bastards" responsible for sorting the mail were to blame; it was easier for them "to make the letters disappear" than to sort them properly. "They are really to blame we who have only this consolation it's the only thing that can restore our morale especially when they are good letters like the one that I have in front of me where you have really expressed all your love and your suffering where I see you as I have always wanted to." The mail service was not uniformly abysmal, as Paul was willing to acknowledge. In mid-January when his battery moved into position high in the mountains, he was delighted (and astonished) to receive a package that Marie had sent only three days earlier. In the main, though, troops complained vociferously about the unreliable postal system that disturbed their well-established epistolary routines.[28]

Inadequate leave, unreliable mail delivery, and uncertain access to stationery combined to intensify a profound homesickness that seems to have been particularly acute among the ranks of French troops serving in Italy. Detailed to a foreign land where everyone spoke an unfamiliar language, they felt their distance from home most keenly in the weeks leading up to and following the new year. New Year's in France has long been an occasion when extended families either gather together or exchange letters with those who are far away. At the beginning of the twentieth century, schoolchildren learned in the earliest grades the importance of New Year's correspondence and of sending affectionate greetings to relatives who could not be physically present for the family gathering.[29] This tradition continued during the war, when the postal service, which usually processed about four million letters each day, dealt with an increase of almost a million letters daily in the last weeks of each year.[30] Troops serving in Italy were not cut off entirely from this bounteous flow, for the postal censors noted in early January: "This time of year has produced the traditional wishes, to which are added hopes for peace in 1918."[31] Paul received letters of this type from several relatives, but they cheered him very little. Homesickness combined with a sinking sense that the war would not soon be won left him despondent. In his own letter to Marie he ignored all the niceties of New Year's correspondence and sounded instead a somber tone: "On the dawn of the new year I am not going to wish you a good year first because I find this stupid and second because I know that this is not going to be a good year that you will spend far from the one who loves you good friends will be those who accelerate the end of the war and I do not see that happening this year."[32]

The package that Paul received in mid-January, welcome though it surely was, only deepened his melancholy, for it made very clear what he was missing out on. Nestled in among the warm clothing that Marie had carefully assembled was a cameo locket with photographs of herself and little "Nenette." Paul was delighted; he reported that his comrades had been quick to admire his charming wife and adorable son. Admitting that he was pleased to receive his comrades' compliments, for he was "very proud" of his family, he admitted nonetheless that he would "have preferred to be home with them." He certainly missed Marie and longed for the love, affection, and sexual solace that he would find in her arms: "How I long to come home again to taste once again those caresses that you have promised and to forget as you say the rest of the world I am keeping your letters and if you don't keep your promises I will show them to you and tell you remember you promised to make a guy really happy." But he missed the simple pleasures of family life as much as the sexual fulfillment that he longed for in restless dreams. "Oh how happy I would be how I love you both you are my hope my faith and my support in difficult times."[33]

Paternal affection, reinforced by touching tales of his son's extraordinary development and by worrisome news when he fell ill, made Paul still more homesick. By January 1918, Serge was a mischievous, chubby little imp with a mind of his own and, like most toddlers, the ability to say no. At the beginning of the year, Marie had dressed him up to show him off to neighbors at the local fair. Suitably impressed by his finery, he had looked at himself admiringly and pronounced (in words he had no doubt heard from his mother and grandmothers), "Nenette is cute." When the women attending the local fair tried to make a fuss over him, however, he would have none of it: "Everyone hugged him which made him impatient and he pushed them aside saying 'Don't.'" Marie took great pride in the fact that the once sickly, pallid infant was now "pink and plump," and she longed for Paul to come home to see how he was thriving under her care. When Serge fell ill in February, presenting as symptoms a high fever and profound lethargy that responded quickly to Marie's ministrations, the doctor (called in promptly as always) opined that perhaps the boy was a little too plump for his own good; this stoutness "made him fragile," the medical man judged. Learning from afar that their son was ill, Paul could do nothing but reassure Marie that he had complete confidence in her ability to care for their little one. Had the baby been gravely ill, Paul could have requested compassionate leave, but otherwise he could not count on being home again until mid-March at the earliest.[34]

Leave, when it came, was a most welcome relief, but afterward Paul suffered the *cafard* that invariably accompanied any return to the front lines after a week of home comforts. In his judgment the tedium and interminable nature of the war seemed worse in Italy than they would have had he been serving in France. Knowing that fighting on the western front was intense in late March and early April 1918, he had no regrets about missing the German offensive that was taxing the resilience of the Anglo-French front and placing Paris in danger: "When the newspapers tell us about the events that are unfolding in France we can't help feeling happy with a good letter giving good news of your little family at home it makes you a little more courageous to know that your family is in good health." Still, time dragged in Italy, and the tedium gave rise to dismal thoughts. An especially loving letter from Marie left him simultaneously delighted "to feel so loved [and] desired," and depressed: "After reading it and reflecting on it it makes you down in the dumps to glimpse happiness so close and not to be able to taste it damned war when will it be over." He mournfully observed, "We are martyrs of the century." Not being able to watch his son grow up aggravated the feelings of martyrdom. "It's impossible the longer it goes on the more I suffer from this separation I constantly imagine my home and the happiness that awaits me there if it were not for this damned war. What a miserable fate!"[35]

As the months wore on and Serge, having recovered from two bouts of illness that had caused his parents anxiety, approached his second birthday, he became increasingly independent-minded. Marie reported in early April that sometimes he behaved badly, which prompted Paul to conclude that he was becoming spoiled. Marie did not doubt it—a little boy recently ill and fussed over by two grandmothers, an aunt, and his mother was probably used to getting his way—but neither she nor Paul seemed overly worried. Paul, who had imagined how charming it would be to take his "little man" on country walks, holding him by the hand as they wandered the winding roads of Nanteuil, was inclined to play the indulgent father: "It's much better," he judged, "to spoil them and make them happy" when you have an opportunity to do so. The letter that Paul received only days later would, no doubt, have reinforced his desire to spoil his son. Twenty-two months old, Serge inscribed in a careful hand (guided of course by his adoring mother) a penitent and poignant message to his absent father: "Nené very cute writes to his daddy that he will be very well-behaved and that he sends big big kisses, Serge." Only a handful of Marie's letters from the spring of 1918 have survived, and those that have are badly decayed and water-damaged, suggesting how difficult it was to preserve them in alpine combat conditions. It therefore seems likely that Paul must have taken special pains to preserve this one letter, in which the affecting words of his winsome "little terror" brought home to him in this fourth year of war the pain of separation from those he loved. As he confessed a few weeks later: "I rejoice to have such a lovely baby such a cute son but when I think that I can't go and see him that I can't enjoy this domestic joy that makes me heart sick." In his most despondent moments, he wondered if his son, who in Marie's considered judgment was "so cute and so smart," would even recognize him the next time he came home on leave.[36]

Not every soldier serving in the French expeditionary force had a young son at home, growing up with only a foggy image of what his father looked like; but nearly all the soldiers remained emotionally connected to families whose living conditions, they knew, deteriorated more with every passing day. In the early months of 1918, fears abounded that families were once again facing economic catastrophe. Comparable concerns a year earlier had abated in the months immediately following the harvest of 1917. Although far from bountiful, it had at least put food on the table for the short term. The longer view was anything but promising. With agricultural production in sharp decline everywhere, grain crops (and especially wheat, for which the 1917 harvest had been less than half that of 1914) were critically deficient. Military requisitioning of cattle, which by the third year of the war had taken more than 2.5 million cows and steers off the land, had also brought about a sharp drop in milk production.[37] Soldiers far from home were neither unaware of nor indifferent to the looming food crisis. As early as January 1918, eight full months before the next harvest, French troops in Italy expressed fear that their families would soon face famine. Letters from home, reinforced by the eyewitness reports of men returning from leave, were filled with disheartening stories of high prices, widespread scarcity, and imminent rationing.[38] One postal censor noted, "A very few soldiers rejoice at seeing civilians forced to live with privation. The greatest number worry about their families."[39]

This was true of soldiers from all parts of France. Those whose families had been forced in August 1914 to flee their homes in the face of the advancing German army were the worst off. One soldier whose wife and children had been evacuated was so upset by the hardships they had to endure as refugees that he resolved to take on extra chores in his spare time. Perhaps he could "do the laundry or other things" that would earn him "a little bit of money to send to [his] wife." When he witnessed the utter destitution to which his family had descended, he was both heartsick and outraged.[40] Refugee families were not the only ones facing deprivation in early 1918. The men serving in Italy who came from the southwest of France seem to have been especially unsettled by tales of escalating hardship and impending famine. They were so upset, in fact, that military commanders ordered a targeted survey of all letters sent from and to the department of the Gironde. What, the officers wanted to know, were families at home saying about the food crisis, and how were men assigned to the Italian front responding?

That the Gironde in particular, and southwest France more generally, should have been a source of particular concern is significant, for it suggests that even regions far removed from the massive disruptions of combat at the front were suffering genuine hardship by early 1918. The unwonted affluence of rural society, so often decried, seems to have been more an illusion than a reality. The police commissioner for the Gironde, a rather crusty individual constantly appalled by any evidence that people in his jurisdiction were not suffering enough, larded his monthly reports with accounts of lavish spending and irresponsible excess. He discounted complaints, heard from late 1917 onward, about bread shortages, because those who complained the loudest were, he noted waspishly, also buying tickets to the local theaters, purchasing Christmas presents with unseemly abandon, and spending money on pastries and other little luxuries. Government officials in the Dordogne who noted that peasants could (and did) buy every piece of jewelry available at a county fair in March 1918 were similarly struck by the unprecedented prosperity of rural society.[41]

What would the officials have thought of Jean Pireaud's gleaming gold pen or Rosa Pireaud's silk scarf, purchased in Italy by a grateful son eager to compensate for all the packages his parents had sent over the years—or of the silk dresses worn by young peasant women whose men were serving in Italy? In April 1918 when Paul purchased his father's pen, he also secured a length of pale blue silk for a comrade who intended to send it to his sister. Paul wondered whether Marie would like something similar. It was, he assured her, a lovely color and surprisingly inexpensive. However much she must have appreciated his generous offer, Marie thought that it would be better if he could send something a little less luxurious; a length of wool for a dress in some dark color might be better, all things considered. After all, she wrote, "We are on the brink of shortages all around." It was no doubt true, as the police commissioner noted in February 1918, that the war had lined the pockets of "businessmen, peasants, and workers." Access to cash had, however, secured a very strange affluence. Those who could buy jewelry could not always buy bread; those who could send their menfolk on shopping expeditions in Italy could not purchase such basic commodities as salt or sugar; and those who could send to Paris for a dress (as Marie did in the summer of 1918) could rarely find kerosene or matches.[42]

Of all the shortages that plagued civilians in 1918, none was more alarming than the scarcity of bread. A regulation introduced in November 1917 but not immediately implemented, to restrict bread consumption for every adult to three hundred grams per day, met with enthusiasm in most cities, but with outrage in rural France. Unlike city dwellers who hoped that rationing would bring about a more equitable distribution of the existing grain supplies, peasant families whose diets were heavily based on bread feared not having the strength to work on such a meager diet. The lament was the same everywhere: "Three hundred grams of bread per day might suffice for people in the cities with sedentary occupations but not for peasants or manual laborers." In Italy French husbands and sons, in receipt of stories from home about government indifference to the lot of peasant laborers, responded angrily to the threat of bread rationing. One young man, representative of many, wrote to his parents in the Gironde: "I have just learned that you are now restricted to 300 grams of bread each day, regardless of the work you do or your age. Do you believe that life can go on like this? Really, no one can get by on such a ration! No matter what his age. That's just enough for a little meal. Really, if this continues, it's not going to encourage farmers very much. Most of them will be happy just to grow what they need for themselves, and I don't blame them."[43]

Conditions in the Dordogne were no better. By January 1918 the question of bread was uppermost in the minds of rural and urban populations alike. Some regions, including most of the communities near Nanteuil, had weathered the earlier food crisis without serious inconvenience, but the specter of rationing alarmed one and all: "In the villages the peasantry is beginning to realize that bread might come to be, if not entirely lacking, then at least difficult to find." Many country people, it seems, had not really believed that the restrictions discussed since the previous November would go into effect, and when local millers and bakers began to enforce the government regulations, residents became angry and, in some cases, violent. Clearly, the stoic patience of the rural population (which the prefect and his local deputies had noted appreciatively throughout the preceding years) had worn thin. Contempt for corrupt politicians, on trial in Paris for financial misconduct and consorting with the enemy, complaints issued by men at the different fronts, and concerns about the ever-increasing cost of living bred malaise in the ranks of the once-uncomplaining peasantry. One village mayor wrote, "The rural population has only one goal: to see the end of the war. It endures patiently but not without complaint the current economic difficulties and especially the manpower shortages that are the root cause of the food shortages; of all the restrictions [in place] the one that concerns them most is the fear that there will not be enough bread."[44]

These concerns, familiar to the people of Nanteuil-de-Bourzac and their neighbors, only intensified in the months immediately preceding the harvest. By May 1918 economic questions, and the issue of bread restrictions more than any other, sparked concern in the rural communities served by the subprefecture of Ribérac. Everywhere in the department peasants feared that three hundred grams of bread per day would not suffice, now that they were working fourteen- or fifteen-hour days. A ration adequate for a city bureaucrat, they were quick to observe, was far from sufficient for a farm laborer putting in fourteen-hour days; and the reduced ration of two hundred grams per day for everyone older than sixty was perhaps enough for a pensioner, but it was completely inadequate for an older man toiling in the absence of his adult sons to maintain a family farm.[45] Paul knew and worried about these distresses. He fretted that Marie would not have enough to get by from day to day, especially as the season of heavy work in the fields approached, and that she would fall ill from overwork and an inadequate diet. Hoping that the rationing would last only until the next harvest, he advised her to do as little as possible in the meantime: "If only you could just live without having to do very much work and not get sick that's all that I ask."[46]

Grain shortages—actual and anticipated—were the most

pressing problem facing the Dordogne in early 1918. Other basic commodities were also in short supply. Sugar and tobacco had been hard to obtain for months, and kerosene was nowhere to be found. In communities like Nanteuil-de-Bourzac, which did not join the electric power grid until the late 1930s, kerosene shortages meant that farmers had to tend their cattle in the dark. Given that candles were prohibitively expensive and almost impossible to find, kerosene lamps were the only means of lighting the barns and stables. As the days grew longer, the lack of kerosene became less of a problem, but inequities in supply were galling even so. Hard-working farmers who noticed elegant women driving through the countryside in fancy cars—and these ladies in the company of young men who, everyone agreed, should have been in uniform—wondered how it was that gasoline was available for the privileged, when basic fuels were lacking for everyone else. And shortages of coal provoked bitter complaints from blacksmiths, rural artisans, and farmers who could not keep essential farm equipment in good repair.[47]

In contrast to the major cities of France, these pretty villages displayed no socialist agitation to alarm government officials; nor did the authorities notice many signs of defeatism. Even so, peasant women whose husbands and sons were now assigned to a foreign country were disconsolate.[48] They were not arming themselves with pitchforks to stage a political insurrection or demanding that peace be negotiated immediately, but they were weary and unhappy. Meanwhile, the misery of families at home wore on men at the front, making them even more despondent and more eager to see an end to the war. As Paul observed, he was beginning to "find that time is damned long."[49]

As long as winter lasted, troops in northern Italy could do nothing to contribute in any direct way to bringing the war to a close. Mountain passes remained perilous; and as intemperate weather lingered well beyond the official start of spring—a meter of snow fell in the Italian Alps during the last week of April 1918—renewal of large-scale fighting had to be delayed into mid-June. Until then the Italian front remained a quiet sector. Soldiers in pitched battle elsewhere dreamed of such places, for military service here was far from onerous. A few hair-raising car rides at what seemed like breakneck speed down mountain roads ill suited for such adventures posed more danger, Paul discovered, than the enemy did during the winter and early spring of 1918. Days went by when he had little to do but answer the battery's telephone, take photographs of the breathtaking scenery, and dream of vacationing in Italy with Marie once the war was over. Who could complain about sleeping late, dining lavishly at noon, and then idling away the afternoon hours until dinner? One especially memorable meal included soup, asparagus vinaigrette, omelet, *steak frites*, salad, cheese, and coffee. As Paul quipped, everyone in the battery ate "like fat cats" and worked "like priests." Even when snow fell and the thermometer plunged below freezing, the mountains of northern Italy were, he conceded, markedly more comfortable than the mudflats of the Somme had been a year earlier.[50]

As everyone knew, the arrival of spring brought with it the certainty that combat would resume. Many anticipated that this battle, slated for late May or early June, would prove decisive, for few French soldiers serving in Italy held their new enemy in high esteem. Indeed, they often spoke with an almost affectionate disparagement of their opponents' fighting capacity. In the quiet winter months, Paul had taken comfort in the idea that the men across the mountain valleys, to whom he invariably referred indiscriminately as the Austrians (whether they were Austrian, German, or from one of the many ethnic minorities making up the Austro-Hungarian Empire), were "not the same kind of soldiers as the Boches." They rarely returned fire and did little to make life difficult for the newly arrived French forces. But even if in Paul's judgment this particular enemy was "not very wicked," seasoned soldiers knew a major offensive in the coming months could not be laughed off. The 112th found itself north of Asiago, with Italian batteries on either side of it. For men who continued to worry more about the fighting spirit of their allies than of the enemy, this situation was far from ideal. Believing that the Italians would retreat at the first sign of Austrian bombardment, the French felt apprehensive that they would be left unprotected, an easy prey for the enemy. Many feared they would be either killed or taken prisoner.[51]

Paul certainly seemed to harbor such concerns, but he grew more and more reluctant to speak openly about the impending battle. In late May he predicted, "We will see all the Austrian shells that are sent our way because we now command a view of all the valley what a din there will be in a few days." Three weeks later, though, he spoke only obliquely of the danger that they would soon confront. He confessed to a profound spiritual malaise but remained unwilling to divulge its cause. Nothing, he avowed, interested him any more, and were it not for Marie's loving letters, he would be at his wits' end: "I have only your letters your good words to support me I beg of you be good gentle loving that is all I have to restore my courage I have got to such a point." With no hope for leave before September or October, he had only fond memories of "familial joy" to sustain him. Unlike many of his comrades, who wrote openly about the anticipated Austrian attack and scathingly about their allies' resolve, he kept his counsel. More attentive now than in previous years to the need for circumspection, Paul was reluctant to indulge in "defeatist talk." Reminding Marie, "We are no longer in 1914," he urged her, "Be careful about what you say at home because many words repeated by an ill-intentioned neighbor can be interpreted as defeatist talk and earn you a year in prison and a 1,000-franc fine and I assure you it doesn't take much for that to happen."[52]

Unaware of Paul's specific anxieties, Marie found his uncharacteristically laconic letters and his elusiveness unnerving. And when she read on 16 June 1918 that on the previous day the Austrians had unleashed a massive offensive in the Italian Alps, she knew that her apprehension had been warranted. The Battle of the Piave was marked by intense fighting and the extensive use of poison gas. French soldiers noted after the fact, with considerable relief, that their gas masks, having been subjected to continuous redesign for more than two years, were now up to the task. Forced to wear their headgear for hours on end, as the poison-gas shells exploded around them, the men remained fully protected from the effects of chemical attack. Nothing, however, could adequately protect them from the deafening roar of heavy guns firing without letup, or from the danger that was at last close and unavoidable, as Paul conceded. As the Austrian shells rained down on his battery, he feared for his life more than once. "It was worse," he claimed, "than Verdun . . . two days and two nights without sleep in a bombardment such as I have never seen before." Unlike Verdun, though, this offensive was of short duration. Within a day or two, the worst had passed and Paul could reassure his anxious wife, "Everything is all right now our situation has been reestablished and we are in perfect safety all danger has been removed." He made no apologies for having said nothing in advance of the attack, for he believed that Marie, by now accustomed to the nuances of daily correspondence, could read between the lines: "You should at least understand what they were meant to say."[53]

Ultimately, the French fears about their allies' resolve in

the face of a renewed onslaught proved unfounded. The Austrians could not break through the French line, and most of the Italians stood firm—more or less. Italian regiments to the left of the French held fast, but those on the right scattered (to the undisguised disgust of their Gallic comrades) without firing a shot. Only when confronted by French troops threatening swift punishment did the fugitive Italians reconsider and return to hold their position. Such experiences soured relations between the allies even more and made the French especially resentful of later Italian claims that they had won the battle single-handedly. When the Italian high command cited their troops' accomplishments in June 1918 as evidence that Caporetto had at last been avenged, their allies were outraged that no mention was made of the French contribution to the victory. Paul was not the only Frenchman angered by this slight, and many of his compatriots would have been quick to agree with his judgment uttered in the thick of battle: "The French greatly deserve the title of the finest soldiers in the world no one can do anything to touch them."[54]

The battle continued for several days more, but any hopes the Austrians had entertained of a decisive victory were soon frustrated. A week after the offensive began, Paul observed, "It's only at night that the 'music' picks up we never know if we should get up and get ready for something big but in the morning everything is calm again." At the very end of the month, Paul warned Marie that he might still be taken prisoner by the Austrians, but other signs suggested that the offensive had failed. Despite the heavy bombardment, French and Italian forces suffered few casualties, while the enemy ranks dissolved under the Entente's counterbarrage. As the French and Italians continued to put pressure on the opposite lines, the Allies' heavy guns creating "a veritable hell" of noise and mayhem, the "Austros" began to "surrender like rabbits." Word had it that the

Italians had taken twenty-four thousand prisoners on 24 June alone, and another twelve hundred five days later. Results of this sort, and the rumor that Austria was facing revolution at home, gave Paul great hope that the end of the war was at last in sight. Yet he did not expect to go home on leave until late October at the earliest.[55]

Under fire a man has no choice but to contemplate death; at all other times, it seems, his thoughts turn instead to sex. Or so Paul's reactions would suggest. When the battery rested, as it did for most of July and August 1918, he had ample opportunity to lose himself in thoughts of home and the joys that awaited him there. As active duty went, staying at a rest camp on the plains north of Venice was pleasant enough. Blissfully exempt now from any immediate danger, Paul appreciated the "superb, magnificent" countryside in a chain of leisurely days spent reading the newspaper, drinking coffee with amiable comrades, and picking wild strawberries. At night he slept in a real bed. He could almost have imagined himself at home, had it not been for sweet dreams whose illusoriness revealed when he woke how far from home—and the passionate embrace of a loving wife—he really was. At the end of July he wrote, "I have just woken up what beautiful dreams I had how happy I would be to be able to make them come true in a few days (but not before a month) I can't tell you how happy you will be I propose to make up to you all the time we have lost how I long for those days to arrive I think of nothing but that now and live only for that. We really must be among the most unfortunate to live under this star where we cannot love each other at our ease." At the same time that such dreams could bring temporary delight, they also gave rise to bitter frustration. "How often I dream of the happiness that I long for with you I see everything through rose-tinted glasses we do the most beautiful

the best things I become happy, more than happy in such moments but when I wake up there is nothing but disappointment.
Oh poor Marquise when will that longed-for leave come because we have to make do with that while waiting for something better but I promise myself that I will make you happy
give you a taste of paradise."[56]

Frustrated though he was that he had to confide his most intimate thoughts to paper, Paul did not hesitate to share with
Marie either his erotic reveries or his most deep-seated fears.
After the travails of battle and the physical exhaustion that was
the inevitable result of frontline service, he worried that he
would be unable to turn his dreams into reality. In his capacity
as the battery's messenger, he had logged many a kilometer on
his bicycle, shuttling back and forth as often as four times a day
down the steep and perilous mountain road that connected the
battery to the command post. Less terrifying than his occasional car trip along ice-clad roads, the bicycle rides nevertheless left him exhausted at the end of the day. When the battery
moved into the rest camp, his most onerous responsibilities
disappeared, but "rest" was, in every soldier's experience, a relative term. Infantrymen complained long and loud about pointless drills that filled their days of rest; Paul regretted that he
had to serve his officers at table. He had done so since at least
1916, and it had always rankled. He was not by nature subser-
vient, and his egalitarian instincts made him an uneasy (but by
no means inept) lackey. By mid-July 1918 he had had enough
and did not hesitate to say so. He wanted a bona fide rest, in
large part because he wanted to be in fine fettle when he finally
returned to Marie's bed. He had observed how despondent
some of his comrades appeared on returning from leave; however ardent their desire, their performance had, they regretted,
often been wanting. "The majority of soldiers come back as
worn out as an old horse unable to fulfill their duties." If such a

sorry outcome awaited Paul and Marie, he joked that they could make do by buying "a wooden one"—the city of Saint-Etienne seemed to specialize in the sale of such things—but he sincerely hoped that such an unsatisfying solution would not be necessary. Suspecting that from such silly talk Marie would think he had "gone mad," he sought to assure her that he was in fact quite sane: "I'm simply full of desire and ardor for my beloved Marquise while watching the time approach when I will be able to prove it to her on that day you will see that I'm not crazy and you will pay me back in kind."[57]

His commanding officers, in whom he confided, sympathized with his concerns and recognized that he deserved some real rest. They agreed to assign someone else to wait on them, if Paul—whose quick mastery of Italian astonished his superiors and made him an ideal candidate for forays into the nearby towns—would continue to take responsibility for purchasing provisions: "It is my mission to make sure that they don't go without their chickens, ducks, rabbits, butter, cheese, champagne, and liqueurs." Such bounty rarely made its way into the mess plates of ordinary soldiers. Only on Bastille Day, when champagne flowed like water and troops enjoyed a day of entertainment and movies, did they too live like princes. This, Paul thought, was all pleasant enough, but leave would have been better, and peace best of all: "None of this is as good as an end to the war oh how fed up with it all I am . . . If only the leave schedule were functioning properly."[58] Leave would allow him to make love to his wife, to escort his "little man" on leisurely walks through the country lanes of Nanteuil, and to help Marie with the harvest.

In the summer of 1918 Paul longed also to do what he could to protect his wife and son from the terrifying virus that was then ravaging the Continent.[59] The "Spanish flu" pandemic of 1918–19, which would ultimately kill more people than the

war itself, added a new layer of anxiety for all who were separated by military service from the families they loved. An enemy against which all known defenses proved inadequate, the
flu, which endangered not only men serving at the front but
their wives, children, parents, and grandparents at home, made
its appearance in Europe in the last weeks of May. Simulta-
neous outbreaks on the western front and in northern Italy
temporarily disabled countless regiments. In the 112th Heavy
Artillery Regiment more than ninety men had to be evacuated
from one battery alone. Paul took sick at the battery's command post, and without stationery or the energy to write, he
was unable to send Marie even a brief note for three days.
When his strength returned sufficiently on the third or fourth
day, he wrote home (on the back of a letter that Marie had
written a few days earlier) to describe his illness. The symptoms seemed similar to malaria: a very high fever (40 degrees
Celsius, or 104 Fahrenheit), aches, shivers, and complete loss
of appetite. He and the other men at the command post who
were laid low had felt absolutely awful for three days and had
then recovered completely. At the time, observers blamed the
unseasonably warm weather that was making life so uncomfortable for men still outfitted in winter uniforms.[60] In retrospect,
however, it seems more likely that the men of the 112th Heavy
Artillery Regiment who fell ill in late May were victims of the
first wave of influenza that arrived in Europe with the disembar-
kation of American troops.

The virus that circulated in spring 1918 was much less lethal
than the mutant strain that would kill so many soldiers and
millions of civilians around the world in fall 1918 and the first
months of 1919. In southwest France the epidemic was most
virulent in October, when the subprefect of Ribérac noted that
every community in his region was suffering its effects. Although young adults in the prime of life often fell victim to it—

Marie noted that a military interpreter and an officer had been buried in a single ceremony in a nearby town—the very young and the old were by no means exempt. In Saint-Martial-Viveyrol, only a few kilometers from Nanteuil, Paul's grandfather succumbed at the end of October, and a third of the community's school-age children fell ill. Since one child in Saint-Martial was dying from the illness, Marie felt more than justified in her refusal to attend the grandfather's funeral. With "the plague everywhere in the countryside, but especially in Verteillac and Saint-Martial," she hesitated to venture out of doors, lest she or Serge be struck by it, too.[61]

Although the epidemic would reach its height in October, it was already under way in August. While awaiting his turn for leave, Paul heard from men returning to Italy of "the ravages the flu [was] causing in France," and he was aware from experience what the symptoms were. Having already suffered something resembling the flu in May 1918, he fell more seriously ill in mid-August. For more than a week he battled a high fever and headache, an upset stomach, sore throat, and a general lethargy that, he avowed, made his legs "feel like rags." Only on 24 August could he report that he was "completely out of danger." Recognizing that this disease was not confined to northern Italy—indeed, soldiers inadvertently served as vectors of illness, by taking the virus with them when they left the front or returned to the lines after a week at home—he worried that Marie and Serge had also fallen ill. His premonition was well founded: both mother and child had indeed caught the flu. They had taken refuge with Marie's sister, Rosa, who did what she could to nurse them back to health.[62] Hard work and an inadequate diet might have weakened the resistance of women and children in rural France, but neither fatigue nor food shortages explained the virulence of this epidemic, for well-fed American soldiers in peak physical condition fell victim to it in training camps in Kansas, too. Still, for those who had endured a summer of backbreaking labor, a spring of deprivation, and four years of unrelieved anxiety, the flu came as a cruel blow.

In August 1918 French men in uniform marked the fourth anniversary of mobilization. The anxiety Paul felt about his family's well-being, combined with the cumulative effects of four years of war, aggravated his yearning for leave. Until the day arrived "when we will no longer need to confide our most intimate thoughts in writing," Paul wrote, only leave would allow him "to forget in the arms of the wife I love this horrible nightmare." By the end of August, this enticing fantasy seemed tantalizingly close to realization. If rumors that leaves would be suspended on or around 26 August proved groundless, he expected to be home sometime in early September. In anticipation of his return, Marie made plans to have Serge, who usually shared her bed and always shared her room, sleep at his Pireaud grandparents' at Moulin du Pont. This arrangement had worked well on previous leaves. Earlier in the year, Paul had complimented her on her foresight: "You are right to take my big Nenette to sleep with his grandpa that way when I have the good fortune to come home on leave we will be able as you say to practice our gentle caresses and *other things that are even better without disturbing him.*" A similar arrangement in September 1918 would, he thought, be ideal. All would be well, if only the annoying aunts would be good enough to stay away.[63]

Paul had heard from his Aunt Irène in Angoulême that she hoped to visit Nanteuil for her summer vacation. Ordinarily, she preferred to spend her holidays in Paris, but a city under intermittent bombardment from March through the end of August was no longer an attractive tourist destination. In the circumstances of 1918, a week in the country acquired a novel charm. That she would be in Nanteuil during Paul's leave was perhaps less than ideal; but Paul felt confident that as long as she stayed with his parents she would interfere little with the young couple's intimate agenda. The threatened arrival of "Tante Rose" was, however, a different story entirely, for the untimely appearance of that aunt could certainly frustrate a couple eager to abandon themselves to "gentle caresses and *other things that are even better.*" When Marie announced that Tante Rose would pay her monthly visit at the beginning of September, coinciding precisely with Paul's arrival, he was at first unconcerned: "As for the possibility of meeting Tante Rose too bad we will have enough time this time around to annoy her and if need be to get rid of her altogether." As his leave drew closer, however, he became noticeably less accepting: "As for Tante Rose she will arrive at the same time I do thanks for the surprise especially in the first days please give her my compliments."[64]

Tante Rose had first emerged as a topic of conversation in the summer of 1916; before that Marie spoke only of being unwell or unable to travel for a few days. Menstruation, a topic considered so taboo at the beginning of the century that even mothers and daughters rarely spoke of it, was certainly not a fit topic for correspondence that could be intercepted by censors and thus read by total strangers.[65] To allude even euphemistically to the subject was to fly in the face of propriety and long-established convention. The circumstances of war, the reality of long-term separation, and the need to plan for precious time together made such niceties increasingly irrelevant, however. The delightful promise of leave and the unnerving possibility of a second pregnancy prompted Paul and Marie to write regularly about Tante Rose, calculating when she would next make an appearance or what her tardiness might signify.

Paul and Marie calculated the optimal times of the month for him to return home; for example, in November 1916 Marie, whose inability to breast-feed had caused her periods to resume shortly after Serge's birth, anticipated that it would be best if Paul could take some leave in mid-January, because Tante Rose showed up around the third or fourth of each month and stayed for four or five days. Because the French army did not go out of its way to accommodate the menstrual cycles of soldiers' wives, it was never entirely certain that careful planning would make much of a difference. Sometimes Tante Rose was good enough not to interrupt a leave at all: in July 1917, for example, Paul was delighted "to learn that Tante Rose has just left she is very kind . . . Now I don't have anything else to do but get ready to go home on leave." In early September 1918, however, she "screwed everything up" for at least a few days. Thinking back on the inconvenience of it all, Paul explicitly hoped that "Tante Rose [wouldn't] come to visit" on his next leave, and even threatened idly that if she did he would "just have to just kick her out for a little while." He reassured Marie that he was only joking. That he would have even considered the possibility of sexual relations during his wife's period, however, suggests that the exigencies of war were slowly undermining long-established cultural practice. According to local lore, sexual intercourse during menstruation would be punished by the birth of a red-headed infant: parents' wanton ways would be thus exposed in the unseemly brilliance of their child's hair.[66]

Shortly after Paul returned to Italy in late September, it became evident to both civilian observers and soldiers on the ground that the war would at last soon be over. Rumors to this effect emerged in Paul and Marie's correspondence in early October, when they both made mention of it for the first time.[67] After four years of grueling combat, enforced separation, and great suffering, it was difficult to grasp the possibility of peace. Indeed, it was perhaps premature to put much store in dreams of peace, appealing though they were, for some hard fighting still awaited those who had survived up to this point. The 112th participated in late October in the Battle of Vittorio Veneto, the final Allied offensive of the Italian war that would push the Austrians into full retreat. They were compelled to cede territory so quickly that the heavy artillery of the French army could not keep pace with its advancing infantry. Although casualties in the French and Italian ranks were sobering—Paul and others were not so hardened by war as to be unmoved by the horrendous sight of fellow soldiers killed by enemy artillery—the numbers paled by comparison with the Austrian losses. Thousands died; hundreds of thousands were taken prisoner.[68] At Vittorio Veneto, the Italians took revenge for the humiliation of Caporetto and redeemed their reputation. Their allies contributed to the cause as well. On 30 October Paul noted with some pride that the French had taken more than thirty-two thousand prisoners (including more than eight hundred officers) and had seized 151 cannon; to critics in the French press who had disparaged the French forces in Italy as layabouts and shirkers, he could rejoin, "We aren't *embusqués* any longer."[69] After the defeat of the Austrians at Vittorio Veneto it was clear that the Italian war would soon be over. Some French feared, Marie among them, that now that this enemy had been beaten, the French expeditionary force would be redeployed to the western front, where Entente troops were at last pushing the Germans out of France and, it was to be hoped, toward full surrender. Most soldiers, however, preferred to repress such thoughts and to dream instead of home and peace—a definitive end to war.

For Paul and Marie, a marital crisis that brought to the surface deep-seated but often suppressed anxieties about fidelity and the permanence of affection marred these last months of war. Only days after Paul left Lescure, Marie described the torment caused by a rash that extended from head to toe and inflamed her face, neck, and ears. The misery she endured led her father to send for the doctor. The patient and her parents alike were unnerved by her affliction. Marie feared that she would be permanently disfigured by the spots and the scars that would remain. She was not by nature unduly vain, but like most young women in love she was by no means immune to the fear that her husband might at some point no longer find her attractive. Paul quickly set her mind to rest on this point: "Naughty girl, why did you tell me that if I were near you I would love you less you know very well how much I love my Marquise she could have spots everywhere and for the rest of her life I would love you as much If it were me would you love me any less certainly not then why do you suppose that others are less capable of loving than you are." When the worst of the illness had passed, she reassured Paul (and herself) that although she had "not become beautiful" in the last few weeks, "at least," she had "not become completely ugly."[70]

Losing her looks had been awful to contemplate, but ultimately losing her hair turned out to be a much more real possibility. Like many women of her generation, Marie took pride in her long hair, which in her case was dark and thick. Sensuous though luxuriant tresses were, they were by no means easy to keep clean in homes that lacked running water, built-in showers, and other modern amenities. The doctor made it clear, however, that Marie would have to wash her hair regularly; otherwise, he warned, she would risk losing it completely. When it became evident how difficult it would be to keep her hair and scalp clean, Marie, on the verge of tears, conceded to having her hair cut. In the 1920s short hair would become the sign of avant-garde female fashion: trendy young women—dubbed garçonnes for their boyish looks—shocked their parents by sporting bobbed cuts that fairly shrieked liberation and sexual ambiguity. Marie, however, was no flapper avant la lettre. In a state of genuine distress, she watched her long locks fall under the shears.[71]

Marie's symptoms prompted deeper fears, more unsettling than any temporary disfigurement. They suggested—to Marie herself, her parents, and any nosy neighbor who might learn of her discomfort—that she had "caught something wicked." Both a full rash with itchy spots and hair loss were symptoms consistent with secondary-stage syphilis. Whether the doctor told her as much or whether the signs of untreated syphilis, which was extremely common in prewar and wartime France, were so well known as to render expert diagnosis unnecessary remains unclear. What is certainly clear is that Marie at first feared the worst. Convinced that her ailment was contagious and that she could only have caught it from Paul, she asked if he too had spots. His response that he "had nothing at all not even a little one" was perhaps reassuring, but suspicions lingered on both sides. Although Paul insisted that whatever ailed Marie was "a sickness that anyone could have," he wondered why the doctor had refused—apparently—to proffer a clear diagnosis. Was he trying to keep something from Marie? Or were the two of them conspiring to keep something from Paul that he had a right to know? Not knowing what to make of all this secrecy, and convinced that the doctor was willfully keeping him in the dark, Paul resolved to write him directly, demanding a clear and honest assessment of Marie's illness: What was it, how would it be treated, and how long would it be before a full recovery could be expected? This step infuriated both Marie and the doctor, for Paul's intemperate letter, which "made all sorts of allusions," simultaneously called into question the doctor's professional integrity and Marie's fidelity. "My little Paul," she lamented when she learned of his letter, "why did you write that why did you think such wicked things?"[72]

The truth of the matter, of course, was that Paul thought

"such wicked things" precisely because Marie had been unusually evasive in her early letters. She had suggested that it was the doctor who refused a clear diagnosis, whereas in fact it was she who refused to pass along his apparently reassuring evaluation until she had received independent verification from Paul that he had no similar symptoms. Even when she became convinced that she had an infection of entirely innocent origin, because her treatment based on the doctor's diagnosis of eczema proceeded successfully, she was absolutely determined to keep her affliction hidden from her neighbors. Forgoing even her daily walk to the village mailbox, she chose to stay indoors until no traces of the suspicious spots remained; when forced to go outside, she hid her new hairdo under a head-scarf; and she swore her parents and Paul to complete secrecy. Whatever reassurances Paul and her doctor might have offered, she feared that gossipy women would quickly jump to more scandalous conclusions. "You know," she confided, "how people are with their tongues some will say that it is this others that it is that I want none of it." Some would "say that it is a present that you have given me." Even the discretion of her closest relatives could not be entirely counted upon: "To tell your mother or my sister you might as well take out a drum" and proclaim her misery to one and all.[73]

Marie knew that village women liked nothing better than to pass along bits of prurient gossip about misbehaving neighbors. If some, saying that he had surely given her a "present," would have blamed Paul for Marie's malady, others might have called into question her own virtue. There was, as she well knew, enough evidence of sexual misconduct in the towns and villages nearby to fuel such rumors. She herself had lamented the licentious ways of women consorting with the soldiers of Ribérac. And she was as scandalized as any of her neighbors to hear that the bereaved fiancée of Léon Videau was, a year after his death, seen riding a bicycle with his brother "every day that he was home on leave as if he were her husband." Women like Paul's cousin who paraded around in décolleté mourning dresses were no better. When loyalty to men at the front was both a moral obligation and a patriotic responsibility, failure to mourn sincerely the death of one's fiancé or husband was deplorable and dishonorable. Women who took steps to remarry before receiving official confirmation of their husband's death at the front were judged to be even more despicable. It seemed astonishing to Paul and Marie alike that such women could persuade a mayor to issue a new marriage license under such circumstances. Most shocking of all, though, was the conduct of a local woman whose three-year-long affair was jeopardized by the imminent return of her betrayed husband. Terrified that her husband, who had been conveniently out of the way in a prisoner-of-war camp until the summer of 1918, would surprise them in a compromising situation, the adulteress officially threatened to kill her lover if he continued to seek her out. To the surprise of no one, her resolve quickly weakened, and she and her lover were soon seen in a secluded spot, up to no good.[74] Such racy tales suggested that the traditional mores of rural society were by 1918 well and truly under assault.

Spreading news of this sort did more than fill a daily letter with juicy gossip. It helped reaffirm rules of moral conduct in village society threatened by the social upheavals and uncertainties of war. Gossip articulated what was and was not acceptable behavior by identifying and castigating those who transgressed the established norms of social decency. Deeply immersed in this village culture, Marie knew that her neighbors would be as quick to criticize her, if they had any reason to believe she had acted inappropriately, as she had been to criticize others. In particular, it was well understood that parents—and mothers, in particular—of men at the front would certainly tell

their son of any misbehavior on their daughter-in-law's part.[75] If
Rosa Pireaud had failed to alert her son to evidence of Marie's
putative misconduct, it is likely that Charlotte, whose affection
for Marie was lukewarm at best and whose newborn son stood
to inherit some of the Pireauds' land, would have done so. Anything that cast doubt on Marie's fidelity would only advance
Charlotte's interests. Marie would not allow such an outcome if
she could help it. Accustomed to sharing with Paul all her most
intimate secrets, she could not permit malicious neighbors or
ill-disposed in-laws to invent stories that would impugn either
her own integrity or her husband's.

   If fear of denunciation kept some women faithful, and genuine loyalty to and love for their men in uniform kept many others true, husbands and wives alike harbored a corrosive *fear* of
infidelity. Knowing that some women misbehaved, could a soldier be blamed for worrying that his own wife might be one of
them? Knowing that some underemployed soldiers far from the
firing line succumbed to the superficial charms of easy women,
could a wife set aside all fears that her husband might also be
tempted? By the last year of the war, these concerns plagued
even Paul and Marie. For years they had taken comfort in the
belief that theirs was a marriage unlike many others. Whereas
marriages that had been built on economic calculation alone
were, in Paul's judgment, bound to fall apart under the stress of
separation, theirs was a union grounded in the freely given
consent of both partners, rooted in a true and abiding love, and
sustained by passion, genuine compatibility, and a deep love of
their infant son. It surely could withstand the buffeting of separation, loneliness, and the occasional marital misunderstanding.
By the summer of 1918, however, Paul's confidence—eroded
more by cumulative recognition of the moral mayhem wrought
by the war than by any evidence of wrongdoing on Marie's
part—began to waver. Convinced that "society [was] heading

with sure and swift steps toward vice and debauchery," he worried whenever he went for more than a day or two without word from Marie that he had been eclipsed in her affections.[76]

An inefficient postal service was a fact of life for soldiers serving in northern Italy, but it was one to which they were never fully resigned. Complaints about the irregular delivery of mail, commonplace in the winter of 1917–18, continued into the following summer and early fall. The flu epidemic was no doubt often to blame for interruptions in the mail service, for neither letter writers nor mail sorters stricken with the virus would have been able to keep up with correspondence at the regular rhythm that soldiers found so reassuring. Paul thus found the absence of letters from home particularly unsettling in August, when he knew that epidemic illness was stalking the land and feared that seductive Americans were not far behind. At the beginning of the month, having gone three days without word from Marie, he despaired that he was "condemned to receive no more letters" from her. He wanted to believe that the fault lay not with his wife, whom he knew to be fully occupied in the fields, but with "those bastards who continue to neglect their duty" by failing to process the mail in a timely manner. Only the subsequent delivery of a cluster of letters, the delayed arrival of which confirmed his worst suspicions about the postal service, calmed his nerves—for the time being.[77] At the end of the month he went once more for several days with no word from home. He alternately fretted that Marie had fallen ill (as was indeed the case) and feared that she had abandoned him. Couching his anxieties in darkly humorous speculations, he prayed that his beloved Marquise had "not gone off with an American"; or if she had, that at least she would return by early September when he expected to be home on leave. He conceded that running off with an American would be preferable to running off with an Englishman, but it was the Americans he really worried about: flush with money, they had, he feared—and Marie concurred—a winning way with French-women.[78]

Many French troops expressed similar anxieties, especially in the months between the arrival of American soldiers on French soil and their full deployment at the front. Once the doughboys had shown that they too could fight, the French allies with whom they stood shoulder to shoulder on the western front tended to look upon them with a more accepting eye.[79] But French troops who served in Italy had no direct knowledge of the Americans as soldiers and thus continued to harbor suspicions and mutter misgivings. Inclined to think of themselves as filling a role very similar to that assumed by American troops on the western front, the French in Italy had to worry about the warm reception that awaited young Yankees recently arrived in France. If Italian girls could smile seductively at battle-weary French soldiers, while throwing flowers in their path, was it unreasonable to believe that French girls would greet Americans with similar enthusiasm? However faithful one's wife or girlfriend, how long could she resist the allure of these American interlopers?

Some French women, of course, did not resist at all. But it was not very likely that Marie would have had much contact with, let alone have been led astray by, any tall, handsome, affluent American soldiers. Even in villages close to the major American troop depots of Nantes and Saint-Nazaire, "the daily occupations of rural girls did not lead them to mix with the 'Sammies.' Contacts between them were exceptional, but for the few villages and farms immediately adjacent to the base camps."[80] Whatever the situation was in and around Nantes, Marie might have heard secondhand of people who had come in contact with Americans, for there certainly were doughboys in the Dordogne by August 1918: a troop garrison was established in Périgueux, a convalescent hospital built in Ménestérol, and an infantry division quartered in villages and towns along the Isle valley, stretching westward from Périgueux through the heart of the department. While it is unlikely that many of these men would have made their way as far afield as Nanteuil-de-Bourzac, it is possible that some American soldiers ventured into the gentle rolling countryside of northwest Dordogne, for inns in nearby towns had contracts with the American forces to provide accommodation for men on leave.[81]

If Paul could suggest, even in jest, that Marie might have been led astray by a seductive Sammy, she, in turn, could beseech him not to be seduced by some irresistible *Italienne*. Although considerably more attention was given at the time and thereafter—in popular song, literature, and judicial proceedings—to female infidelity, wives and girlfriends were by no means immune to the fear that their husbands or fiancés might succumb to the charms of another woman. Often expressed in gentle banter that served more to remind a distant husband that he was still loved than to upbraid him for imagined offenses, women's apprehensions were nonetheless real.[82] And Marie was as tormented by such demons as many another young wife. There were, as she well knew from stories Paul recounted, men in his battery who found some of the Italian girls catastrophically seductive. That many of the "professional girls" in Italy were infected with venereal disease was much lamented by those French soldiers who had availed themselves of the girls' services. The brothels were, the troops complained, as "rotten as a dung heap."[83] One of Paul's comrades learned the hard way. Having caught a venereal infection, he had been forced to spend his leave more than a hundred kilometers from his wife, "for fear of infecting her"; having been unable to catch even a glimpse of his family, he had, upon his despondent return to the front, been immediately dispatched to the local hospital.[84] Paul recounted this morality tale to reassure Marie that he had no intention of suffering a similar fate and that her misgivings—more acute when the battery was idle than when it was isolated high in the mountains—were unwarranted.

In early August, when the regiment moved into rest positions on the Lombardy plain, Paul had occasion to visit many of the charming towns and beautiful cities that stretched from the foothills of the Dolomites to the Venetian coast. While he went in search of luxurious gifts for his wife, son, and parents, Marie agonized that his eye might be drawn to something more nubile than the lengths of silk he enthusiastically described in letters home. This notion, Paul assured her, was utter nonsense: "You know very well that it's not Italian girls that I love but you my beloved Marquise and if I am so proud it is in thinking of my Marquise because leave is coming soon and not with the Italian girls. I want to keep everything for you." Unlike his philandering companion, who had clearly paid a high price for his errant ways, Paul felt that faithfulness had its own rewards. "I don't want to go home on leave with such a fear and to be worried all the time instead of being happy in the arms of my little wife." Neither as foolhardy nor as fickle as some of his companions, he took comfort in the strength of his marriage: "It will not be some passing fling that will ever destroy the happiness that awaits me at home . . . How I love you how happy I will be to see you how happy I am to be loved by you that is my only sustenance and my only comfort."[85]

Such passionate, heartfelt words did Marie a world of good, until the rash appeared. Then an underlying anxiety, all but effaced for most of the war, resurfaced: Could it be that Paul, in spite of his undeniable passion for her, had strayed again, as many believed he had done in his unmarried youth? Years earlier, when a young woman known to have many casual admirers was whisked away in the middle of the night with a new-born baby, rumors had circulated that Paul had fathered the child. What village gossips insinuated, he had assured Marie at the time, was both outrageous and, more to the point, impossible. Whatever his previous sins and misdemeanors, he could offer doctor's proof of his assertion: "Since 14 November 1911 no woman or girl [*fille*, which means both "girl" and "prostitute"] can blame me in these conditions."[86] But even if he was not the sometime lover of the unhappy Mademoiselle M., his past had been, as he readily conceded and Marie well knew, by no means blameless. A year before that incident, having recently turned twenty-one, he had found himself away from home (perhaps for the first time) in Limoges, where he had reported for military service. Madly in love with the enchanting Marie Andrieux but not yet formally engaged, he seems to have followed in the footsteps of many a young man called to complete his military service in a town sufficiently far from home to afford a tempting anonymity: he went out on the town and ended up in the bed of a local prostitute. This not quite innocent escapade had some very unfortunate consequences, as became evident five months later.

At the end of April 1912, Paul wrote that he had recently been hospitalized with a case of German measles and would soon be coming home on convalescent leave. Once he returned, the young couple, unofficially engaged since the beginning of the year, when Paul had told his father of his intention to marry Marie, would have some things to talk about. Perhaps they discussed his German measles, but diagnoses of German measles rarely jeopardize an engagement or alienate prospective in-laws. Given the crisis that unfolded when he returned home, it is likely that he had recently been treated for something much more compromising than German measles. In heartbreaking conversations (subsequently alluded to in several letters) he revealed to Marie that his recent illness might have consequences so severe as to undermine their future happiness. However much it pained him to say so, it might be better that she forget him, for he was no longer worthy of her affection and might prove an unfit husband. His doctors had warned that his health might continue to suffer in the future, and Paul preferred that Marie know this now, rather than confront him with his dishonesty years later. He thus offered to call off their engagement: "For your sake for fear of one day making you unhappy I made this proposition to you to find out what effect these revelations had on you and so that being warned about them you would not one day reproach me." All things considered, it seemed impossible to him "that a woman as chaste as [she was] would accept a husband like that."[87]

Had Marie decided to break their engagement, she would have done so, it seems clear, with her parents' approbation, for no one else in her family was very fond of her intended in May 1912. "Everyone," Paul observed, "blames me." Indeed, the chilly reception that must have awaited him at Lescure after he divulged his secret made him reluctant to face his future in-laws anytime soon: "I will never cross the threshold of your door until my sixteen months [of remaining military service] are over." Thus when he returned to his barracks to find no reassuring letter awaiting him, he was convinced that Marie had heeded her parents' counsel. The appearance of a very loving letter a few days later showed how much he had underestimated both her affection and her independence of mind.[88]

Marie willingly forgave Paul, for she loved him to distraction. But neither she nor he could entirely forget the youthful indiscretion that had marred their engagement. Its physical and emotional consequences were serious and enduring. If he had contracted syphilis in late 1911, he would have been either fully cured (if he was given the new arsenic-based injections

that had become available in 1909) or at the very least no longer contagious when he and Marie married in February 1914.
But if at the same time he had also (perhaps unknowingly)
contracted gonorrhea, which before the discovery of antibiotics could not be cured, then it is likely that he passed the
gonorrhea on to Marie after their marriage. The eye infection
that afflicted Serge so soon after birth might certainly suggest
that he did: conjunctivitis in infants is highly indicative of congenital gonorrhea. Marie's subsequent childlessness could be
another sign of untreated gonorrhea, which can spread to the
uterus during childbirth and render a woman sterile thereafter. Doctors of the early twentieth century used the term "one-
child sterility."[89] The letters, although they clearly suggest that
Paul and Marie took precautions to prevent her becoming
pregnant a second time, also give the impression that the couple's contraceptive methods were not entirely reliable. Whenever Tante Rose was a few days late (as was the case in October
1918), Marie fretted that she might be pregnant again. That
she never again conceived gives rise to the suspicion that she
was in fact sterile.

Emotional scars also remained. Marie worried in 1912, and
intermittently thereafter, that perhaps Paul loved her if not
less ardently then perhaps less exclusively than she loved him.
When she inquired in spring 1912 about his true feelings, he
did not hesitate to set her mind at ease: "I love you I adore you
too much not to want to belong to you I am now like your toy
you can do with me what you want but you understand well
that I had to know if you loved me as much after these revelations." Suitably penitent, he promised, "No one else will ever
take possession of my heart." Marie, won over by her errant
love's genuine remorse, obvious affection, and resolve to be
true to her alone, was reassured by his heartfelt assertion that
she should never "have even a shadow of a doubt about [his]

faithfulness"; she could not, however, fully conquer her nagging fear that she was in some way his second choice. This made her hesitant when first married to express the fullness of her affection. As Paul would observe in the spring of 1917, when she had at last taken to calling him "my little Paul," he was delighted to read such "tender words of loving friendship which you seemed hesitant to give me at the beginning of our marriage." He wanted more than anything to see her "fully confident in [his love for her] and without any bitter thoughts none." Marie in turn confessed that unresolved jealousy on her part had given rise to her earlier inhibitions: "To think that others had written you [these things] I couldn't write them to you, tell you so many things I couldn't bear to think that others had said them to you . . . Now that I know that you have no more secrets from me I will love you even more I will no longer have this fear that made me suffer so much before."[90]

When the "fear that made [her] suffer so much" returned in October 1918, Marie could do nothing but wait for reassurances that her anxieties were unfounded. As the rash subsided, giving credence to the doctor's diagnosis that she had nothing untoward to worry about, she recovered her physical strength and her loving ways. Delighted to learn in mid-October that she was well on the way to recovery, Paul took great pleasure in reading letters from her (most of which unfortunately have not survived) that were once again filled with uninhibited expressions of ardor. "I am very happy to see that you are much better . . . You must have really suffered psychologically because I find you so much more free loving and tender in your letters . . . Rest assured that you will never be surpassed in my affections." Indeed, her most recent letters had been so "long good and completely imprinted with tenderness and love" that Paul cherished every word. When he received one of her letters, he wanted only to "hide away to read them all alone so as not to be disturbed in order to be able to savor their good and tender words of love and confidence I am happy too to see that you like it when you get several letters from your little guy love him well for you cannot ever love him more than he loves you."[91]

Reconciliation could not have come at a timelier moment. The prospect of peace, long dreamed of but tangible enough by late October 1918 to make one's mouth water, prompted Paul to reflect on what an end to the war would mean to him. Unlike the statesmen who looked to create a peace that would simultaneously (and not always compatibly) defend French security, protect British commercial interests, extract financial reparations from the defeated enemy, and honor the idealistic vision enshrined in Woodrow Wilson's Fourteen Points, Paul expressed little interest in Great Power politics. His definition of peace, in keeping with his reasons for fighting the war, was essentially domestic: "Ever since I've heard talk of peace I think about it morning and night of that return home when I will be able to hug my beloved Marquise [and] all those I love." His simple expectations for a world without war moreover revealed how dreary and uncomfortable day-to-day life at the front was, even for those safe from enemy fire. Peace would mean returning to a house where "in the evening I will find my bed made and a real bed not a pallet where the rain won't come through the roof where I will have a table a chair a plate with a spoon and fork to eat with a table to write at instead of being seated on the ground in the mud and faces that will make me smile and finally freedom love and happiness." Until that day arrived (and the slow pace of demobilization delayed its advent into 1919), he took comfort in reflecting, "I have there at home a Marquise and a little angel who love me and who are waiting for me with just as much impatience a little wife who suffers as much as I do from this separation all that gives me courage."[92]

On 4 November 1918, a full week before the war ended

Le 11 Novembre 1918

Marguerite bien aimée

C'est une paie malchance
en ayant de si bonnes
nouvelles au sujet des évène-
ments de ne pas même oui
une lettre de Mon aimée depuis
trois jours J'espère que tu va
bien quand même ainsi que
mon gros Yvette. Si tu
voyait la joie qui règne ici

Letter from Paul to Marie Pireaud, 11 November 1918. Service historique de la défense, France.

depuis ce matin ayant le jour
que nous ayant appris que
c'était fini en France les Italiens
n'ont pas l'air de partager notre
joie et nous regardent même
d'une manière... enfin ou s'en
moque ou je les quitte pour
aller se faire en Autriche le
poser en paiement...
... que j'aime la paix pour
revenir à ma Marquise que
j'adore tu dois être bien contente
maintenant que tu es rassurée
sur mon sort que tu dois être
heureuse de penser que maintenant tu es sure que ton ... vaut
que tu auras ... reviendras te
rappeler que je t'avais toujours

on the western front, peace came to northern Italy. Paul's delight knew no bounds, for everyone was saying that the Kaiser would soon abdicate, thus bringing to an end a war that had taken more than four years out of his life, that had forced him to live apart from his wife and son, and that had exposed him to unimaginable horror. "What happiness can you believe that you will have your little guy with you forever that we will be happy I can hardly believe it I have wanted it so much and we have suffered for such a long time." He knew that they were luckier than many: "In spite of all our suffering we will still be together forever and will no longer ever have to be apart." The last full week of the war was marked, in Italy at least, by spontaneous celebrations. French and Italians took to the streets to celebrate the armistice with Austria-Hungary: "The streets and houses are filled with people singing fireworks are going off everywhere it's indescribable." Then, two days later, premature rumors that an armistice had been signed in France prompted further revelry. Nothing compared with the "joy that reigned" on 11 November when definitive word arrived in Italy that Germany had signed the armistice that morning. Only the Italians seemed grudging in their enthusiasm for a distant development that, they thought, made little difference to them. For Paul, however, the true celebration still awaited him: once home in the arms of his beloved wife they would both "remember the hours of anguish the suffering endured" and lose themselves in "kisses that would be all the better caresses more tender as if to blot out this nightmare." Remarking that he was "mad with joy," he laid plans to be home in time to plant the next potato crop. The war was over, and real life awaited them once more.[93]

Conclusion

*F*or Paul and Marie the armistice of November 1918 brought with it exuberant joy, profound relief, and intense frustration. The war was won; Paul had survived; they now had only to wait, with undisguised impatience, for his safe and definitive return. In her ebullient letter of 14 November, Marie wrote of the relief that had for the last few days suffused her daily life: "We can all breathe freely now"; of the joy that accompanied the end of the war: "I am so happy that it seems as if I don't even need to write you that you can guess my thoughts my joy"; and of her hope that Paul would soon be home: "Oh that that blessed day may come quickly."[1] The thirteen families in Nanteuil who had lost a son, a husband, or a father knew neither such joy nor excited anticipation of what the future would bring. They knew only grief. Paul and Marie, however, were among the fortunate ones. Over the course of the war they had experienced profound suffering sometimes, discomfort frequently, and anxiety almost constantly. They had witnessed and to some extent shared in others' bereavement. But their marriage had survived more than four years of enforced separation; their son had successfully negotiated the perils of infancy; and their future—as a couple, as a family, and as citizens of a now victorious nation—appeared blessedly uncomplicated by any crisis comparable to the one they had just weathered. Their joy was as understandable as it was hard-won.

Assured for the first time in fifty-two months that her husband would indeed come home, Marie's relief was that of a prisoner reprieved. The gnawing anxiety that had been her constant companion since August 1914 was at last laid to rest. Without doubt she wanted Paul home as quickly as military necessity and diplomatic negotiations would allow. She was, however, willing to be patient. Through the winter of 1918 and the spring of 1919, when newspapers were filled with stories of international leaders convening in Paris to hammer out a peace settlement, she repeatedly calculated and then recalculated when her husband would be home for good. At first, she thought that January 1919 was a genuine possibility. The "Boches," in her judgment, had no appetite left for war: "I think that [they] aren't going to want to start everything up again tomorrow." Very soon, though, she had to accept that there would be no early demobilization, for most French soldiers would be free to go home only after the conclusion of the peace conference. Until Germany accepted the victors' terms, however draconian and unjust they might have seemed to the defeated nation, France would remain a nation under arms: two million French soldiers were still in uniform through June 1919, to maintain the threat, implicit throughout the months of the Paris peace conference, that if Germany did not sign the treaty, the war would resume.[2]

Having abandoned her hope that Paul would be home by the new year, Marie spent the early months of 1919 scouring the papers for any sign that a settlement was imminent. The recognition that wild rumors were repeatedly controverted by hard facts taught her not to get her hopes up. And unsettling stories of significant casualties following derailments of trains transporting troops made her increasingly jittery. When, in March, Paul came eligible for his second leave in three months, she worried about the wisdom of his coming home. Should he

come home, even if only for a few days, or remain safely en-
sconced in his barracks? Paul, of course, was ready to head
home: the potatoes had yet to be planted, for bad weather was
delaying all work in the fields, and in any case delights awaited
him indoors, whatever the weather. Marie was not so sure. Although another leave would have been wonderful, Marie—
finally free of worries about Paul's survival—fretted that an accident might befall him on his way home. The thought that her
beloved husband, having so long survived enemy fire, might
fall victim to a chance train derailment was too much to bear.
She could relish the relief brought by the end of war only if she
knew for sure that Paul was and would remain safe. Better that
he stay in his barracks than that he venture unnecessarily out
into the dangerous No Man's Land of civilian transportation.[3]

Paul, not surprisingly, saw things very differently. If the
great torment of Marie's life during wartime had been her persistent fear for Paul's safety, the great anguish of his existence
had been his enforced separation from those he loved. He had
tolerated this for as long as the war lasted, for he told himself
that he was fighting to protect his family and his home from
the horrific consequences attendant on French defeat. When
the war was at last won, separation seemed well-nigh unendurable. Peace, in his mind, meant the right to return home, resume his civilian life, and abandon once and for all the disci-
plined subjugation of life in uniform. It rankled, therefore, that
he had to remain under arms with no prospect of demobilization any time soon. He and his companions in the French expeditionary force, more keenly aware than ever of their separation from home, were enervated by their enforced idleness on
the now tranquil Italian front. Biding their time in makeshift
billets in northern Italy was, admittedly, somewhat more pleasant than postcombat service in the devastated and distressingly

damp villages of northern France, but only just. Inadequate food, irregular mail service, extortionate locals eager to extract a little more profit from French soldiers soon destined for home, and evidence that the Italian army was demobilizing with unseemly haste all combined to demoralize and depress French troops remaining in Italy. The movie screenings, soccer matches, and musical concerts organized by commanding officers intent on maintaining morale made life marginally better, but nothing could compare with the comforts of home. Soldiers unable to resume their civilian duties grumbled at their forced inability to do anything useful. Factory workers fearful that demobilized Italians would head to France, where they would steal positions rightly belonging to French veterans, wanted to go home and reclaim their jobs. Educated men thought they had better things to do than "sit around with their arms crossed and their brains asleep." And peasants wanted, more than anything, to return to their land, "which was dying for lack of labor." Whatever his vocation, everyone wanted to go home. As one of Paul's companions in the 112th confessed: "I have had enough of Italy and lots of others are just like me."[4]

Relocating to France was therefore an improvement of sorts. When the expeditionary force dissolved and its component parts decamped to northeastern France at the end of February 1919, Paul was moved to find himself once again "in France this dear France." War, deprivation, and separation from those he loved, none of these had lessened his love for and identification with his homeland. Thus, it pained him to see the destroyed cities and devastated countryside around the French front lines. In March 1919, as the regiment moved through the Champagne region, where it had served two years earlier, Paul noted with bitterness all the ruination the war had wrought: "On the second day we passed through Reims where we saw the unfortunate cathedral most of Reims is razed to the ground and forms nothing more than a mass of stone ruins." He thought, "It will definitely take more than twenty years to rebuild everything if it can be done at all." The countryside "where there was not one house left standing" had been equally laid waste, and evidence of last-minute German looting and gratuitous destruction of the few remaining houses did nothing to soften his longstanding antipathy for the now defeated enemy. Although the national press spoke of promising developments at the peace conference, and the possibility of a preliminary settlement by the end of March, Paul was not convinced. "The bellicose character of the Boches" would, he feared, delay the proceedings and put off "demobilization which is already moving at a slow enough pace." Rumors that the 112th would be sent to Germany as part of the French occupation force only intensified his melancholy.[5]

Marie did what she could to restore Paul's good humor. Even her promises ("In a month you will see how happy we will be") could not, however, dispel his deepening gloom. He had, he confessed, been overwhelmed of late by an "indescribable depression, unlike anything [he] had ever known." Remaining under arms while politicians postured in Paris strained his patience and left him perpetually out of sorts. "I can no longer stand it everything annoys me everything I eat makes me sick to my stomach I have a headache that nothing will take away." He knew that his moaning was immature; he acknowledged that he should be "more courageous" as he cooled his heels in a barracks far from home. Yet homesickness always got the better of him. It was easy for Marie to counsel patience, for she was at home surrounded by those who loved her: "You have your son your parents your home your house you are mistress of your own life in short there is nothing that you need." He, by contrast, was deprived of everything that he held dear: "I am without everything that I love all my family my home my house where I would be able to say I am at home free and master of my own life free to do what I want to do." Life in the barracks, where soldiers were bossed and berated by officers who, he charged, had made a good career for themselves out of the war and were loath to see it come to an end, was anything but free. It was, in truth, "a kind of vile slavery."[6] Paul had always chafed under the yoke of military discipline. In wartime he had accepted it as an unpleasant necessity; in peacetime, it seemed a violation of his fundamental rights as a citizen and free man.

If true freedom would have to wait until the peace treaty was signed—an event that would take place on 28 June 1919, five years to the day after the assassination that had provoked the war—perhaps Paul could secure an extended agricultural leave that would take him home and keep him there, while the diplomatic process crept along. Other men in his regiment, especially those with advantageous political connections, had already benefited from such leave. One comrade whose uncle was a senator had applied, unsuccessfully at first, for early demobilization. When the influential uncle had interceded with the Ministry of War directly, the much-desired authorization had soon appeared. Paul had no uncles elected to high office, but his father was the mayor of Nanteuil. Surely that might make a difference. Could Marie prevail upon his father to file a petition requesting the early release of his only son? Jean Pireaud could indicate, truthfully enough, that he was now elderly and no longer physically able to keep up the family farm; that his official responsibilities were growing ever more onerous because the village schoolteacher, who (like so many other women teachers) had served as acting secretary of the commune for the duration of the war, was ready to unburden herself of her extra duties; and that Paul was thus urgently needed to work the family's sizable farm and to assume some of the administrative duties of the mayor's office.[7] Such a petition, if ever filed, had no noticeable effect.

The wonderful news that the regiment would relocate to Angoulême in mid-May made life somewhat easier. Since Nanteuil was only thirty-five kilometers away, Marie could surely leave Serge with her parents and get away for a long weekend or two. Marie, however, found herself in a situation similar to that of 1915: having been forced to work out of doors in miserable weather, she had come down with a cold that made travel impossible. Even when she was fully recovered, there was work to be done every day of the week: an unusually wet spring—which caused severe flooding in the north of France and delayed planting in the southwest—made it essential that everyone pitch in whenever the weather allowed. Idleness would destroy prospects, already bleak, for an adequate harvest. The knowledge of all that he could be doing at home—and he had, in Marie's absence, almost nothing worth doing in Angoulême—merely added to Paul's frustration. Increasingly impatient at the plodding pace of demobilization, he fumed at "the bastards," who, he charged, "moved a lot faster to get us mobilized."[8] Indeed they had. After having been mobilized within hours, Paul remained in uniform for more than eight months after the armistice. In late July, as France approached the fifth anniversary of the outbreak of war, Paul was still hoping to be granted an agricultural leave that would allow him to help with the harvest, cuddle his son, and make love to his wife. Regretting that she had had to spend yet another season on heavy farmwork, he promised Marie that he would "find work [for her to do] without going into the fields," and it would be, he assured her, "a lot more interesting." Passionate as ever, he closed his last love letter of the war with words of deep affection: "Receive from your little guy the expression of all his desires his tenderest kisses he who loves you desires you with all his strength all his flesh and his heart."[9] Within days, he was home for good.

The Pireaud correspondence, together with much directly or indirectly corroborating evidence, powerfully suggests that the generation of men who served in the First World War, and the women who awaited their return, had both the ability and the need to remain in close contact with those they loved. Civilian and combatant France were not isolated, mutually indifferent communities, unaware of and unmoved by each other's suffering and anxiety; rather, they remained for the duration of the war intimately connected by networks of correspondence that kept the horrors of combat vividly present to mind and the refuge of home never entirely remote. Letters united parents and children, husbands and wives, and kept affection alive, family almost palpably present. If the military front was not so much an island physically cut off from contact with the French home front, but rather a peninsula permanently linked to civilian society, then correspondence constituted the causeway that brought these two societies together.[10]

For more than four years the French people—the semiliterate soldier as well as the highly educated fellow, the peasant and the rural artisan as well as the urban worker—wrote of material suffering, psychological torment, and emotional longing. Horror, pain, desire, and love left their mark not only on the letters that Paul and Marie Pireaud so faithfully exchanged, but (as the records of the postal censors reveal) on the letters of thousands of other correspondents from all over France. With a war to be waged, the French did not, of course, devote themselves to nothing but writing. At the front, soldiers manned the guns, huddled in trenches, obeyed orders (sometimes grudgingly or selectively), scrounged for food, contemplated death, and complained about the indolence of shirkers, the indifference of civilians, and the idiocy of commanding officers. At home, women labored long and hard to plant and harvest crops, care for children, and look after the elderly. In their idle hours, they squabbled, gossiped, and consoled and comforted one another. And at the end of the day, in dimly lit rooms and even darker dugouts, civilians and soldiers alike recaptured their experiences—the mundane and the momentous—in writing.

Correspondence allowed even simple men with minimal schooling to write honestly and poignantly of the ordeal of war. Censorship notwithstanding, soldiers like Paul Pireaud wrote openly about where they were, described what they were doing, and calculated whether the campaigns in which they participated were bringing victory and the much-desired return home any closer. Realizing that sanitized newspaper reports overlooked much that was happening, frontline combatants resolved to bear testimony through daily correspondence to the war as they experienced it. Regular letter writing also allowed women overburdened with unfamiliar chores and traditional responsibilities to speak of their hardships, confess their anxieties, and lament the disturbing ways in which village life, disrupted by four years of war, was being transformed before their very eyes: harvests, despite the women's best efforts, were inadequate, essential supplies scarce, medical care hard to find; and some women forgot their marriage vows and found distraction in adulterous affairs.

Such open, honest, extensive communication allayed some fears, while exacerbating others. A letter from the front reassured those at home that their loved one still lived, and—with its stark descriptions of combat—gave ample reason to fear for his survival. A letter from home offered evidence of a wife's fidelity, and yet never fully allayed fears of future abandonment.

During the war, Paul had worried that the sexual immorality he deplored among his fellow soldiers and despised in their occasional companions would create a crisis of broken marriages and family disintegration. Many shared such fears. Newspaper columnists, novelists, and sociologists, who raised a chorus of lamentation in the closing years of the war and the early years of the postwar era, proclaimed a "crisis of marriage." Divorce data seemed to bear out their worst fears. Whereas divorce had by modern standards been relatively rare in France before 1914, it became more common and hence more disconcerting after 1918. The statistics for 1920 and 1921 were especially alarming. Furthermore, men were for the first time more likely than women to initiate divorce proceedings: more than half of all divorce petitions filed in 1919 originated with an aggrieved husband. The rush to dissolve an unhappy marriage was most evident in Paris, where the divorce rate was twice the national average.[11] Social commentators, sitting in their Parisian studies, therefore seemed justified in warning that an "epidemic" of divorce was stalking France. Some believed that female infidelity was to blame; others feared that women's newfound financial independence made them increasingly indifferent to their family obligations. Everyone, however, agreed that the institution of the family would not survive the cultural cataclysm brought on by more than four years of war-enforced separation.[12] Novels and the popular press recounted stories of faithless wives, betrayed husbands, and the violence that sometimes ensued when an unsuspecting soldier returned from the front in such cases. The philandering wife—like the heartless Mme Sulphart in Roland Dorgelès's best-selling novel *Les Croix de bois*, who ran off with a Belgian refugee, leaving her husband to return to an empty apartment after demobilization—thus became a stock villain denounced both in popular literature and high-minded scholarship.[13]

Such women certainly existed, even in the depths of the Dordogne. In November 1918, months before men still serving at the front were eligible to return home, Marie wrote to Paul of a local man (presumably the prisoner of war whose wife had been conducting a scandalous affair until the very end of the war) who arrived home to discover that she had walked out on him and had taken everything she could carry with her. Distraught and disillusioned, the deceived husband left for Ribérac on the following morning, to file suit for divorce. In Marie's judgment, women like that "deserved to be shot," but what could one expect? Behavior of this sort was, she lamented, becoming "the fashion."[14] She was right, in part. In the Dordogne, where only eighty-seven divorces had taken place in 1913, marital disintegration was, as elsewhere in France, more common after the war than before it. Two hundred divorces finalized in 1921 proved the point. The "fashion" that Marie deplored was not, however, as widespread as many feared. The putative disintegration of the French family appeared critical in part because divorce statistics from the early twenties represented the concentration in a short period of all the marital misery that had built up over several years. During the war, when legal obstacles and social opprobrium made it almost impossible to initiate divorce proceedings against a man in uniform, divorce had been all but unknown: the Dordogne recorded only fifteen divorces in 1915 and thirty-two in 1916. Many marriages that might have fallen prey to the ordinary stresses of incompatibility or the extraordinary stress of physical or psychological abuse remained intact, then, until demobilization brought the ill suited and the intemperate back together again. Incompatibility did not, however, account for all divorces after the war. Some husbands, like the poor fellow Marie wrote about, clearly did seek to end their marriages because their wives had betrayed them. Indeed, 17 percent of all divorce petitions filed in France after the war named female infidelity as the motivating cause.[15] Nevertheless, divorce in rural France remained a rare occurrence. When calculated on a per capita basis, the two hundred divorces registered in the Dordogne in 1921 translated into one divorce for every two thousand residents. Paul and Marie knew of couples whose marriages had not survived the stresses of war, but (if the statistics tell us anything), not many.

Marriage, by contrast, had lost none of its romantic luster. More than twelve thousand couples exchanged marriage vows in the Dordogne in 1919 and 1920. The marriage rate remained robust through the mid-1920s, increasing from 75 marriages for every 10,000 residents in 1912 to 118 for every 10,000 in the five years following the war. Many of these marriages, especially in 1919 and 1920, were (like a significant number of the divorces granted in the same years) the expression of deferred intention. Presumably, many of the newlyweds in the Dordogne resembled the patient couple from the Haute-Savoie whose engagement had lasted for the duration of the war. In April 1919, Marie-Louise Donche married Jean-Marie Paccot, the no longer young man with whom she had maintained a faithful correspondence since August 1914.[16] The postwar marriage boom led, not surprisingly, to a small-scale baby boom. Couples who had postponed marriage during the war and married couples who had found little opportunity for procreation made up for lost opportunities once the war was over. In a population 10 percent smaller than that of 1911, more babies were born in the Dordogne in each of the six years after demobilization than in any year immediately prior to the war. Paul and Marie did not participate in this rush to repopulate rural France, but Charlotte and Joseph did: their second (and last) child was born in 1923.

Babies born in the aftermath of the war fared better than ever before. By the early 1920s (that is, even before 1923, when child and infant care became a mandatory part of girls' elementary education in France) parents' familiarity with the causes of infant death was making a significant difference. Parents could either call a doctor in the event of a medical emergency or, like Marie, follow the sensible, scientific advice set forth in child-care manuals. Of course, their ability to protect their children from premature death was not complete. Infants born with severe congenital disabilities could not be saved; children who fell ill with most contagious diseases might or might not recover. Scarlet fever could not be cured without antibiotics; German measles still lacked an effective vaccination. By contrast, in those years diphtheria, which could be remedied through timely medical intervention, almost disappeared as a cause of death among children, presumably because parents were aware that a cure existed and were willing to call in a doctor to effect it.

The greatest improvement in infant health, however, resulted from significant reductions in infant deaths due to diarrhea. One of the most widespread causes of early death, infant diarrhea was—as Marie had learned in 1916—one of the few afflictions parents could combat through careful attention to cleanliness and basic hygiene. Michel Huber, the national statistician for France, observed that simple efforts to improve hygiene paid real dividends with infants: on the decline since 1915, infant diarrhea did not disappear as a major cause of death, but its lethal power diminished significantly during and after the war. Even during the exceptionally hot summer of 1921, when many infants fell critically ill with heat-related diarrhea, progress was evident in relation to the prewar record. In

1911, when France had experienced a comparably hot summer, four out of every ten babies that died had succumbed to diarrhea, and the infant mortality rate spiked to an abnormally high 15.7 percent; ten years later, one in three babies that died were victims of diarrhea and the overall infant mortality rate was a more modest 11.6 percent. When temperatures were not so high, infants were more likely than ever before to survive the summer months unscathed. The killing season for newborns had at last receded.[17]

Improvements in infant health were, I believe, significantly abetted by parents' heightened sensitivity to their own mortality. That certainly seems to have been the case for Paul and Marie, whose determination to keep their infant son alive was reinforced by their realization that if Paul were to die in combat, Serge would be their only child. Other couples in similar circumstances probably felt the same way. In their understandable eagerness to protect their children from the deadly diseases that had plagued previous generations, wartime parents turned for advice to child-care manuals. The printed word, rather than oral tradition, became the source of authority and instruction for young parents, whose everyday lives were unusually dependent upon their ability to read and write. By turning peasants into writers, the Great War effected in the heart of rural France a cognitive transformation of profound consequence.

Peasant society became, during and because of the First World War, one that relied as never before on writing. To sustain a marriage or manage a family enterprise, to raise a child or reassure an anxious spouse, men and women separated by force of circumstance turned to writing. Correspondence made possible both the communication of simple news—this young man has been wounded, that calf has been sold, this village has been deprived of a doctor's attention—and the articulation of complex emotions and aspirations. The fears, beliefs, and hopes of forty million people had to be expressed in writing, for without regular correspondence, the citizens of France would have sunk into a swamp of ignorance, incomprehension, and mutual indifference. In rural France, as in the nation at large, what citizens believed to be true, feared might be true, and hoped would come true was communicated in writing.

Marriage by correspondence, complicated as it was by inadvertent miscommunication, was, everyone would have agreed, a poor substitute for the real thing. When a husband was going into pitched battle, when a baby was battling illness, letters hastily written and subject to unpredictable delays in delivery could either allay or heighten anxiety exacerbated by wartime separation. In the days that passed between the writing and the receipt of a letter, much could have changed for the worse. Letters written on the run could give rise to anger or hurt feelings. At home, all could have been settled by a sympathetic word, a soothing gesture, a smile of reconciliation. In the strained circumstances of war, when kisses and caresses were conveyed only in writing, the misunderstandings sometimes deepened. Yet no one would have forgone correspondence. A letter was as essential as food, as longed-for as leave.

As the conflict progressed, rural men and women, who had often been awkward correspondents in the first months of the war, became ever more comfortable with the task of daily writing. One soldier from the south of France, whose young son loved to receive illustrated postcards from his father, mastered a script that by the last years of the war allowed him to fill each card with two hundred words or more.[18] Similarly, when Paul was under fire in June 1918, even a critical shortage of stationery did not silence him: determined to describe the Battle of Piave, he filled both sides of a military-issue postcard with tiny handwriting, and then rotated the card and continued to write at ninety degrees to the original lines. These postcards were a far cry from the preprinted cards distributed, for example, in the British ranks; on those, any individual expression was prohibited and a checked box indicated, at best, that a soldier remained as yet unharmed.

Peasant women, like their men at the front, became more adept at writing out of necessity. Few children born in the 1880s and 1890s had been exposed to more than five or six years of schooling. Young girls from poor families often suffered an even more abbreviated education. This was true, for example, of both Claire Ferchaud and Anna Cuzacq, young peasant girls who before 1914 wrote either hesitantly or not at all. Claire was a saintly visionary (or, depending on one's point of view, a psychotic simpleton) who believed that the war could be won and France saved if the nation were to dedicate itself to the Sacred Heart. When taken out of school at the age of eleven, she had only imperfectly mastered the art of writing. Anna, the impoverished child of an unwed mother, had attended school for less than a year before being put to work full-time as shepherdess at the age of eight. Yet Claire, Anna, and countless others became modestly proficient writers during the war—Claire because writing allowed her to convey her religious visions to believers and nonbelievers alike; Anna because literacy allowed her to stay in touch with her husband at the front.[19] For the first years of the war, Anna had relied on others to read her husband's letters aloud to her and set down her dictated responses. Frustrated by an arrangement that precluded any intimate communication, Anna took it upon herself to learn to read and write. In February 1916 she sent her husband the first letter written in her own hand. In a response written soon after, he urged her henceforth to confide to him "these little things" that would remain, he assured her, "entre nous."[20] After September 1916 Anna Cuzacq had less need for her self-taught literacy, for her husband died at Verdun; but over the course of the war other peasants, men and women alike, became increasingly capable correspondents, whose letters were detailed and descriptive, and often impassioned and intimate.

Descriptions of battle such as the ones that Paul sent home from Verdun and northern Italy show that peasant soldiers were capable of conveying in prose as poignant as it was unpretentious the horror of war. Writing was not, however, confined to documentary accounts of combat. Rather, it became an intensely confessional enterprise that prompted self-reflection and self-revelation. Nowhere was this more evident than in Paul and Marie's willingness to write openly about sexual desire. On the occasion of their first wedding anniversary, Marie wrote of her regret that she and Paul were not in a position to reenact their wedding night, for she would have loved to give him once again the pleasure they had savored a year earlier. When the baby was expected, she assured her husband that she would continue to love him, sensually and physically, for years to come. And in the midst of Verdun, when Paul wrote mournfully that he was surrounded by men convinced that when the war was over they would be too old to enjoy sex ("Some fellows say that . . . when we get home we will be old and disgusted by the pleasures of the flesh that used to make us so happy"), Marie roundly rejected such nonsensical notions. "When people say that there will come a time when we will no longer enjoy each other's caresses As for me I believe that that will never happen not even a baby will prevent us from caressing each other as we did before. How I would love to see you again."[21]

The habit of writing, whether about sex, suffering, or seasonal chores, transformed rural France. Before 1914 the written word had made real inroads into country life: newspapers, invoices, doctors' prescriptions, and report cards were all part of

the fabric of peasant routine.[22] Yet peasant France was still more
passively than actively literate. Paul's experience suggests that
peasant boys probably wrote home (as their teachers had insisted they should) during their mandatory military service.
Most of the time, however, they were at home, on the land,
within hailing distance of anyone who really mattered. Writing, which in such a situation was not so much a luxury as an ir-
relevance, became a necessity during wartime.

Peasants also became increasingly comfortable with other
habits long taken for granted in urban society. In 1915 when
Marie wanted to purchase a new blouse, she went to the village
fair; in 1918, she sent to Paris, ordering directly from a department store catalogue.[23] This constituted something more than
an extravagance; it revealed the emergence of a new conscious-
ness. Roger Thabault, who grew up in a village approximately
150 kilometers from Nanteuil, recalled that prior to the war
only town girls felt confident enough to place an order from a
catalogue. Farm girls "might well know how to read and write
but, to place an order with a big store, one needs to have a certain familiarity with symbols—pictures and writing—and a certain confidence in them which these girls lacked. They would
only buy materials and things which they had seen, touched,
and felt in their hands."[24] When Paul contemplated how he
could become a truly modern farmer—a goal that he set for
himself in the spring of 1919—he did not turn to his father for
advice. Instead, he wrote directly to the national agricultural
college and asked for titles of books that would give him the
most up-to-date information about everything from improving
crop yields to animal husbandry. No one book covered everything Paul wanted to know, but his inclination, as much as his
ability, to make such an inquiry speaks volumes.[25] Having relied for more than four years on reading and writing, he was no
longer content with local lore and oral culture.

Regular letter writing thus changed the way residents of rural France perceived and mastered their world. Writing became the means by which they defined their identity, interacted with the world beyond their village boundaries, and made plans for the future. We are now able to know not only that this occurred, but why. Recent scholarship in cognitive science demonstrates that cognition—the way we make sense of the world and ourselves—is shaped not just by the innate capacity of the human brain to gather, categorize, and assimilate information. Rather, cognition is an interactive process in which human beings employ simple tools, such as pens and paper, to make sense in ever more complex ways of themselves and the world in which they function. Not only do these "cognitive props" help rational beings think, but they make possible thought that is more complex than that unmediated by written expression. In the same way that an individual who has memorized the multiplication tables can solve more sophisticated mathematical problems when she is armed with pencil and paper than when she is relying on mental arithmetic alone, an individual who describes his experiences in writing engages in a cognitive process that by its nature allows for the development and assimilation of ever more sophisticated ideas.[26] Writing thus becomes a mechanism for rendering a complicated, confusing, and often disorderly world more comprehensible. The transformation of rural France that became evident after the Great War, and which has been much commented upon by scholars since, was, it seems clear, made possible by a cognitive revolution effected by writing.

When Paul returned home, he, Marie, and Serge continued to live in the stone cottage of Lescure (to which all his letters had been addressed throughout the war) through the early 1920s, when they moved to the more spacious house at Moulin du

Pont that Paul's parents had purchased years before. Paul was at last master of his own home. A man remembered twenty-five years after his death for his avid appetite for learning, he read newspapers voraciously (even during the last years of his life, when he could have stayed abreast of world events by watching television instead). In the 1930s, when electrification made oil lamps a thing of the past, Paul was happy to see progress come to the village. Much admired for his fair-mindedness, he served as mayor of Nanteuil-de-Bourzac for many years in the 1950s and 1960s. Although his suspicion of organized religion remained unabated, he did not hesitate, in his capacity as mayor, to make funds available to restore the medieval church. Moreover, years earlier he had gone out of his way to save the village priest from vigilante justice. During the Second World War, the priest, an ardent supporter of the repressive Vichy regime, had denounced a local woman for some sexual transgression; at the liberation, resistance groups targeted the priest and, it seems clear, would have killed him if Paul had not personally intervened to save his life.[27]

Paul and Marie lived well into old age: Paul died in June 1970, only a few months shy of his eightieth birthday, and Marie eight years later. Serge, having learned his letters at an early age, must have found school to his liking, for he became a teacher and moved to Angoulême. He married late, had no children, and predeceased his mother by five years. Having done so much all those years earlier to keep him alive, Marie wept bitter tears when, accompanied by family friends, she laid her only child to rest. With Marie's death in September 1978, the Pireaud family perished too. With no grandchildren to remember them, the couple's remarkable story of love and longing, war and interminable waiting, would have been lost forever; but the letters they had exchanged, and then stored away, survived. And in the final analysis the letters are legacy enough.

NOTES

INDEX

NOTES

INTRODUCTION

1. Section Historique de l'Armée de Terre [hereafter SHAT], 1Kt T458, Correspondance entre le soldat Paul Pireaud et son épouse, 10 janvier 1910–1927, Letter from Paul Pireaud to Marie Andrieux, 3 September 1913. All subsequent references to the Pireaud correspondence will be to this collection.

2. Paul Pireaud to M. and Mme Andrieux, 16 October 1912; Paul Pireaud to Marie Andrieux, 21 March 1913.

3. Archives départementales de la Dordogne [hereafter ADD], 6 M 147, "Recensement de 1891: Liste nominative des habitants de la commune de Nanteuil-de-Bourzac, 1891"; 6 M 335, "Recensement de 1901: Liste nominative des habitants de la commune de Nanteuil-de-Bourzac, 1901." All subsequent statistical evidence relating to Nanteuil before the war is drawn from these two census records. The detailed census record (*liste nominative*) for 1911 does not exist.

4. There were eighteen such foster children living in Nanteuil-de-Bourzac at the turn of the century. They were neither nurslings farmed out in the countryside to live with wet nurses (there were no children thus designated in the 1901 census for Nanteuil) nor apprentices or servants. On the social status of *enfants de l'hospice*, see Ivan Jablonka, "Paths towards Autonomy: The Living Conditions of Fostered Children in Western France in the Early 20th Century," *History of the Family* 6 (2001): 401–421.

5. ADD, 4 Z 106, "Elections municipales, 1909–1919."

6. ADD, 1 M 86, "Mobilisation et état de siège," Circular from the prefect of the Dordogne to all mayors in the department, confirming contents of a telegram sent earlier in the day, 31 July 1914.

7. Edward Berenson, *The Trial of Madame Caillaux* (Berkeley: University of California Press, 1992), 3; Jean-Jacques Becker, *1914: Comment les*

Français sont entrés dans la guerre (Paris: Presses de la Fondation nationale des sciences politiques, 1977), 131–35.

8. *Historique du 21ème Régiment de Chasseurs, 1914–1918* (Limoges: L. Queyment, 1920); *Campagne 1914–1918, 12ème escadron du train des équipages militaires* (Paris: Lavauzelle, 1920).

9. Gérard Bacconnier, André Minet, and Louis Soler, "Quarante millions de témoins," *Mémoire de la Grande Guerre: Témoins et témoignages*, ed. Gérard Canini (Nancy: Presse universitaire de Nancy, 1989), 141.

10. Jules Romains, *Verdun*, trans. Gerard Hopkins (London: Prion, 2000), 74.

11. Michel Huber, *La Population de la France pendant la guerre*, Publications de la Dotation Carnegie pour la paix internationale (Paris: Presses universitaires de France, n.d.), 426.

12. One significant exception to this general rule is Henri Gerest's detailed study of the rural region of Montbrisonnais: *Les Populations rurales du Montbrisonnais et la Grande Guerre* (Saint-Etienne: Centre d'études Foreziennes, 1975).

13. Ernest Pérochon, *Les Gardiennes* (Paris: Gestes Editions, 1993 [1924]); Jean Giono, *To the Slaughterhouse*, trans. Norman Glass (London: Peter Owen, 1969), first published as *Le Grand Troupeau* (Paris, Gallimard, 1931).

14. *Annuaire statistique*, vol. 33 (1913) (Paris: Imprimerie nationale, 1914).

15. ADD, 1 T 145, "Dossier: Nanteuil-de-Bourzac."

16. I develop this argument at greater length in "A Republic of Letters: The Epistolary Tradition in France during World War I," *American Historical Review* 108, no. 5 (December 2003): 1338–1361.

17. Paul Pireaud to Marie Andrieux, 6 September 1913.

18. Paul Pireaud to Marie Andrieux, 13 October 1911, 29 October 1911, 24 December 1911.

19. Paul Pireaud to Marie Andrieux, 11 September 1912, 7 November 1912, 10 July 1913.

20. Henri Barbusse, *Under Fire*, trans. Robin Buss, intro. Jay Winter (New York: Penguin Books, 2004), 69.

21. Pierre Barral, "La Paysannerie française à l'arrière," *Les Sociétés européennes et la guerre de 1914–1918*, Actes du colloque organisé à Nanterre et à Amiens du 8 au 11 décembre 1988 (Paris: Publications de l'Université de Nanterre, 1990), 237–243.

22. For an important analysis of the postal censorship records, see Jean Nicot, *Les Poilus ont la parole: Dans les tranchées, lettres du front, 1917–1918* (Paris: Editions Complexe, 1998).

23. Fernand Maret, *Lettres de la guerre 14–18* (Nantes: Siloë, 2001); Germain Cuzacq, *Le Soldat de Lagruelet: Lettres de Germain Cuzacq écrits du front entre août 1914 et septembre 1916*, ed. Pierre et Germaine Leshauris (Toulouse: Eché, 1984).

24. SHAT, T682, "Mémoire rédigé par Alexandre Lefebvre concernant les lettres écrites par son père adressées à son épouse." Marie Catherine Santerre, whose village was destroyed in the German advance of 1914, also experienced a very different war from that of Marie Pireaud. See Louise Tilly, "Individual Lives and Family Strategies in the French Proletariat," in *Family and Sexuality in French History*, ed. Robert Wheaton and Tamara K. Hareven (Philadelphia: University of Pennsylvania Press, 1980): 201–223.

25. Jacques Meyer, *Les Soldats de la Grande Guerre* (Paris: Hachette, 1966), 37; Barbusse, *Under Fire*, 114.

1. HOW SAD THE COUNTRYSIDE IS

1. Archives départementales de la Charente [hereafter ADC], J 94, "Histoire des communes par les instituteurs (1914–1918): Salles La Valette"; J 84, "Histoire de la commune Juignac (Charente) pendant la guerre."

2. Marie to Paul, 15 January 1915.

3. On the nature of agricultural production in late nineteenth- and early twentieth-century France, see Hugh D. Clout, *The Land of France, 1815–1914*, London Research Series in Geography (London: Allen and Unwin), 1983. I am grateful to Mme Arlette Durand who shared with

me her study of Nanteuil-de-Bourzac. In it she pays particular attention to the agricultural character of Nanteuil from the early twentieth century through the 1960s.

4. ADD, 4 Z 137, "Enquête sur les vides causés par la guerre parmi les agriculteurs," July 1920.

5. ADD, 1 M 86, Report of the prefect of the Dordogne to the minister of the interior, 12 August 1914.

6. Marie to Paul, 20 September 1914.

7. Michel Augé-Laribé, L'Agriculture pendant la guerre, Histoire économique et sociale de la Guerre mondiale (Paris: Presses universitaires de France, [1925]), 125–126.

8. ADD, 1 M 86, Report of the subprefect, arrondissement of Ribérac, 3 August 1914.

9. Marie to Paul, 26 October 1914; ADD, 1 M 86, Report of the subprefect, arrondissement of Ribérac, 5 August 1914.

10. ADD, 1 M 86, Reports of the prefect of the Dordogne to the minister of the interior, Reports dated 2 August 1914, 5 August 1914, 9 August 1914.

11. Ibid., Reports of the subprefect, arrondissement of Ribérac, August–September 1914, Reports dated 7 August 1914, 8 August 1914, 24 August 1914, 25 August 1914.

12. Ibid., Reports dated 3 August 1914, 5 August 1914, 8 August 1914, and 14 August 1914.

13. Alain Corbin, Village of Cannibals (Cambridge, Mass.: Harvard University Press, 1992).

14. Ralph Gibson, "The Périgord: Landownership, Power, and Illusion," Landownership and Power in Modern Europe, ed. Ralph Gibson and Martin Blinkhorn (London: HarperCollins Academic, 1991), 90.

15. ADD, 1 M 86, Reports of the prefect of the Dordogne to the minister of the interior, Report dated 5 August 1914; Reports of the subprefect, arrondissement of Ribérac, Reports dated 5 August 1914, 21 August 1914.

16. Ibid., Reports of the subprefect, arrondissement of Ribérac, August–September 1914, Reports dated 8 August 1914, 14 August 1914; ADC, J 87, "Historique de la guerre: Montignac-le-Coq."

17. ADD, 1 M 86, Daily reports of the prefect of the Dordogne to the minister of the interior, August 1914, Reports dated 8 August 1914, 9 August 1914.

18. Ibid., Report dated 9 August 1914; Poster dated 8 August 1914, issued by the military commandant, 12th Region (Limoges).

19. Ibid., Report dated 27 August 1914.

20. Hew Strachan, *The First World War*, vol. 1: *To Arms* (Oxford: Oxford University Press, 2001), 230.

21. ADD, 1 M 86, Reports of the prefect of the Dordogne to the minister of the interior, August 1914, Reports dated 27 August 1914, 7 September 1914.

22. ADD, 1 M 89, Letter dated 9 August 1914 from the mayor of Montignac to the director of posts in Périgueux; ibid., letter dated 13 August 1914 from the director of posts to the prefect of the Dordogne.

23. ADD, 1 M 86, Reports of the prefect of the Dordogne to the minister of the interior, August 1914, Report dated 27 August 1914.

24. Paul to Marie, 9 August 1914, 16 August 1914, 18 August 1914.

25. Marie to Paul, 25 August 1914.

26. Paul to Marie, 19 August 1914, 9 September 1914; Marie to Paul, 1 September 1914, 4 September 1914; *Campagne 1914–1919, 12ème escadron du train des équipages militaires* (Paris: Lavauzelle, 1920), 4.

27. ADC, J 94, "Histoire des communes par les instituteurs (1914–1918): Salles La Valette."

28. Marie to Paul, 20 September 1914, 23 October 1914.

29. Rosa Pireaud to Paul Pireaud, 15 January 1915.

30. Marie to Paul, 26 February 1915, 28 May 1915.

31. Marie to Paul, 1 March 1915, 2 February 1915, 6 April 1915, 27 May 1915.

32. Marie to Paul, 2 June 1915.

33. ADD, 3 R 40, "Allocations militaires: Instructions et affaires générales, 1914–1919," Report from the prefect of the Dordogne to the minister of the interior, 10 May 1915.

34. Marie to Paul, 4 June 1915. On agricultural wages in southwest France, see Augé-Laribé, *L'Agriculture pendant la guerre*, 85–86.

35. Marie to Paul, 14 August 1915.

36. Marie to Paul, 9 July 1915, 29 July 1915, 11 August 1915.

37. ADD, 1 M 86, Reports of the prefect of the Dordogne to the minister of the interior, August 1914, Report dated 12 August 1914; Ibid., Reports of the subprefect, arrondissement of Ribérac, August–September 1914, Report dated 18 August 1914.

38. Ibid., Reports of the prefect of the Dordogne to the minister of the interior, August 1914, Report dated 12 August 1914; ADC, J87, "Historique de la guerre: Montmoreau."

39. ADC, Br 8435, Jean Escande, Le Journal de Mathieu: La Guerre de 14, vécue par un charpentier de Labruguière, sapeur au 2ème Génie (Castres: n.p., 1986).

40. ADD, 3 R 40, "Allocations militaires: Instructions et affaires générales, 1914–1919," Ruling from the minister of the interior, 9 December 1915.

41. Marie to Paul, 21 June 1915; Jean Pireaud to Paul Pireaud, 6 May 1915; Marie to Paul, 8 May 1915.

42. Teachers in Brittany made this point during the war, as did economists afterward. Jean-Jacques Becker, The Great War and the French People (New York: Berg, 1985), 122; Charles Gide and William Oualid, Le Bilan de la guerre pour la France: Histoire économique et sociale de la Guerre mondiale (Paris: Presses universitaires de France, n.d. [1931]), 140–141.

43. ADD, 3 R 40, Letter from the prefect of the Dordogne to the minister of the interior, 10 May 1915; ADC, J 84, "Histoire de la Commune Juignac (Charente) pendant la guerre"; J 87, "Historique de la guerre: Montignac-le-Coq"; Archives départementales du Rhône [hereafter ADR], 4 M 234, "Etat moral de la population," Report of the prefect, March 1916.

44. ADC, J 94, "Historique de la guerre, août 1914–août 1916: Vaux Lavalette."

45. ADD, 1 M 89, Letter dated 4 November 1914 from the minister of commerce, industry, post, and telegraph to the prefect of the Dordogne.

46. Marie to Paul, 20 September 1914.

47. Marie to Paul, 14 February 1915, 28 May 1915; Paul to Marie, 9 August 1915.

48. ADD, 1 M 89, Newspaper clipping (date not included) concerning mailing of packages for Christmas and New Year.

49. Marie to Paul, 10 January 1915, 24 January 1915, 25 January 1915, 8 February 1915, 27 March 1915, 15 June 1915; Paul to Marie, 16 February 1915, 18 June 1915; Rosa Pireaud to Paul Pireaud, 29 May 1915.

50. Paul to Marie, 30 May 1915.

51. *Historique du 21ème Régiment de chasseurs, 1914–1919* (Limoges: Queyment, 1920).

52. Marie to Paul, 20 September 1914, 23 October 1914, 9 October 1914.

53. Marie to Paul, 8 February 1915, 8 March 1915.

54. Marie to Paul, 22 January 1915, 31 January 1915, 24 February 1915.

55. Marie to Paul, 14 February 1915, 21 February 1915.

56. Jean-Yves Le Naour, *Misères et tourments de la chair durant la Grande Guerre: Les Moeurs sexuelles des Français, 1914–1918* (Paris: Aubier, 2002), 361.

57. See, on the details of the Hérail case, ibid., 362–364; on the Caillaux trial, see Edward Berenson, *The Trial of Mme Caillaux* (Berkeley: University of California Press, 1992).

58. André Kahn, *Journal de guerre d'un juif patriote, 1914–1918* (Paris: Jean-Claude Simoën, 1978), 134, 141, 142.

59. Paul to Marie, 3 February 1915; Marie to Paul, 8 February 1915; Paul to Marie, 12 February 1915.

60. Paul to Marie, 16 August 1914; Marie to Paul, 1 September 1914, 4 September 1914.

61. Paul to Marie, 9 September 1914, 17 September 1914; note dated 22 September 1914, which appears to be the text of a telegram Marie was to send to Paul, announcing that she would leave Angoulême that evening at 11 P.M. and would arrive in Paris the next day.

62. Françoise Loux, *Le Jeune Enfant et son corps dans la médecine traditionnelle* (Paris: Flammarion, 1978), 32–33; Martine Segalen, *Love and Power in the Peasant Family: Rural France in the Nineteenth Century,* trans. Sarah Matthews (Chicago: University of Chicago Press, 1983), 125.

63. Marie to Paul, 26 September 1914.

64. Paul to Marie, 30 September 1914; Marie to Paul, 4 October 1914, 9 October 1914.

65. Marie to Paul, 27 October 1914; Paul to Marie, 29 October 1914.

66. Paul to Marie, 5 January 1915; Marie to Paul, 6 January 1915.

67. Marie to Paul, 6 January 1915, 18 January 1915.

68. Marie to Paul, 21 February 1915, 13 May 1915.

69. Marie to Paul, 13 May 1915, 18 May 1915.

70. Paul to Marie, 19 May 1915.

71. Marie to Paul, 21 May 1915, 15 June 1915; Paul to Marie, 18 June 1915.

72. Marie to Paul, 21 June 1915.

73. Paul to Marie, 20 June 1915.

74. Marie to Paul, 20 June 1915.

2. HERE IT IS EXTERMINATION ON THE GROUND

1. On the importance of religion to French troops, see Annette Becker, *La Guerre et la foi: De la mort à la mémoire, 1914–1930* (Paris: Armand Colin, 1994).

2. General Herr, *L'Artillerie: Ce qu'elle a été, ce qu'elle est, ce qu'elle doit être* (Paris: Berger-Levrault, 1924), 37.

3. Herr, *L'Artillerie,* 42; Colonel Alvin et Commandant André, *Manuel d'Artillerie lourde (matériel),* 4th ed. (Paris: Henri Charles-Lavauzelle, 1919), 50–54.

4. Alden Brooks, *As I Saw It* (New York: Knopf, 1930), 99.

5. Lieutenant Thibault, *Notions d'artillerie lourde: A l'usage des sous-officiers et candidats sous-officiers,* 2nd ed. (Paris: Henri Charles-Lavauzelle, 1918).

6. SHAT, 26 N 1130, "Journaux des marches et opérations du 112ème Régiment d'artillerie lourde."

7. For a description of the work of a heavy artillery battery, see Arsène Le Breton, *Campagne de 1914–1918: Mon Carnet de route* (Rennes: Ennoïa, 2004), 88–89.

8. France, Armeé, Service historique, *Les Armées françaises dans la Grande Guerre*, vol. 3 (Paris: Imprimerie nationale, 1923), 602–615.

9. Paul to Marie, 6 February 1916.

10. André Kahn, *Journal de guerre d'un juif patriote, 1914–1918* (Paris: Jean-Claude Simoën, 1978), 142; Benjamin Simonet, *Franchise militaire: De la bataille des frontières aux combats de Champagne, 1914–1915* (Paris: Gallimard, 1986), 66; Fernand Maret, *Lettres de la guerre 14–18* (Nantes: Siloë, 2001), 183; Paul to Marie, 12 February 1915.

11. Paul to Marie, 16 February 1916.

12. Paul to Marie, 16 February 1916, 21 February 1916.

13. Paul to Marie, 3 March 1916, 5 March 1916.

14. *General Notes on the Use of Artillery*, trans. and ed. Army War College, November 1917 (Washington, D.C.: Government Printing Office, 1917), 16. This manual was the translation of one in use by the French army before the entry of the United States into the war.

15. Paul to Marie, 23 February 1916, 11 March 1916; SHAT, 26 N 1130, "Journaux des marches et opérations du 112ème Régiment d'artillerie lourde"; Paul to Marie, 23 March 1916; Marie to Paul, 8 March 1916.

16. Paul to Marie, 23 February 1916.

17. Ian Ousby, *The Road to Verdun: France, Nationalism and the First World War* (London: Pimlico, 2003); Antoine Prost, "Verdun: The Life of a Site of Memory," in *Republican Identities in War and Peace: Representations of France in the 19th and 20th Centuries*, trans. Jay Winter with Helen McPhail (New York: Berg, 2002): 45–71.

18. Robert A. Doughty, *Pyrrhic Victory: French Strategy and Operations in the Great War* (Cambridge, Mass.: Harvard University Press, 2005), 260–263.

19. France, Armée, Service historique, *Les Armées françaises dans la Grande Guerre*, vol. 4, bk. 1 (Paris: Imprimerie nationale, 1926), 541–543.

20. Paul to Marie, 3 March 1916.

21. Marie to Paul, 18 March 1916; Paul to Marie, 30 March 1916.

22. Augustin Cochin, *Le Capitaine Augustin Cochin: Quelques lettres de guerre* (Paris: Bloud et Gay, 1917), 45–47.

23. Paul to Marie, 14 April 1916.

24. Paul to Marie, 10 April 1916, 11 April 1916, 16 April 1916.

25. France, Armée, Service historique, *Les Armées françaises dans la Grande Guerre*, vol. 4, bk. 1, supplement 3 (Paris: Imprimerie nationale, 1931), 725.

26. SHAT, 26 N 1130, "Journaux des marches et opérations du 112ème Régiment d'artillerie lourde."

27. Paul to Marie, 16 April 1916, 15 April 1916, 25 April 1916.

28. Paul to Marie, 23 May 1916.

29. Paul to Marie, 23 May 1916.

30. Paul to Marie, 24 May 1916.

31. Leonard V. Smith, *Between Mutiny and Obedience: The Case of the French Fifth Infantry Division during World War I* (Princeton, N.J.: Princeton University Press, 1994), 141–154.

32. Paul to Marie, 24 May 1916, 27 May 1916.

33. Paul to Marie, 27 May 1916.

34. Paul to Marie, 27 May 1916. It is likely that very few soldiers spoke openly of such bodily functions; see Frédéric Rousseau, *La Guerre censurée: Une Histoire des combattants européens de 14–18* (Paris: Seuil, 1999), 159.

35. Paul to Marie, 27 May 1916, 31 May 1916.

36. Ousby, *The Road to Verdun*, 101.

37. Marie to Paul, 1 June 1916; Paul to Marie, 4 June 1916, 5 June 1916; Marie to Paul, 1 June 1916; Paul to Marie, 4 June 1916, 5 June 1916.

38. Paul to Marie, 20 June 1916, 16 June 1918.

39. Paul to Marie, 28 May 1916; Marie to Paul, 10 April 1916.

40. L. V. Haber, *The Poisonous Cloud: Chemical Warfare in the First World War* (Oxford: Clarendon Press, 1986), 73, 76.

41. Marie to Paul, 10 April 1916.

42. Paul to Marie, 27 May 1916.

43. Marie to Paul, 6 June 1916; Paul to Marie, 9 June 1916, 21 June 1916.

44. Paul to Marie, 12 April 1916, 23 May 1916, 24 May 1916.

45. Paul to Marie, 28 March 1916, 19 April 1916, 28 May 1916, 31 May 1916.

46. Paul to Marie, 25 April 1916, 26 May 1916, 31 May 1916, 3 June 1916.

47. Paul to Marie, 17 April 1916, 5 May 1916.

48. Paul to Marie 27 May 1916, 5 May 1916.

49. Paul to Marie, 21 June 1916.

50. Paul to Marie, 1 May 1916, 18 May 1916, 19 April 1916, 25 April 1916, 4 June 1916.

51. Paul to Marie, 13 May 1916.

52. Paul to Marie, 10 November 1916, 13 May 1916; Marie to Paul, 19 May 1916.

53. John Horne and Alan Kramer, *German Atrocities, 1914: A History of Denial* (New Haven, Conn.: Yale University Press, 2001), 196–197.

54. Paul to Marie, 23 March 1915, 28 March 1916.

55. Marie to Paul, 21 April 1916, 1 June 1916.

56. Paul to Marie, 17 May 1916; Jean-Yves Le Naour, *The Living Unknown Soldier: A True Story of Grief and the Great War* (London: Heinemann, 2005), 81–85.

57. Marie to Paul, 21 May 1916; Paul to Marie, 26 May 1916.

58. Paul to Marie, 2 June 1916.

3. OH, HOW I SUFFERED, MY POOR PAUL

1. Françoise Loux, *Le Jeune Enfant et son corps dans la médecine traditionnelle* (Paris: Flammarion, 1978), 32.

2. Marie to Paul, 18 January 1915; Paul to Marie, 18 September 1915, 11 October 1915, 2 January 1916.

3. Loux, *Le Jeune Enfant et son corps*, 69.

4. Marie to Paul, 7 August 1915.

5. Loux, *Le Jeune Enfant et son corps*, 66.

6. Maternal mortality rates in wartime France were calculated by dividing the number of pregnancy-related deaths by the total number of births, as given in two separate tables for 1921 in the *Annuaire statistique*: "Décès suivant les causes par catégories de communes: 1914, 1915, 1916," and "Mouvement de la population, 1915, 1916, 1917, 1918, 1919, 1920," *Annuaire statistique*, vol. 37 (Paris: Imprimerie nationale, 1922): 63–64, 10–14. Contemporary data relating to maternal mortality are taken from *Human Development Report: Deepening Democracy in a Fragmented World*, United Nations Development Programme (New York: Oxford University Press, 2002), 174–177.

7. Jacques Gélis, *A History of Childbirth: Fertility, Pregnancy, and Birth in Early Modern Europe*, trans. Rosemary Morris (Boston: Northeastern University Press, 1991), 227.

8. Marie to Paul, 9 April 1915, 7 December 1916.

9. Marie to Paul, 7 February 1916.

10. Dr. Sicard de Plauzoles, *La Maternité et la défense nationale contre la dépopulation* (Paris: V. Giard et E. Brière, 1909), 145; Adolphe Pinard, *L'Enfant de sa naissance à la fin de la première enfance: Des soins à lui donner par toute personne étrangère à la médecine*, (Paris: Colin 1924 [1914]).

11. Pinard, *L'Enfant de sa naissance à la fin de la première enfance*, 52.

12. Loux, *Le Jeune Enfant et son corps*, 67.

13. Marie to Paul, 9 March 1916; Loux, *Le Jeune Enfant et son corps*, 29, 185.

14. Sicard de Plauzoles did recommend that pregnant women drink milk: "A pregnant woman should insist particularly on bread, vegetables, eggs, milk, meat, and fish." De Plauzoles, *La Maternité et la défense nationale contre la dépopulation*, 145. As Mary Lynn Stewart has noted, however, other experts insisted that "milk hardened fetal bones, making for a difficult delivery. Competing advice may have meant little change in pregnant women's eating habits." *For Health and Beauty: Physical Culture for Frenchwomen, 1880–1930s* (Baltimore: Johns Hopkins University Press, 2001), 127.

15. Irvine Loudon points out that anemia, a common side effect of poor diet, increased the risk of hemorrhage during delivery. *Death in*

Childbirth: An International Study of Maternal Care and Maternal Mortality, *1800–1950* (Oxford: Clarendon, 1992), 378.

16. Paul to Marie, 3 March 1916; Marie to Paul, 9 March 1916.

17. Paul to Marie, 28 March 1916, 29 March 1916.

18. Marie to Paul, 26 March 1916, 28 May 1915; Paul to Marie, 30 May 1915; Marie to Paul, 9 July 1915, 29 July 1915.

19. ADC, J94, "Historique de la guerre, août 1914–août 1916: Vaux Lavalette." The price of calves went from fifty-five centimes per livre to one franc; that of pigs went from sixty centimes per livre to one franc, twenty-five centimes. The schoolteacher for Salles-Lavalette did not provide the prewar prices, but the prices he gave for wartime cattle stock—one franc, seventy centimes for cows and one franc, fifty centimes for calves—suggest comparable increases in the village closest to Nanteuil-de-Bourzac. Michel Augé-Laribé, *L'Agriculture pendant la guerre: Histoire économique et sociale de la Guerre mondiale,* Publications de la Dotation Carnegie pour la paix internationale (Paris: Presses universitaires de France, [1925]), 59.

20. Augé-Laribé, *L'Agriculture pendant la guerre,* 149, 59.

21. SHAT, 16 N 1448, GQG, 2e Bureau, Contrôle postal créé de Abbeville, Amiens, 1916–1918, Report of 16 August 1917.

22. Marie to Paul, 2 April 1916; Rosa Pireaud to Paul, 17 April 1916; Marie to Paul, 27 April 1916; Paul to Marie, 1 May 1916.

23. Marie to Paul, 8 April 1916.

24. Paul to Marie, 12 April 1916, 5 June 1916.

25. ADD, 5 M 27, Report to the prefect prepared by Dr. Jammes, medical inspector for public health, Dordogne [1918]; 1 M 92, "Liste des médecins, officiers de santé, 18 chirurgiens, dentistes et sages-femmes diplômés exerçant dans le département de la Dordogne, 1 janvier 1914." Handwritten notations indicate members of the medical profession who were mobilized.

26. ADC, J 94, "Histoire des communes par les instituteurs (1914–1918), Salles La Valette."

27. ADC, J 87, "Historique de la guerre: Montignac-le-Coq"; J 84, "Histoire de la Commune Juignac (Charente) pendant la guerre."

28. Paul to Marie, 28 May 1916, 19 June 1916.

29. Sicard de Plauzoles, *La Maternité et la défense nationale contre la dépopulation*, 140–141, 144. The average birth weight for a baby born to a mother who did not work in her final trimester was 3.25 kilograms (7.16 pounds); babies born to women who worked to full term weighed 2.90 kilograms (6.39 pounds); babies born to peasant women who continued to work through the last trimester had an average birth weight of 2.81 kilograms (6.19 pounds).

30. Loux, *Le Jeune Enfant et son corps*, 80–81, 90.

31. Gélis, *A History of Childbirth*, 98.

32. Extrapolating from prewar patterns, we can say that the number of children who should have been born in the five years between 1915 and 1919 (from the point when conceptions during wartime that resulted in births would have first become evident, up through the nine-month period marking the end of the war) was 3.5 million, or 700,000 per year. Only 2.1 million French children were born during this period—420,000 births per year. This constitutes a deficit of 1.4 million births, or a drop in the birthrate of 40 percent. Patrick Festy, "Effets et répercussions de la Première Guerre mondiale sur la fécondité française," *Population* 39, no. 6 (1984): 979.

33. Françoise Thébaud, *La Femme au temps de la Guerre de 14* (Paris: Stock, 1984), 150.

34. Gélis, *A History of Childbirth*, 132–133; Marie to Paul, 13 July 1916, 15 July 1916, undated fragment.

35. Gélis, *A History of Childbirth*, 162.

36. Marie to Paul, 15 July 1916, undated fragment, 16 July 1916.

37. Marie to Paul, 15 July 1916, 16 July 1916, 23 July 1996.

38. Marie to Paul, 29 July 1916.

39. Marie to Paul, 19 October 1916, 23 October 1916.

40. Paul to Marie, 17 July 1916.

41. Marie to Paul, 16 July, 1916, 21 July 1916; Loux, *Le Jeune Enfant et son corps*, 68.

42. Marie to Paul, 21 July 1916.

43. Pinard, *L'Enfant de sa naissance à la fin de la première enfance*, 113; Gasto Variot, *Comment sauvegarder les bébés: Enseignement de l'hygiène donné à*

l'Institut de puériculture et à la Goutte de Lait de Belleville (Paris: Doin, 1922), 28.

44. Marie to Paul, 18 July 1916.

45. Pinard, *L'Enfant de sa naissance à la fin de la première enfance*, 109.

46. Marie to Paul, 21 July 1916; Paul to Marie, 22 July 1916.

47. Michel Huber, *La Population de la France pendant la guerre, avec un appendice sur les revenus avant et après la guerre*, Publications de la Dotation Carnegie pour la paix internationale (Paris: Presses universitaires de France, [1931]), 303. Huber claims that infant diarrhea accounted for 29 percent of infant deaths; Sicard de Plauzoles cites a figure of 385 per 1,000 infant deaths, and Pinard claims that 50 percent of all infant deaths were caused by diarrhea or other intestinal illnesses. Sicard de Plauzoles, *La Maternité et la défense nationale contre la dépopulation*, 100; Pinard, *L'Enfant de sa naissance à la fin de la première enfance*, 69.

48. Sicard de Plauzoles, *La Maternité et la défense nationale contre la dépopulation*, 95, 198; ADD, 5 M 20, "Enquête sur la mortalité infantile, 1917."

49. Pinard, *L'Enfant de sa naissance à la fin de la première enfance*, 69, 100.

50. Marie to Paul, 23 July 1916.

51. Marie to Paul, 8 August 1916, 31 July 1916.

52. Loux, *Le Jeune Enfant et son corps*, 192; Pinard, *L'Enfant de sa naissance à la fin de la première enfance*, 125.

53. Pinard, *L'Enfant de sa naissance à la fin de la première enfance*, 126–127.

54. Paul to Marie, 30 August 1916; Marie to Paul, 7 September 1916, 10 September 1916, 11 September 1916.

55. Marie to Paul, 14 September 1916, 16 September 1916, 19 September 1916, 23 September 1916.

56. Pinard, *L'Enfant de sa naissance à la fin de la première enfance*, 123–124.

57. Marie to Paul, 30 September 1916.

58. Marie to Paul, 12 October 1916.

59. ADD, 5 M 20, "Enquête sur la mortalité infantile, 1917."

60. Marie to Paul, 30 September 1916.

61. Evelyn Ackerman, *Health Care in the Parisian Countryside, 1800–1914* (New Brunswick, N.J.: Rutgers University Press, 1990), 98–100.

62. Marie-France Morel, "Les Soins prodigués aux enfants: Influence des innovations médicales et des institutions médicalisées, 1750–1914.

Médecine et déclin de la mortalité infantile," *Annales de démographie historique* (1989): 157–181.

63. Marie to Paul, 23 July 1916, 24 July 1916.

64. Marie to Paul, 2 August 1916, 5 August 1916, 13 August 1916.

65. Marie to Paul, 31 October 1916, 8 November 1916, 11 November 1916, 15 October 1916, 23 November 1916, 30 November 1916.

66. Marie to Paul, 7 or 8 February 1917, 10 February 1917, 11 February 1917, 13 February 1917, 22 February 1917.

67. Marie to Paul, 7 or 8 February 1917, 10 February 1917, 13 February 1917, 3 March 1917, 13 March 1917; Paul to Marie, 4 August 1917.

68. Loux, *Le Jeune Enfant et son corps*, 136–149.

69. Paul to Marie, 31 May 1916; Marie to Paul, 6 June 1916; Paul to Marie, 23 July 1916; Marie to Paul, 31 July 1916; Paul to Marie, 4 August 1916.

70. Paul to Marie, 28 September 1916.

71. Ralph Gibson, *A Social History of French Catholicism, 1789–1914* (London: Routledge, 1989), 171, 175, 179, 165. In 1906 only 38.5 percent of men (but 69.4 percent of women) living in the diocese of Périgueux received Easter communion. In rural parishes, 56.2 percent of all residents, male and female, received Easter communion. Thus it would seem likely that many rural men were, like Paul, very indifferent Catholics.

72. Marie to Paul, 19 September 1916, undated letter from September 1916; Paul to Marie, 2 October 1916, 25 February 1917.

73. Marie to Paul, 10 October 1916; Michel Gervais, Marcel Jollivet, and Yves Tavernier, *La Fin de la France paysanne, de 1914 à nos jours: Histoire de la France rurale*, vol. 4, ed. Georges Duby and Armand Wallon (Paris: Seuil, 1976), 185.

74. Marie to Paul, 6 October 1916, 7 October 1916. On the advantages (and greater expense) of a live-in wet nurse, see Pinard, *L'Enfant de sa naissance à la première enfance*, 107.

75. Eugen Weber, *Peasants into Frenchmen: The Modernization of Rural France, 1870–1914* (Stanford, Calif.: Stanford University Press, 1976).

76. Paul to Marie, 26 October 1916.

77. Paul to Marie, 19 June 1916, 2 August 1916, 30 August 1916.

78. Paul to Marie, 4 October 1916.

79. Marie to Paul, 23 July 1916, 3 September 1916, 5 September 1916; Paul to Marie, 24 July 1916, 6 September 1916.

80. Marie to Paul, 7 or 8 February 1917; Marie and Serge to Paul, 13 May 1918.

81. Huber, *La Population de la France pendant la guerre*, 247.

82. Ibid., 303, 267.

4. NO ONE IS HAPPY IN WAR

1. SHAT, 16 N 1452, Commission de contrôle postal, Boulogne-sur-Mer, Report of the week of 11–17 June 1917.

2. Paul to Marie, 5 October 1916, 8 October 1916.

3. Lieutenant Marcel Etévé, *Lettres d'un combattant, août 1914–juillet 1916* (Paris: Hachette, 1917), 235, 246–247, 248, 249.

4. Hew Strachan, *The First World War: A New Illustrated History* (London: Simon and Schuster, 2003), 187.

5. SHAT, 26N 1130, "Journaux des marches et opérations [JMO] du 112e Régiment d'artillerie lourde," JMO for the Twenty-seventh Battery of the 112th Heavy Artillery Regiment.

6. Paul to Marie, undated letter, 1916.

7. Paul to Marie, undated letter (probably 17 September 1916), 19 October 1916.

8. Paul to Marie, 18 October 1916, 19 October 1916; Marie to Paul, 9 December 1916; Paul to Marie, 24 October 1916; SHAT, 26N 1130, "Journaux des marches et opérations du 112e Régiment d'artillerie lourde," JMO for the Twenty-seventh Battery of the 112th Heavy Artillery Regiment.

9. Paul to Marie, 24 November 1916, 26 November 1916, 7 December 1916. Concerning the intensification of hostilities between major battles, Leonard Smith writes: "British commanders had a particularly keen interest in constantly harassing the enemy *before* they had a large field army on the continent; French commanders acquired

this interest after they had spent much of theirs." Leonard V. Smith, *Between Mutiny and Obedience: The Case of the French Fifth Infantry Division during World War I* (Princeton, N.J.: Princeton University Press, 1994), 158.

10. SHAT, 16N 1440, Commission de contrôle postal, Xe Armée, Report of 10 January 1917, Thirty-third Artillery Regiment; 16N 1452, Commission de contrôle postal, Boulogne-sur-Mer, Report of 12–18 February 1917; 16N 1440, Commission de contrôle postal, Xe Armée, Report of 21 January 1917, 108th Heavy Artillery Regiment, Fourth Engineers; Report of 8 January 1917, 141st Territorial Regiment.

11. SHAT, 16N 1440, Commission de contrôle postal, Xe Armée, Report of 26 January 1917, 112th Heavy Artillery Regiment.

12. SHAT, 16N 1448, Contrôle postal créé de Abbeville, Amiens, 1916–1918, Report of 27 January 1917; Paul to Marie, 17 January 1917, 24 January 1917, 20 January 191[7]. (Like many check writers in the first weeks of a new year who absentmindedly date them to the previous year, Paul dated his letter—clearly written in 1917—as 20 January 1916.)

13. SHAT, 16N 1440, Commission de contrôle postal d'Amiens, Xe Armée, Reports of 10 January 1917, 19 January 1917.

14. Ibid., Report of 8 May 1917.

15. Ibid., Reports of 10 January 1917, Thirty-third Artillery Régiment; 19 January 1917, First Engineers; summary of 8 May 1917; Paul to Marie, 30 January 1917, 20 February 1917.

16. SHAT, 16N 1448, Contrôle postal créé de Abbeville, Amiens, 1916–1918, Report of 19 July 1917.

17. SHAT, 16N 1449, Commission de contrôle postal de Bar-le-Duc, Report of 26 April–2 May 1917.

18. Ibid., Reports of 26 April–2 May 1917, 3–9 May 1917; 16N 1451, Commission de contrôle postal de Besançon, Report of 20–27 October 1917; 16N 1452, Commission de contrôle postal, Boulogne-sur-Mer, Report of 24–31 December 1916.

19. SHAT, 16N 1451, Commission de contrôle postal de Besançon, Report of 20–27 October 1917.

20. Paul to Marie, 6 May 1917, 16 March 1917, 18 May, 1917, 6 May 1917, 11 March 1917; Marie to Paul, 11 March 1917.

21. Michel Augé-Laribé, *L'Agriculture pendant la guerre: Histoire économique et sociale de la Guerre mondiale*, Publications de la Dotation Carnegie pour la paix internationale (Paris: Presses universitaires de France, [1925]), 86.

22. Archives départementales de la Gironde [hereafter ADG], 1 M 413, Reports of the police commissioner, July 1914–January 1918, Report of the subprefect of the arrondissement of Lesparre to the prefect of the Gironde, 17 July 1916.

23. ADC, J 84, "Histoire de la Commune Juignac (Charente) pendant la guerre, renseignements fournis par Mmes Pinassaud et Gerbaud, institutrices."

24. SHAT, 16N 1440, Commission de contrôle postal d'Amiens, Xe Armée, Report of 6 January 1917.

25. SHAT, 16 N 1441, Report of the Thirtieth Artillery Regiment, 11 May 1917.

26. Jean-Jacques Becker, *The Great War and the French People*, trans. Arnold Pomerans (Providence, R.I.: Berg, 1985), 120–123.

27. ADR, 4 M 234, "Etat d'esprit de la population," Report of the prefect of the Rhône to the minister of the interior, 1 March 1916; Marie to Paul, 11 March 1917; ADC, J 94, "Histoire des communes par les instituteurs, 1914–1918, Salles La Valette"; J 84, "Histoire de la Commune Juignac (Charente) pendant la guerre"; J 87, "Historique de la guerre: Montignac-le-Coq"; ADD, 8 R 51, "Correspondance générale sur la situation du ravitaillement en céréales," arrondissement de Ribérac, Decree of the mayor of Montpon, 22 May 1917; ADD, 1 M 82, Report of the prefect of the Dordogne, 17 June 1917.

28. Barbara Engel, "Not by Bread Alone: Subsistence Riots in Russia during World War I," *Journal of Modern History* 69 (December 1997): 696–721.

29. Augé-Laribé, *L'Agriculture pendant la guerre*, 75.

30. Yves Pourcher, *Les Jours de guerre: La Vie des Français au jour le jour, 1914–1918* (Paris: Plon, 1994), 132; SHAT, 16 N 1448, GQG, 2e Bu-

reau, contrôle postal créé de Abbeville, Amiens, 1916–1918, Report of 24 May 1917. The postal censors in Besançon noted similar complaints about the poor quality of bread in spring 1917: 16 N 1451, Report of the president of the postal censorship commission of Besançon, 9–15 June 1917.

31. ADD, 8 R 51, "Correspondance générale sur la situation du ravitaillement en céréales," Letter from the subprefect of Ribérac to the prefect of the Dordogne, 19 May 1917.

32. SHAT, 7 N 985, Commission militaire de contrôle postal de Bordeaux, 1915–1918, Report of March 1917.

33. Stéphane Audoin-Rouzeau, *Men at War, 1914–1918: National Sentiment and Trench Journalism in France during the First World War*, trans. Helen McPhail (Providence, R.I.: Berg, 1992), 134–35.

34. SHAT, 16 N 1452, Commission de contrôle postal, Boulogne-sur-Mer, Report of 12–18 March 1917.

35. ADC, J 87, "Historique de la guerre: Montignac-le-Coq."

36. ADG, 1 M 413, Reports of the police commissioner, Report dated 17 July 1916; 1 M 414, "Etat moral de la population, 1916–1917," Report from the police commissioner to the prefect of the Gironde, 7 June 1917; Report from the subprefect of the arrondissement of La Réole to the prefect of the Gironde, 8 June 1917.

37. SHAT, 16N 1452, Commission de contrôle postal, Boulogne-sur-Mer, Reports of 2–8 April 1917, 9–15 April 1917.

38. Paul to Marie, 13 April, 1917, 14 April 1917.

39. Paul to Marie, 16 April 1917.

40. For more detail on the Nivelle offensive, see Leonard V. Smith, Stéphane Audoin-Rouzeau, and Annette Becker, *France and the Great War, 1914–1918* (Cambridge: Cambridge University Press, 2003), chap. 4; Strachan, *The First World War*, chap. 8; and Robert A. Doughty, *Pyrrhic Victory: French Strategy and Operations in the Great War* (Cambridge, Mass.: Harvard University Press, 2005), chap. 7.

41. SHAT, 7 N 985, Commission militaire de contrôle postal de Bordeaux, 1915–1918, Report of April 1917.

42. Paul to Marie, 12 May 1917.

43. SHAT, 16 N 1452, Commission de contrôle postal, Boulogne-

sur-Mer, Report of 7–15 May 1917; 16N 1441, Commission de contrôle postal, Xe Armée, Report of the 162nd Infantry Regiment, 17 May 1917.

44. Paul to Marie, 25 April 1917.

45. Paul to Marie, 30 April 1917; Fernand Maret, *Lettres de la guerre 14–18* (Nantes: Siloë, 2001), letter of 1 May 1917.

46. Paul to Marie, 18 May 1917.

47. Paul to Marie, 21 May 1917.

48. Henry Bordeaux, "Les Zouaves au Cornillet," *La Terre de France reconquise*, as quoted at *http://vinny03.club.fr/gg/leshistos/1erzouavescornillet.htm.*

49. Patrick Facon, "La Tragédie du Mont Cornillet (avril–mai 1917)," *Revue historique des armées* 2, no. 3 (1975): 53–72.

50. Maret, *Lettres de la guerre 14–18*, letters of 26 May 1917, 29 May 1917.

51. Paul to Marie, 29 May 1917, 31 May 1917.

52. Paul to Marie, 1 June 1917, 27 May 1917, 4 July 1917, 7 July 1917.

53. Paul to Marie, 4 July 1917, 29 May 1917.

54. Paul to Marie, 27 June 1917.

55. Paul to Marie, two letters, both dated 17 July 1917.

56. Guy Pedroncini, *Les Mutineries de 1917* (Paris: Presses universitaires de France, 1967), 235.

57. Paul to Marie, 8 January 1917, 9 January 1917.

58. SHAT, 16 N 1441, Commission de contrôle postal, Xe Armée, May–June 1917, Reports of the 267th Infantry Regiment, 17 May 1917; the 162nd Infantry Regiment, 17 May 1917; Fifty-seventh Infantry Regiment, 22 May 1917.

59. Smith, *Between Mutiny and Obedience*, 182. Leonard V. Smith, Stéphane Audoin-Rouzeau, and Annette Becker suggest that "the total number of 'mutineers' is most reliably estimated at 25,000–30,000." Smith, Audoin-Rouzeau, and Becker, *France and the Great War*, 122.

60. Maret, *Lettres de la guerre 14–18*, letter of 16 June 1917.

61. Paul to Marie, 29 May 1917, 31 May 1917.

62. Paul to Marie, 29 May 1917, 21 May 1917, 1 June 1917.

63. Paul to Marie, 27 May 1917.

64. SHAT, 16 N 1448, GQG, 2e Bureau, contrôle postal créé de Abbeville, Amiens, 1916–1918, Report of 23 August 1917.

65. SHAT, 16 N 1452, Commission de contrôle postal, Boulogne-sur-Mer, Reports of 2–8 July 1917, 16–22 July 1917.

66. Paul to Marie, 8 July 1917.

67. Paul to Marie, undated letter [summer 1917].

68. SHAT, 16 N 1452, Commission de contrôle postal, Boulogne-sur-Mer, Report of 11–17 June 1917.

69. ADR, 4 M 234, "Etat d'esprit de la population," Report of the prefect of the Rhône to the minister of the interior, 5 January 1918.

70. ADD, 4 Z 65, "Rapports mensuels sur l'état moral de la population, 1916–1918," arrondissement de Ribérac, Report of 15 June 1917 to the prefect of the Dordogne; Report prepared by squadron commander Violland, 29 July 1917; ADG, 1 M 414, "Etat moral de la population, 1916–1917," Report from the special commissioner to the prefect of the Gironde, 7 June 1917.

5. WE ARE MARTYRS OF THE CENTURY

1. Hew Strachan, The First World War: A New Illustrated History (London: Simon and Schuster, 2003), 251.

2. Paul to Marie, 12 November 1917.

3. Jean Nicot, Les Poilus ont la parole: Dans les tranchées: lettres du front, 1917–1918 (Paris: Editions Complexe 1998), 78.

4. France, Armée, Service historique, Les Armées françaises dans la Grande Guerre, vol. 6, bk. 1, chap. 3: "Les Troupes françaises en Italie pendant l'hiver 1917–1918 (26 octobre 1917–23 mars 1918)" (Paris: Imprimerie nationale, 1931), 93–94.

5. Leonard Smith, Stéphane Audoin-Rouzeau, and Annette Becker, France and the Great War, 1914–1918 (Cambridge: Cambridge University Press, 2003), 130.

6. Guy Pedroncini, Les Mutineries de 1917 (Paris: Presses universitaires de France, 1967), 236; Nicot, Les Poilus ont la parole, 45–60.

7. France, Armée, Service historique, *Les Armées françaises dans la Grande Guerre*, vol. 6, 1:93–94.

8. Henri Guichard, *La Grande Guerre du soldat Guichard: Itinéraire peu commun d'un poilu—Carnets de route, 1916–1919* (Charenton-le-Pont: Presses de Valmy, 2000), 42.

9. Ibid., 63.

10. SHAT, 16N 1443, Commission de contrôle postal, Xe Armée, Armée d'Italie, September–December 1917, Report of the Seventy-eighth Infantry Regiment, 3 December 1917.

11. Paul to Marie, 7 December 1917, 7 January 1918.

12. SHAT, 16N 1443, Commission de contrôle postal, Xe Armée, Armée d'Italie, September–December 1917, Report of the Twenty-first Artillery Regiment, 6 December 1917.

13. Paul to Marie, 7 December 1917.

14. SHAT, 16N 1443, Commission de contrôle postal, Xe Armée, Armée d'Italie, September–December 1917, Report of the 203rd Artillery Regiment, 11 December 1917; Report of CVAD and COA Escorte, 8 December 1917; 16N 1444, Commission de contrôle postal, Xe Armée, Armée d'Italie, January–April 1918, Report of the Sixty-fourth and Twenty-fourth Infantry Divisions, 11–18 March 1918.

15. SHAT, 16N 1443, Commission de contrôle postal, Xe Armée, Armée d'Italie, September–December 1917, Report of the 311th Infantry Regiment, 12 December 1917.

16. Ibid., Report of the 261st Infantry Regiment, 14 December 1917; 16N 1444, Commission de contrôle postal, Xe Armée, Armée d'Italie, January–April 1918, Report of the Thirty-fourth Artillery Regiment, 4 January 1918, and Summary report for 5–12 January 1918.

17. Paul to Marie, 23 December 1917.

18. On widespread French indignation at the Russian defection, see Nicot, *Les Poilus ont la parole*, 72–78.

19. SHAT, 16N 1443, Commission de contrôle postal, Xe Armée, Armée d'Italie, September–December 1917, Report of the 311th Infantry Regiment, 12 December 1917.

20. Pedroncini, *Les Mutineries de 1917*, 236.

21. SHAT, 16N 1443, Commission de contrôle postal, Xe Armée, Armée d'Italie, September–December 1917, Report of the 203rd Infantry Regiment, 11 December 1917.

22. Ibid., Report of the 255th Regiment, 14 December 1917.

23. Paul to Marie, 23 December 1917.

24. Paul to Marie, 7 February 1918.

25. Lionel Lemarchand, *Lettres censurées des tranchées, 1917: Une Place dans la littérature et l'histoire* (Paris: L'Harmattan, 2001), 199; Paul and Marie made use of this stratagem at several junctures during the war.

26. Marie to Paul, 2 October 1916; Paul to Marie, 11 October 1916.

27. SHAT, 16N 1444, Commission de contrôle postal, Xe Armée, Armée d'Italie, January–April 1918, Report for the week of 5–12 January 1918; 16N 1443, Commission de contrôle postal, Xe Armée, Armée d'Italie, September–December 1917, Report for the week of 1– 7 December 1917.

28. SHAT, 16N 1443, Commission de contrôle postal, Xe Armée, Armée d'Italie, September–December 1917, Report for the week of 1– 7 December 1917; Paul to Marie, 22 December 1917; SHAT, 16N 1444, Commission de contrôle postal, Xe Armée, Armée d'Italie, January–April 1918, Report for the week of 5–12 January 1918; Paul to Marie, 17 December 1917, 18 January 1918.

29. Martha Hanna, "A Republic of Letters: The Epistolary Tradition in France during World War I," *American Historical Review* 108, no. 5 (December 2003): 1344.

30. France, Armée, Service historique, *Les Armées françaises dans la Grande Guerre*, vol. 11: *La Direction de l'arrière*, chap. 38, "Services des Postes et du Trésor" (Paris: Imprimerie nationale, 1937), 394–395.

31. SHAT, 16N 1444, Commission de contrôle postal, Xe Armée, Armée d'Italie, January–April 1918, Report for the week of 30 December 1917–5 January 1918.

32. Paul to Marie, 1 January 1918.

33. Paul to Marie, 16 January 1918, 9 January 1918.

34. Marie to Paul, 4 January 1918, 6 February 1918, 7 February 1918; Paul to Marie, 14 February 1918.

35. Paul to Marie, 25 March 1918, 3 April 1918, 1 April 1918, 4 April 1918, 18 April 1918.

36. Paul to Marie, 5 April 1918, 11 May 1918; Marie and Serge to Paul, 13 May 1918, 8 June 1918, 23 June 1918.

37. Michel Augé-Laribé, *L'Agriculture pendant la guerre: Histoire économique et sociale de la Guerre mondiale*, Publications de la Dotation Carnegie pour la paix internationale (Paris: Presses universitaires de France, [1925]), 56, 59.

38. SHAT, 16N 1444, Commission de contrôle postal, Xe Armée, Armée d'Italie, January—April 1918, Report for the week of 5–12 January 1918.

39. Ibid., Report for the week of 25 January–3 February 1918.

40. Ibid., Report of the 227th Artillery Regiment, 13 January 1918.

41. On purchasing of jewelry at the county fair, see ADD 1 M 82, Report of the squadron commander, "Commandant la compagnie sur l'état moral de la population," 12e Région, Gendarmerie nationale, Compagnie de la Dordogne, 23 March 1918. On lavish Christmas spending, see ADG, 1 M 414, Report of the police commissioner to the prefect of the Gironde, 29 December 1917.

42. Marie to Paul, 13 May 1918; ADD, 1 M 82, Report of the squadron commander, "Commandant la compagnie sur l'état moral de la population," 12e Région, Gendarmerie nationale, Compagnie de la Dordogne, 24 February 1918. On Marie's purchase of a dress from Le Printemps, receipt dated 19 August 1918, for one dress, sold to Mme Pireaud, for ten francs, forty centimes.

43. SHAT, 16N 1444, Commission de contrôle postal, Xe Armée, Armée d'Italie, January—April 1918, Surveillance ordered by telephone communication from military headquarters, 11 February 1918, of correspondence emanating from the 120th postal sector and destined for Bordeaux and the Gironde, poll conducted 11 February 1918.

44. ADD, 4 Z 65, Report from the commune of Cherval to the subprefect of Ribérac, 28 February 1918.

45. Ibid., Report of 21 May 1918 from the subprefect of Ribérac to

the prefect of the Dordogne; 1 M 82, Report of squadron commander Lacaze, "Commandant la Compagnie de la Dordogne sur l'état moral de la population," 12e Région, Gendarmerie nationale, Compagnie de la Dordogne, 23 May 1918.

46. Paul to Marie, 11 May 1918.

47. ADD, 1 M 82, Report of the prefect of the Dordogne, 27 November 1917; Report of the squadron commander, "Commandant la compagnie sur l'état moral de la population," 12e Région, Gendarmerie nationale, Compagnie de la Dordogne, 23 March 1918.

48. Ibid., Report of the prefect of the Dordogne, 27 December 1917; Report of squadron commander Lacaze, "Commandant la compagnie de la Dordogne sur l'état moral de la population," 12e Région, Gendarmerie nationale, Compagnie de la Dordogne, 23 May 1918.

49. Paul to Marie, 18 April 1918.

50. Paul to Marie, 27 January 1918, 29 January 1918, 31 January 1918, 28 April 1918, 29 April 1918.

51. Paul to Marie, 29 January 1918, 22 May 1918; SHAT, 16 N 1445, Commission de contrôle postal, Xe Armée, Armée d'Italie, April–November 1918, Report of the 112th Heavy Artillery Regiment, 28 May 1918.

52. Paul to Marie, 18 May 1918, 8 June 1918, 3 June 1918.

53. Paul to Marie, 16 June 1918.

54. Paul to Marie, 16 June 1918; SHAT, 16 N 1445, Commision de contrôle postal, Xe Armée, April–November 1918; Reports for the weeks of 15–21 June 1918, 22–28 June 1918.

55. Paul to Marie, 21 June 1918, 24 June 1918, 29 June 1918, 31 [sic] June 1918.

56. Paul to Marie, 5 August 1918, 30 July 1918.

57. Paul to Marie, 19 July 1918, 28 July 1918.

58. Paul to Marie, 19 July 1918, 13 July 1918.

59. Paul to Marie, 28 July 1918, 29 July 1918.

60. Paul to Marie, 2 May [sic—should be June] 1918, 3 June 1918; SHAT, 16N 1445, Commission de contrôle postal, Xe Armée, Armée d'Italie, April–November 1918, Report of the 112th Heavy Artillery Regiment, 28 May 1918.

61. ADD, 5 M 27, "Epidémies: La Grippe, 1918–1920"; Marie to Paul, 29 October 1918.

62. Paul to Marie, 24 August 1918, 25 August 1918.

63. Paul to Marie, 12 August 1918, 16 August 1918, 29 February 1918.

64. Paul to Marie, 18 August 1918, 27 August 1918.

65. On the subject of menstruation being taboo, see Jacques Gélis, *A History of Childbirth: Fertility, Pregnancy, and Birth in Early Modern Europe*, trans. Rosemary Morris (Boston: Northeastern University Press, 1991), 10–11; Mary Lynn Stewart, *For Health and Beauty: Physical Culture for Frenchwomen, 1880s–1930s* (Baltimore: Johns Hopkins University Press, 2001), 81–83.

66. Marie to Paul, 4 November 1916, 20 July 1917; Paul to Marie, 5 October 1918; Gélis, *A History of Childbirth*, 15.

67. Marie to Paul, 6 October 1918, Paul to Marie, 9 October 1918.

68. SHAT, 16N 1445, Commission de contrôle postal, Xe Armée, Armée d'Italie, April–November 1918, Report of the 112th Heavy Artillery Regiment, 5 November 1918; Paul to Marie, 1 November 1918.

69. Paul to Marie, 30 October 1918.

70. Marie to Paul, 24 September 1918, 22 October 1918; Paul to Marie, 3 October 1918.

71. Marie to Paul, 6 October 1918, 8 October 1918; Mary Louise Roberts, *Civilization without Sexes: Reconstructing Gender in Postwar France, 1917–1927* (Chicago: University of Chicago Press, 1994), chap. 3: "'Women Are Cutting Their Hair as a Sign of Sterility.'"

72. Paul to Marie, 2 October 1918, 3 October 1918; Marie to Paul, 13 October 1918. On syphilis in early twentieth-century France, see Claude Quétel, *History of Syphilis*, trans. Judith Braddock and Brian Pike (Baltimore: Johns Hopkins University Press, 1990), chap. 6.

73. Marie to Paul, 8 October 1918, 21 October 1918.

74. Marie to Paul, 8 December 1916; Paul to Marie, 23 June 1918; Marie to Paul, 13 May 1918.

75. Jean-Yves Le Naour, *Misères et tourments de la chair durant la Grande Guerre: Les Moeurs sexuelles des Français, 1914–1918* (Paris: Aubier, 2002), 227–228.

76. Paul to Marie, 10 October 1916, 23 June 1918, 20 August 1918.

77. Paul to Marie, 7 August 1918, 8 August 1918.

78. Paul to Marie, 20 August, 22 August, 1 September 1918.

79. Nicot, *Les Poilus ont la parole*, 429–431.

80. Yves-Henri Nouailhat, *Les Américains à Nantes et Saint-Nazaire, 1917–191* (Paris: Belles Lettres, 1972), 185.

81. ADD, 8 R 172, "Guerre de 1914–1918: Troupes américaines, 1917–1921."

82. Le Naour, *Misères et tourments de la chair durant la Grande Guerre*, 224–225.

83. SHAT, 16N 1444, Commission de contrôle postal, Xe Armée, Armée d'Italie, January–April 1918, Report of the 108th Infantry Regiment, 21 January 1918.

84. Paul to Marie, 8 August 1918.

85. Paul to Marie, 8 August 1918.

86. Paul to Marie, 7 November 1912.

87. Paul to Marie, 30 April 1912, 14 May 1912.

88. Paul to Marie, 4 June 1912, 14 May 1912.

89. Allan M. Brandt, *No Magic Bullet: A Social History of Venereal Disease in the United States since 1880*, expanded edition (New York: Oxford University Press, 1987), 16.

90. Paul to Marie, 17 May 1912, 24 May 1912, 10 July 1912, 30 April 1917; Marie to Paul, 4 May 1917.

91. Paul to Marie, 16 October 1918, 20 October 1918.

92. Paul to Marie, 25 October 1918.

93. Paul to Marie, 4 November 1918, 6 November 1918, 11 November 1918.

CONCLUSION

1. Marie to Paul, 14 November 1918.

2. Colin Dyer, *Population and Society in Twentieth-Century France* (New York: Holmes and Meier, 1978), 58.

3. Marie to Paul, 18 November 1918, 10 March 1919.

4. SHAT, 16 N 1445, Commission de contrôle postal, Xe Armée, Armée d'Italie, April–November 1918, Report of 17 December 1918; Report of the 112th Heavy Artillery Regiment, 13 December 1918.

5. Paul to Marie, 27 February 1919, 25 March 1919, 12 March 1919.

6. Paul to Marie, 4 March 1919, 13 March 1919.

7. Paul to Marie, 7 May 1919, 8 May 1919.

8. Paul to Marie, 26 May 1919.

9. Paul to Marie, 21 July 1919.

10. Stéphane Audoin-Rouzeau, *Men at War, 1914–1918: National Sentiment and Trench Journalism in France during the First World War*, trans. Helen McPhail (Providence, R.I.: Berg, 1992), 135.

11. Michel Huber, *La Population de la France pendant la guerre*, avec un appendice sur les revenues avant et après la guerre (Paris: Presses universitaires de France [1931]), 243; "Divorces et séparations de corps: Année 1919," *Annuaire statistique*, vol. 37: *1921* (Paris: Imprimerie nationale, 1922), 107.

12. Mary Louise Roberts, *Civilization without Sexes: Reconstructing Gender in Postwar France, 1917–1927* (Chicago: University of Chicago Press, 1994), 138.

13. Roland Dorgelès, *Les Croix de bois* (Paris: Albin Michel, 1919), 243.

14. Marie to Paul, 18 November 1918.

15. Huber, *La Population de la France pendant la guerre*, 246.

16. Bernard Paccot, *Marie-Louise Donche et Jean-Marie Paccot, Saint André de Boëge, 1909–1919* (Annecy: Centre généalogique de Savoie, 1994).

17. Huber, *La Population de la France pendant la guerre*, 54, 303, 693, 736–739, 741–743.

18. Luc Capdevila, "L'Expérience de guerre d'un combattant ordinaire: Une Histoire de la souffrance et de la résignation à partir des sources privées (France 1914–1918)," *Modern and Contemporary France* 11, no. 1 (2003): 59.

19. Raymond Jonas, *The Tragic Tale of Claire Ferchaud and the Great War* (Berkeley: University of California Press, 2005), 23; Germain Cuzacq, *Le Soldat de Lagraulet: Lettres de Germain Cuzacq écrites du front entre août 1914*

et septembre 1916, ed. Pierre et Germaine Leshauris (Toulouse: Eché, 1984), 111.

20. Cuzacq, *Le Soldat de Lagraulet,* 111–112.

21. Paul to Marie, 16 May 1916; Marie to Paul, 19 May 1916.

22. Martyn Lyons, *Readers and Society in Nineteenth-Century France: Workers, Women, Peasants* (New York: Palgrave, 2001), 154–155.

23. Marie to Paul, 26 July 1915; receipt from Le Printemps, dated 19 August 1918.

24. Roger Thabault, *Education and Change in a Village Community: Mazières-en-Gâtine 1848–1914,* trans. Peter Tregear (New York: Schocken, 1971), 158.

25. Undated draft of a letter from Paul Pireaud to the Ecole nationale d'agriculture de Grignon (Seine-et-Oise) and response from the Ecole nationale d'agriculture, dated 7 May 1919.

26. Andy Clark, *Mindware: An Introduction to the Philosophy of Cognitive Science* (New York: Oxford University Press, 2001), chap. 8: "Cognitive Technology: Beyond the Naked Brain."

27. I am grateful to M. Rémy Lachaise and Mme Arlette Durand for sharing with me these memories of Paul, Marie, and Serge Pireaud.

INDEX